新 时 代 大 学 应 用 英 语
New Era Applied College English

总主编 胡开宝

综合教程
Integrated Course

主　编　吴　勇　　赵晓红　　胡开宝
副主编　潘之欣
编　者　李晓倩　　江任鱼　　江　峰
　　　　张丽莉　　黑　黔

2

教师用书

上海外语教育出版社
外教社 SHANGHAI FOREIGN LANGUAGE EDUCATION PRESS

图书在版编目（CIP）数据

综合教程2教师用书/吴勇,赵晓红,胡开宝主编;
潘之欣副主编. -- 上海：上海外语教育出版社，2022
（新时代大学应用英语/胡开宝总主编）
ISBN 978-7-5446-7245-0

Ⅰ.①综… Ⅱ.①吴…②赵…③胡…④潘… Ⅲ.
①英语—高等学校—教学参考资料 Ⅳ.①H319.39

中国版本图书馆CIP数据核字（2022）第112219号

出版发行：**上海外语教育出版社**
　　　　　（上海外国语大学内）　邮编：200083
电　　话：021-65425300（总机）
电子邮箱：bookinfo@sflep.com.cn
网　　址：http://www.sflep.com
责任编辑：蔡一鸣

印　　刷：上海信老印刷厂
开　　本：850×1168　1/16　印张 11.25　字数 287 千字
版　　次：2022 年 8 月第 1 版　　2022 年 8 月第 1 次印刷
书　　号：ISBN 978-7-5446-7245-0
定　　价：53.00 元

本版图书如有印装质量问题，可向本社调换
质量服务热线：4008-213-263　电子邮箱：editorial@sflep.com

总 序

　　近年来，随着我国参与全球治理的深度和广度不断增强，国家对广大高校毕业生的英语综合应用能力尤其是职场英语应用能力提出了更高的要求，而承担培养外语人才重任的大学英语教学则被寄予越来越高的期望。2020年，教育部高等学校大学外语教学指导委员会正式颁布了《大学英语教学指南》（2020版）（以下称《指南》），对新时代大学英语教学提出了新的要求。《指南》指出，大学英语课程"兼具工具性和人文性"。工具性要求强调大学英语课程教学不仅要重视学生听、说、读、写、译能力的提升，而且应"让学生学习与专业相关的学术英语或职业英语"。人文性要求明确规定大学英语课程教学应使学生"了解国外的社会与文化，增进对不同文化的理解，加强对中外文化异同的认识，培养跨文化交际能力"。《指南》指出人文性的核心是"以人为本，弘扬人的价值，注重人的综合素质培养和全面发展。社会主义核心价值观应有机融入大学英语教学内容"。此外，包括语料库技术在内的信息技术日益广泛地应用于外语教育之中，大大推动了大学英语教学的发展。在这一历史语境下，外教社组织了上海交通大学、北京交通大学和上海外国语大学等高校的师资，编写了"新时代大学应用英语"系列教材，包括《综合教程》和《视听说教程》。

　　本系列教材紧扣《指南》关于大学英语课程性质、教学目标和教学要求、评价与测试及教学方法和教学手段等方面的要求，充分反映国家对于外语人才培养的要求，体现我国大学英语教学改革与发展的最新趋势和动向。

一、教材特色

　　本系列教材的编写凸显大学英语教学的人文性和应用性，注重课程思政与教学内容的有机融合，重视语料库技术在大学英语教学中的应用。本系列教材的特色主要表现为以下三方面：

1. 人文性与应用性并重

　　本系列教材注重提供人文、社会与自然等方面的阅读材料和听力材料，包括关于中国文化内容的文章，尤其是与西方文化习俗或概念既有关联又有差异的中国文化内容的文章，并适当选择科普或相关专业方面的文章。课文内容强调贴近现实，反映学校生活，且具有趣味性、应用性和思想性，能够引领学生的思想发展，有助于培养学生的批判性思维。

　　本系列教材还重视练习设计的应用性，相关练习的设计着眼于实际问题的解决，尽量结合真实的语言应用场景和学习者的个人生活体验。《综合教程》的语言功能板块（Language Functions），着重介绍和操练与实际生活场景相关的英语知识和技能，包括如何作自我介绍、如何制定日程等；写作板块（Writing）不仅介绍了基本的写作技能，帮助学生学习传统形式的作文，还介绍了邀请信、投诉信、申请信、简历、通知、会议备忘录、收据、产品介绍和产品使用说明等应用文的写作技能。《视听说教程》的工作技能板块（Work Skills）和功能板块（Functions）的语言素材源自实际生活和工作中的语言应用场景，如处理投诉和视频会议等，培养学生的语言实操能力。

2. 全方位体现课程思政元素

本系列教材的编写强调全方位体现课程思政元素。一方面，选材和练习题均蕴含课程思政元素。其中部分练习题含体现中国文化要素、反映中国社会巨大进步的内容。教师用书注重课程思政的教学指导，方便老师组织相关讨论和活动。另一方面，每个单元均提供与主题密切相关的中外名言警句，以帮助学生领悟古今贤能的智慧和思想，形成正确的世界观、人生观和价值观。其中，中国名言警句帮助学生领会中国思想和中国文化的精华并掌握其英语表达。

3. 以语料库的应用为基础

本系列教材的《综合教程》编写以自主研发的"应用学科英语学习语料库"（Corpus of Applied Disciplines for English Learning，简称为CADEL）的应用为基础。首先，我们利用语料库技术，在对课文难易度进行量化分析的基础之上，控制课文难度，并根据难易度编排课文顺序，从而确保课文编排的科学性。其次，我们借助语料库技术统计文章所含单词的词频，生成每篇课文的词表。最后，我们应用语料库，提取每篇课文的高频词、重点词汇或短语以及相关句法结构，并在分析这些语料的基础上编写相关练习题，保证课文练习的真实性和针对性。每个单元均设有基于语料库的语言知识训练练习（Corpora in Language Learning），考察和培养学生运用语料库学习英语的能力，考察的内容包括构词法、词汇搭配、词汇应用、句法、主题和体裁等。

二、教材架构

本系列教材由《综合教程》和《视听说教程》组成，总主编为上海外国语大学胡开宝。

《综合教程》旨在全面提高学生的英语语言技能及英语综合应用能力，从而能够运用英语解决生活或工作中遇到的实际问题。

《综合教程》共4册，由吴勇、赵晓红、胡开宝主编。《综合教程》学生用书每册设8个单元。每个单元包括Lead-in、Reading to Learn、Corpora in Language Learning、Writing、Language Functions、Reading to Explore等部分。每个单元包含A、B两篇阅读课文，选文兼具人文性和应用性，并尽量保持原汁原味。每个单元的Lead-in部分采用视频、音频、图片、问答等多种形式激发学生的学习兴趣。针对课文，设计了丰富多样的练习，聚焦语言基本功及应用能力训练，不仅包括课文主题讨论、篇章结构分析，还包括重点词汇、构词法、搭配、语法的练习。基于语料库的应用，设计了与构词、搭配、句型、篇章相关的练习。写作板块则侧重应用英语写作技能的训练。此外，每单元提供思政话题讨论，以帮助学生提高团队合作能力和思想素养。针对Corpora in Language Learning这一部分，配有CADEL语料库。

《视听说教程》旨在提高学生在真实生活或工作场景中的英语听说能力，培养学生的批判性思维。

《视听说教程》共4册，由李京平主编。《视听说教程》学生用书每册设8个单元，每个单元由Lead-in、Focus Listening、Work Skills、Functions、Viewing和Extended Listening等部分组成。Lead-in部分采用多样形式导入每单元的内容。Focus Listening、Viewing和Extended Listening等部分侧重于训练学生在真实生活和工作场景中的英语听力技能。Work Skills和Functions等部分侧重于提升学生职场英语听力及口语交际能力。本教程练习的设计强调多样、有趣、真实，从而激发学生的学习兴趣，培养学生的英语应用能力。

三、教材使用建议

本系列教材可充分满足《指南》提出的基础级和提高级的教学要求，适用于应用型高校及职教本科，其他类型的高校可以根据本校学生的实际情况和教学目标选择使用。

本系列教材中的《综合教程》和《视听说教程》可以作为主干教材用于大学英语教学。新生英语基础较好的学校可以选用该系列教材中的3-4册或2-4册。新生英语基础较弱的学校可以使用该系列教材的1-4册。

本系列教材在策划和编写过程中得到了上海外语教育出版社高等教育事业部策划编辑、文字编辑、美术编辑的大力支持。在此谨向他们表示感谢。

由于编者水平有限，加之时间仓促，教材中难免有疏漏与不足，敬请广大师生予以批评指正。

胡开宝

编者的话

  《综合教程》系"新时代大学应用英语"的主干教材，根据《大学英语教学指南》（2020版）（以下称《指南》）编写，旨在让学生在听、说、读、写、译等方面得到系统训练，以提高学生英语综合应用能力，尤其是职场英语交际能力，培养学生的自主学习能力和批判思维能力，并对学生进行思想政治引领。本教程秉承建构主义教学理念，强调让学生在语言应用和自主探索过程中提高英语综合应用能力。

一、编写目标

  本教程的编写旨在帮助学生打下扎实的英语语言基本功。

  首先，通过本教程的系统学习，学生的英语听、说、读、写、译能力能够达到《指南》提出的基础目标及提高目标。通过学习，学生能够较好地应用英语语音、词汇、语法及语篇结构等语言知识，了解中外不同的文化价值观，掌握必要的英语学习策略，提高英语理解能力以及口头和书面交流能力。

  其次，提升学生的英语应用能力和职场英语交际能力，尤其是邀请信、投诉信、产品介绍和产品使用说明等英语应用文的写作能力，为学生今后从事相关工作打下坚实的基础。

  再次，通过基于语料库的英语语言知识训练，培养学生运用语料库技术对英语构词法、词汇搭配、句法结构以及语篇等语言知识进行自主探索和归纳的能力。

  最后，本教程介绍中西文化知识，培养学生的跨文化交际能力和批判思维能力，提高学生使用英语介绍中国文化的能力。

二、编写理念

1. 秉承建构主义原则，以学生为中心

  本教程在课文内容和练习设计两方面，均体现以学生为中心的教学理念。课文内容充分考虑学生的认知能力与知识结构，选择生活话题及一般社会话题的文章。练习设计不仅包含基本知识点的操练与巩固，还强调学生自主学习、自主探究能力培养，通过鼓励学生独立学习、配对讨论、小组讨论、完成项目等方式，提高学生语言应用能力、批判性思维及解决问题的能力。

2. 突出应用性

  本教程编写强调英语的应用性，即工具性。无论是课文的选文，还是知识技能的

介绍以及课文练习的设计，均以英语的实际使用为导向，尽量切合学生生活和未来工作的需要，着力培养学生的英语应用能力。

3. 尽量保持课文的原汁原味

本教程的选文注重趣味性、人文性与应用性，并依据文章的难易度，确定课文的编排顺序，尽量不对课文进行改编。

4. 重视信息技术的应用

本教程的编写重视多媒体、语料库等信息技术的应用。除了传统纸质教材，该教程还配有网络学习平台以及语料库。借助于这些信息技术，学生可以根据学习兴趣选择个性化的学习材料，进行自主学习和探索式学习。

5. 重视课程思政元素与教材内容之间的有机融合

本教程的编写强调将课程思政元素融入教材内容。课程思政元素蕴含于教材内容的方方面面。无论是课文内容的选择，还是课后讨论题和练习题的设计，均蕴含着课程思政元素。

三、教材构成

《综合教程》共4册，由学生用书和教师用书组成。每册8个单元。

学生用书每个单元包括6个部分：

1. Lead-in

Lead-in部分是根据单元内容而设计的导入练习。练习内容生动有趣，形式丰富多彩，包括插图、视听材料、调查问卷、游戏等，帮助学生初步了解单元内容，激发学生学习兴趣，为接下来的学习做好准备。

2. Reading to Learn

Reading to Learn是课堂教学的重点部分，包括Text A、课文生词与短语注释、专有名词注释、课文背景知识介绍以及课文配套练习。Text A涵盖的主题多种多样，不仅介绍人文、社会与自然等方面的知识，而且力求反映实际生活和工作。配套练习形式多样，富有趣味性，避免程式化；练习用例尽量保持原汁原味。练习设计一方面注重英语语言及英语学习策略等知识的传授，一方面侧重于英语综合应用能力的培养。包括：

- 课文理解练习，包括问答题、多项选择题、课文结构分析填空题等
- 词汇练习，包括课文重点生词和词组的练习题
- 构词法练习，包括构词法知识介绍和构词法练习题
- 搭配练习，包括课文关键词的搭配知识介绍和搭配练习题
- 语法练习，包括语法知识介绍和语法练习题
- 翻译练习，包括英译汉和汉译英练习题

3. Corpora in Language Learning

Corpora in Language Learning部分是本教程的特色之一。该部分练习要求学生利用语料库工具，根据特定条件检索语料库，探究构词法、词汇搭配、句式结构、篇章主题等内容，从而学习如何根据真实的语料探索语言使用的规律。基于语料库的英语知识训练有助于提高学生的自主学习能力，加深对英语语言规律及知识的了解。

4. Writing

Writing部分也是本教材的特色之一。一、二册主要介绍基本的英语写作技能，包括如何写主题句、如何用不同方法展开段落、如何写开头段、如何写结尾段等；三、四册侧重应用文写作，包括邀请信、投诉信、申请信、简历、通知、产品使用说明等的写作。在介绍写作技巧的同时还提供写作范例，便于学生理解所学内容，并在练习时模仿参考。写作练习话题切合学生生活，形式多样，帮助学生学以致用，提高英语应用写作能力。

5. Language Functions

Language Functions部分是本教材的又一特色。该部分着重介绍和操练实际生活中的英语知识和技能，包括如何作自我介绍、如何制定日程、如何谈论价格、如何描述食品、如何使用机场英语等，内容丰富，形式活泼，旨在培养学生的英语实际应用能力。

6. Reading to Explore

Reading to Explore部分主要是Text B的学习，包括Text B、课文生词与短语注释、专有名词注释、课文背景知识介绍以及课文配套练习。配套练习包括：

- 课文理解练习，包括问答题、多项选择题、对错题、段落信息匹配题等
- 词汇练习，包括课文重点生词、词组填空练习题

建议每个单元的教学以Text A为主，Text B为辅。两篇课文的观点有时相辅相成，有时互相对立，目的在于拓宽学生视野，加深学生对主题思想的了解。在组织Text A教学时，老师可布置学生提前阅读课文，并要求他们根据课文阅读理解练习和课文结构练习了解课文主题思想和重要细节，理清作者思维脉络；课堂上则可先检查学生对课文思想和结构的把握，然后帮助学生基于课文进行英语学习，比如解释难词难句、操练生词用法、讲解典型句式、讲解构词法等，最后可组织学生就课文相关的话题或教参提供的相关思政话题进行小组讨论，培养学生使用英语的能力和批判性思维能力。对Text B，老师可以布置学生课外自学，并要求他们完成课后练习，以备课堂检查。

另外，对于每单元的Corpora in Language Learning，Writing以及Language Functions部分，老师需要安排一定的课堂时间进行专门教学，并要求学生课后进行练习。

教师用书主要包括以下5个部分：

1. Introduction

该部分为课文总体介绍，简要介绍课文主题、篇章结构和写作方法。

2. Teaching Suggestions

该部分就课堂教学环节和教学方法提出建议。主要包括Sayings、Lead-in、Text A 及部分练习（包括课程思政讨论题）、Corpora in Language Learning、Writing、Language Functions的教学目标和教学步骤，以及Text B的教学目标、教学步骤及课文概要。

3. Detailed Study of Text A

该部分提供Text A的详细教学资料，主要包括：

1) Background Information：与Text A相关的背景资料，如历史语境和文化信息等；

2) Understanding the Text：Text A课文内容的段落大意和细节的理解，主要以问答方式对课文的整体结构和内容进行梳理；

3) Language Points：Text A长难句解释、重要生词释义与举例、重点句式讲解以及句子所涉文化背景知识的介绍等。

4. Keys to Exercises

该部分提供单元练习的答案。

5. Text Translation

该部分提供Text A和Text B的译文。

四、编写团队

《综合教程》主编为上海交通大学的吴勇、赵晓红和上海外国语大学的胡开宝，副主编为上海交通大学的李玲、潘之欣、顾凯。主编及副主编为上海交通大学外国语学院英语系和大学英语国家级教学团队以及上海外国语大学语科库研究院的骨干教师。这些教师教学经验丰富，曾参加过多部国家级规划教材的编写工作。在本教程的编写过程中，上海外语教育出版社给予了大量的支持，国内外多名专家给予了指导，教材也凝聚了他们的经验和智慧。对以上同仁的支持和帮助，编写组表示由衷的感谢。

胡开宝

Table of Contents

1 SPREAD YOUR IDEAS

PART I Introduction

Public speaking has always been a big concern for many people. Stepping out onto the stage and putting yourself under the spotlight can be a terrifying experience. It requires both courage and skill to be a good speaker. In this unit, we shall learn how we can start with an idea worth sharing and make an impressive speech. Text A is a story about the speech made by Chris Anderson, the head of TED, in 2002, in which he tried hard to persuade TED attendees that the conference would continue just fine. Through his story, he tries to show that content is more important than style. Text B continues to elaborate on this idea. Chris Anderson argues that the most important thing for a speaker is not confidence, stage presence or smooth talking but to say something that is worth saying. In this unit, we shall also discuss the importance of sharing ideas with the world, the benefits of communicating effectively and the ways to develop good communication skills. Hopefully, after learning this unit, you will embark on your journey towards becoming a good speaker and a successful communicator.

In this unit you will:
1 Read a story about making a speech poor in style but strong in idea;
2 Learn the importance of making an effective speech with a great idea;
3 Learn the benefits of sharing ideas and developing good communication skills;
4 Learn how the suffix -y or -ly combines with a noun to form an adjective;
5 Learn nouns that collocate with the verb "preserve";
6 Learn about the use of the past perfect subjunctive mood in different situations;
7 Learn nouns that collocate with *dense/intense/tense* by using CADEL;
8 Learn to write a paragraph using the problem-solution pattern;
9 Learn to speak convincingly by using persuasive expressions.

PART II Teaching Suggestions

Sayings

Learning objectives:

- Get a general idea of the unit
- Get inspirations from the sayings
- Get useful advice and guidance from famous people or books
- Learn to develop a positive attitude toward life

Teaching steps:

1. Ask students to translate the two sayings into Chinese.

    Reference translations for the sayings:

    - 听君一席话，胜读十年书。 ——《增广贤文》
    - 若你口吐心声，便可侃侃而谈。 ——约翰·福特

2. For the first saying, tell students the importance of sharing ideas with others. The saying is quoted from *The Wisdom of Ancient Aphorisms*, a book which collects aphorisms（格言）, folk proverbs, sages' sayings, as well as insightful expressions. The quote suggests that sharing ideas with others is an important way to learn more about the world and improve oneself. Only through sharing and communicating with others can people become well-informed, well-learned and more open-minded. Sharing ideas leads to not only individual progress but also societal progress. Encourage students to reflect on how cultural exchanges can contribute to a deeper understanding and a stronger relationship between China and the rest of the world.

3. The second saying is a quote from John Ford, an American film director. Ask students to think about what it takes to create a successful speech. One key to a successful speech is to show the audience your true ideas and feelings as well as your own goals and needs. In other words, authenticity and sincerity are important. If you do things with authenticity and sincerity, people will trust you, and you will find it easier to get across your ideas.

Lead-in

Learning objectives:

- Learn about what TED talks are
- Learn about some TED talks and different views on the talks

Teaching steps:

1. Make a brief introduction to the unit and explain its learning objectives.
2. Ask students to do Exercises I and II. Encourage students to share the best TED talk they have ever watched.

Reading to Learn

Text A

The Day TED Might Have Died

Learning objectives:

- Learn the importance of making an effective speech with a great idea
- Learn about the text organization pattern: the pattern of presenting a problem and then a solution

Teaching steps:

1 Introduce the topic of Text A: How a good idea made a great speech, which helped with the smooth transition of TED.
2 Ask students to read the first two paragraphs to see what difficult situation the author had to face.
3 Ask students to go through the whole text and divide it into three parts. After that, ask them to look at the Text Organization exercise to check if they have made the same division. The text can be divided as follows: Part 1 (Paras. 1–2), Part 2 (Paras. 3–8) and Part 3 (Paras. 9–11).
4 Go to Part III Detailed Study of Text A. Help students understand difficult sentences in the text accurately. Introduce important new words and expressions with explanations and examples.
5 Ask students to do the exercises following the text.

Critical Thinking

Learning objectives:

- Discuss what makes a successful speaker
- Reflect on the importance of sharing ideas with others
- Discuss the benefits of communicating effectively and the ways to improve communication skills

Teaching steps:

1 Ask students to read the questions first and then give them some ideas on how to approach each question.
2 For Question 1, ask students to discuss the importance of conveying a good idea in a speech. Your audience is giving you their time and expects to get some unique information or idea from you. A speech that has no point is a waste of time. An idea worth sharing will make the speech interesting, convincing and powerful. Encourage students to think of more advantages a good idea brings to a speech.
3 For Question 2, introduce the following quote from Thomas Watson, who was chairman and CEO of IBM: "The great accomplishments of man have resulted from the transmission of ideas of enthusiasm." Ask students if they agree with this quote and encourage them to think about

the benefits of sharing ideas with each other, particularly among their fellow classmates. Sharing ideas deepens our own knowledge, makes us a good team member, opens wider possibilities, and makes our dreams come true. Encourage students to discuss the benefits of sharing ideas in study groups, during conferences, on forums, in blogs, and so on.

4   For Question 3, ask students to discuss the benefits of communicating effectively and the ways to develop good communication skills. Being able to communicate effectively is one of the most important life skills. Successful communication helps us get our ideas across to others and better understand people and situations. It helps us to build trust and respect and is conducive to preventing or solving problems. It enables us to be more creative and productive. It leads to success both in life and work. The following are a few ways to develop good communication skills:

- Show respect
- Be a good listener
- Try to understand the feelings of those around you
- Be aware of your body language and tone of voice
- Be ready to collaborate with others
- Always have an open mind

5   Ask students to work in pairs or small groups to share their opinions. Encourage each pair or group to present their favorite ideas in class.

Corpora in Language Learning

Learning objectives:

- Learn to search CADEL for nouns that collocate with *dense/intense/tense* with "dense/intense/tense *" as the search terms, using the "Concordance" function of AntConc
- Learn to translate the collocations of "dense/intense/tense + noun" into Chinese
- Learn to complete the given sentences with *dense/intense/tense* based on the contexts in which they appear

Teaching steps:

1   Demonstrate how to search CADEL for nouns that collocate with *dense/intense/tense* with "dense/intense/tense *" as the search terms, using the "Concordance" function of AntConc. Ask students to identify the nouns that begin with the given letters. Remind students that some collocating nouns may not come right next to *dense/intense/tense*, and that they should search the context for the collocating nouns.

2   Demonstrate how to sort the search results by setting KWIC sort.

3   Compare the use of *dense*, *intense* and *tense*.

4   Discuss the use of the collocations "dense/intense/tense + noun" and their Chinese translations.

Writing

Learning objectives:

- Learn to identify the problem-solution pattern in a paragraph
- Learn to write a paragraph using the problem-solution pattern

Teaching steps:

1 Introduce the problem-solution pattern and illustrate it through the given example.
2 Ask students to do Exercise I in class to reinforce the idea of the problem-solution pattern in writing.
3 Ask students to do Exercise II after class.

Language Functions

Learning objectives:

- Learn some persuasive expressions
- Learn to discuss the advantages and disadvantages of taking a minor in college and use persuasive expressions to convince others

Teaching steps:

1 Ask students to read the given persuasive expressions.
2 Ask students to work in groups to discuss the advantages and disadvantages of taking a minor in college. Encourage students to give their own opinions.
3 After finishing group discussion, each group should choose one side: either for or against the idea of taking a minor in college. The key is to use as many persuasive expressions as possible.

Reading to Explore

Text B

Start with the Idea

Learning objectives:

- Understand the use of new words and expressions based on the context and through related exercises
- Collect the most important information in each paragraph
- Learn the importance of making a powerful speech with an idea worth sharing
- Learn to make an accurate assessment of one's own strengths
- Learn to keep searching for a unique idea to share

Teaching steps:

1   Ask students to read the text and finish the exercises following the text before class.

2   Check answers to the exercises.

3   Ask students to read Paras. 7–9. Ask them to check if they have something unique to share and what problems they have about themselves in sharing a good idea. Ask students to double-check their self-assessment with the help of their partner.

4   Encourage students to share with their partner a unique experience of theirs regarding a successful or unsuccessful communication/persuasion and the lesson they can draw from the experience, if they have one.

Summary of Text B

The excerpt introduces the main thesis of the book *TED Talks: The Official TED Guide to Public Speaking* by Chris Anderson: the key to a powerful talk is not confidence, stage presence, or smooth talking, but an idea worth sharing with the audience. The idea can range from a scientific breakthrough to a simple method or a simple story, as long as it can change people's way of seeing the world. Undoubtedly, anyone can have some unique experiences to share, only many don't know how to tell a good story. Therefore, in order to win the audience, one has to explore their own strengths and keep searching for something that has some depth.

PART III   Detailed Study of Text A

The Day TED Might Have Died

Background Information

1   **TED:** TED大会

Beginning in 1984, TED was a conference where Technology, Entertainment and Design converged. It is now a nonprofit organization aiming to spread ideas through short and powerful talks, which are usually under 18 minutes long. Today TED talks cover various topics from science to business to global issues in over 100 languages.

2   **Richard Saul Wurman:** 理查德·索尔·沃尔曼

Richard Saul Wurman, born in 1935, is an American architect and graphic designer. Wurman has created the TED conference, the EG conference, TEDMED, and the WWW Conference. Moreover, he has written, designed and published nearly a hundred books on divergent topics.

3   **Jeff Bezos:** 杰夫·贝佐斯

Jeff Bezos, born in 1965 in New Mexico, is an American technology entrepreneur, investor, and philanthropist. He is best known as the founder and CEO of Amazon.

4   **Amazon:** 亚马逊公司

Founded in 1994, Amazon is an American electronic commerce company based in Seattle, Washington. At first Amazon was just an online bookstore, but now it sells a large variety of products, such as software, electronics, furniture, food, and jewelry.

5   **dot-com:** 网络公司

A dot-com company, using a website with the top-level domain ".com", conducts most of its business on the Internet.

Understanding the Text

Part 1 (Paras. 1–2)

Ask students to read Paras. 1–2 and answer the following question:

What difficult situation did the author have to face? (Richard Saul Wurman, the owner and host of TED, was leaving. The TED community was concerned that TED probably couldn't survive after Wurman left. The author, as the new leader, had to persuade the community to support him. He had one chance and one chance only to persuade them.)

Part 2 (Paras. 3–8)

1   Ask students to read Paras. 3–5 and find out what makes the author weak as a public speaker. (He says *um* and *you know* far too often and pauses frequently. He can sound overly earnest, soft-spoken, and conceptual. He tries to be humorous but often in vain. That day, he was very nervous and he wasn't dressed appropriately either.)

2   Ask students to read Paras. 5–8 and find out how the author made a successful speech. (He had prepared carefully, spoke sincerely, tried hard to be open, and expressed his strong belief that TED was such a unique place for sharing wonderful ideas that we couldn't let it die.)

3   Ask students to share what weaknesses or strengths they have in making a public speech.

Part 3 (Paras. 9–11)

Ask students to read Paras. 9–11 and answer the following question:

What was the key to the success of the author's speech? (Question 4 in Exercise II of Reading Comprehension) (He convinced the audience that TED was unique not only because the founder was great but also because it was a good place to share ideas.)

Language Points

1   When I first **took over** leadership of TED in late 2001, I was **reeling from** the near **collapse** of the company I had spent fifteen years building, and I was terrified of another huge public failure. (**Para. 1**)

Paraphrase: Near the end of 2001, when I first took charge of TED, I was still feeling shocked and upset because the company I had spent fifteen years building nearly failed. So I was extremely afraid of facing another big failure in public.

take over: take control of sth. 接管，接任

Some asserted that it was only a matter of time before robots **took over** most human jobs.

reel: *v.* be confused or shocked by a situation 茫然，震惊

Her mind **reeled** when she learned she had failed the test.

reel from: feel very confused or shocked about sth. 因……而晕头转向，心烦意乱

While still **reeling from** the deadly flooding last month, the local residents had to face a major typhoon in two weeks.

collapse: *n.* a sudden failure in the way sth. works, so that it cannot continue 突然失败，倒闭，崩溃

The oldest bridge was in danger of **collapse** after the worst storm in 30 years hit the city.

2 I had been struggling to persuade the TED **community** to back my **vision** for TED, and I feared that it might just **fizzle out**. **(Para. 1)**

Paraphrase: I had been trying hard to convince the TED group to support my idea for TED, and I was afraid that they might just become less interested and thus TED might gradually disappear.

community: *n.* a group of people of the same interests, religion, race, etc. 群体，团体

The Chinese business **community** will continue to promote fair trade and international cooperation.

vision: *n.* an idea of what you think sth. should be like 构想，设想，念头

The school has been set up with the **vision** of providing the best education facilities to its students.

fizzle out: gradually stop happening, esp. because people become less interested 渐停，夭折

Most of us have a group of best friends in college but some friendships **fizzle out** in the end.

3 Back then, TED was an annual **conference** in California, owned and hosted by a **charismatic** architect named Richard Saul Wurman. **(Para. 1)**

Paraphrase: At that time, TED was a large meeting held in California once a year, and it was owned and organized by Richard Saul Wurman, a charming architect.

conference: *n.* a large formal meeting for discussion or exchange of views（大型、正式的）会议

This important **conference** is attended by all the leading companies and professionals.

charismatic: *adj.* having the power to inspire devotion and enthusiasm 有超凡魅力的，有感召力的

With such a **charismatic** personality, he always makes people around smile along with him.

4 About 800 people attended every year, and most of them seemed **resigned** to the fact that TED probably couldn't **survive** once Wurman **departed**. **(Para. 2)**

Paraphrase: About 800 people went to the meeting every year, and most of them seemed to be ready to accept the situation that once Wurman left TED, it probably couldn't continue to exist.

resigned: *adj.* being willing to calmly accept sth. unpleasant or difficult that you cannot change 逆来顺受的，顺从的

be resigned to (doing) sth. 无奈地接受某事物

At the age of 40, Bill was **resigned** to the fact that his football career was over and accepted an offer to work as a TV host.

survive: *v.* continue to live or exist 生存，存活；继续存在

The box of glasses **survived** the long journey and arrived safe and sound.

depart: *v.* leave an organization or job 脱离（某组织），离（职）

In the following season, many ageing soccer players will **depart** after years of service.

5　The TED conference of February 2002 was the last one to be held under his leadership, and I had one chance and one chance only to persuade TED **attendees** that the conference would continue just fine. (**Para. 2**)

Paraphrase: The TED conference of February 2002 was the last conference to be held with Richard Saul Wurman as the leader, and this was the only chance for me to convince the TED conference participants that TED would be just fine after Wurman left.

attendee: *n.* sb. who is at an event such as a meeting or a course 出席者

The **attendees** must wear their admission badge throughout the conference.

6　I had never run a conference before, however, and despite my best efforts over several months at marketing the following year's event, only 70 people had **signed up for** it. (**Para. 2**)

Paraphrase: I had never organized a large meeting before, however, and although I spent quite a few months trying my best to persuade people to attend the next year's TED event, only 70 people arranged to take part in it.

sign up (for): put your name on a list for sth. because you want to take part in it 报名

Runners, joggers and even walkers can all **sign up for** the charity race to raise funds for the children's hospital.

7　I will stop **halfway** through a sentence, trying to find the right word to continue. (**Para. 3**)

Paraphrase: I will pause in the middle of a sentence, and try to find the proper word to go on.

halfway: at a middle point in space or time between two things 在……的中间，在中途

It's going to be a long ride, so the tour bus will have a stop for food and break **halfway**.

8　I can sound overly earnest, **soft-spoken**, and **conceptual**. (**Para. 3**)

Paraphrase: I can sound too serious, too tender, and too abstract.

soft-spoken: *adj.* having a gentle and quiet voice 声音柔和的，说话温柔的

After we chose our table, a very nice **soft-spoken** waitress came over and took our order.

conceptual: *adj.* relating to ideas and principles 概念（上）的

This plan is only a **conceptual** design now, and there will be several public hearings in the future to decide on the details.

9　My **quirky** British sense of humor is not always shared by others. (**Para. 3**)

Paraphrase: I try to be funny with my unusual British sense of humor, but others do not always get it.

quirky: *adj.* unusual, esp. in an interesting way 离奇的，古怪的，奇特的

Buck is a **quirky** guy who always drinks brandy before his shows.

10　I look back at that talk now and **cringe** — a lot. (**Para. 5**)

Paraphrase: Now when I think about that talk, I feel embarrassed — greatly.

cringe: *v.* feel very embarrassed and uncomfortable about sth. 感到尴尬不安；觉得难为情

I **cringe** when I think of the poems I wrote then.

11　If I were **critiquing** it today, there are a hundred things I would change, starting with the **wrinkly** white T-shirt I was wearing. (**Para. 5**)

Paraphrase: If I were reviewing the talk today, there are many things I would change, the first being the wrinkled white T-shirt I was wearing.

critique: *v.* say how good or bad a book, play, painting, or set of ideas is 评论

As a teacher, I **critique** my students' work for their good.

wrinkly: *adj.* covered in wrinkles 有皱纹的

Have you ever stayed in a pool so long that your fingers got **wrinkly**?

12 And yet ... I had prepared carefully what I wanted to say, and I knew there were at least some in the audience **desperate** for TED to survive. **(Para. 5)**

Paraphrase: But I had prepared my talk carefully, and I knew at least some of the listeners wanted TED to continue to exist very much.

desperate: *adj.* needing or wanting sth. very much 非常需要，极想

After having lost three games, the team is **desperate** for a win.

13 If I could just give those supporters a reason to get excited, perhaps they would **turn things around**. **(Para. 5)**

Paraphrase: If I could just provide the supporters with one reason that could make them excited, perhaps they would help TED start being successful again.

turn (sth.) around: stop being unsuccessful and start being successful（使）好转

You should **turn** your life **around** before it's too late.

14 Because of the recent dot-com **bust**, many in the audience had suffered business losses as bad as my own. Maybe I could connect with them that way? **(Para. 5)**

Paraphrase: Since recently Internet-based companies had suffered complete failures, many people in the audience had experienced losses in their business like I did. Perhaps I could reach them by sharing this common experience?

bust: *n.* a complete failure 彻底的失败

Her mom's real estate business turned out to be a **bust**, as she never sold a single house.

15 I spoke from the heart, with as much openness and **conviction** as I could **summon**. **(Para. 6)**

Paraphrase: I spoke sincerely, trying my best to be honest and show my strong belief in TED.

conviction: *n.* the feeling of being sure about sth. and having no doubts 深信，坚信，肯定

There can be no teamwork unless we have the **conviction** that every person matters.

summon: *v.* try very hard to have enough of sth. such as courage, energy, or strength 鼓起（勇气），振作（精神），使出（力气）

If you **summon** all the energy that you have, nothing is ever so hard.

16 I told people I had just gone through a **massive** business failure. That I'd **come to** think of myself as a complete loser. That the only way I'd survived mentally was by **immersing myself in** the world of ideas. **(Para. 6)**

Paraphrase: I told people that I had just experienced a huge business loss. I told them that I had begun to think I was a total failure. I told them that in order to avoid a mental breakdown, the only way I could do is to become completely involved in the field of ideas.

Note: Following the sentence "I told people I had just gone through a massive business failure", there are six clauses starting with "that". These clauses are elliptical clauses（省略句），each having "I told people" left out. The author leaves out "I told people" to highlight the information that he told others.

massive: *adj.* unusually large, powerful, or damaging 巨大的，强大的，强烈的

The Three Gorges Dam is a **massive** project which greatly increases China's electricity production capacity.

come to do sth.: begin to have a feeling or opinion 开始认为，开始觉得

Gradually he **came to** realize that something was seriously wrong.

immerse: *v.* put sb. or sth. deep into a liquid so that they are completely covered 使浸没

To get an accurate temperature reading, the thermometer must be **immersed** in the water.

immerse oneself in: become completely involved in an activity 使沉浸在，使专心于

As a young architect, Catherine visits museums every week as she wants a chance to **immerse herself in** the arts.

17 That TED had come to **mean the world to** me — that it was a unique place where ideas from every discipline could be shared. That I would do all in my power to **preserve** its best values. **(Para. 6)**

Paraphrase: I told people that TED had become very important to me — that it was a rare place where people can share with each other ideas from different fields. That I would try as much as I can to maintain its best values.

mean the world to: used for emphasizing that sb./sth. is very important to sb. 对……来说至关重要，是……的一切

Tony says it **means the world to** him to be able to inspire those kids.

preserve: *v.* make sth. continue without changing 保持，维持

China has taken increasingly tough measures to **preserve** the panda's habitat.

18 That, **in any case**, the conference had brought such intense inspiration and learning to us that we couldn't possibly let it die … could we? **(Para. 6)**

Paraphrase: I told people that, whatever happened, TED had been so inspiring and educational that we could by no means let it die ... could we?

in any case: whatever happens or happened 无论如何，不管怎样

It's important to have a lawyer check the contract for you to make sure that you will not be responsible for any loss **in any case**.

19 **To my utter amazement**, at the end of the talk, Jeff Bezos, the head of Amazon, who was seated in the center of the audience, **rose to his feet** and began clapping. **(Para. 7)**

Paraphrase: I was completely surprised that, at the end of the talk, Jeff Bezos, the head of Amazon, who was sitting in the middle of the audience, stood up and began to clap his hands.

utter: *adj.* complete 完全的，十足的，彻底的

What he said is **utter** nonsense as he knows nothing about it.

to sb.'s amazement/surprise/annoyance/... in a way that amazes/surprises/annoys/... sb. 使某人诧异/吃惊/烦恼……的是

To my amazement, the restaurant is still full at 9 p.m.

rise to one's feet: stand up after you have been sitting 站起身来

As soon as Linda put down her book and **rose to her feet**, Clegg stood up too.

20 It was as if the TED community had collectively decided, in just a few seconds, that it would support this new chapter of TED **after all**. **(Para. 7)**

Paraphrase: It was as if the TED people had made a group decision in a very short time that they would support this new phase of TED despite earlier doubts.

after all: in spite of what has been said, done or expected 毕竟；终究；究竟

Certain parts of the show were quite entertaining, and perhaps it wasn't so bad **after all**.

21 And in the 60-minute break that followed, some 200 people **committed to** buying passes for the following year's conference, guaranteeing its success. **(Para. 7)**

Paraphrase: During the 60-minute break after my talk, about 200 people promised sincerely that they would definitely buy tickets for the next year's TED meeting, and this ensured the success of the conference.

commit: *v.* (**commit to (doing) sth.**) promise sincerely that you will definitely do sth. 承诺；向……保证

I **commit to** spending at least an hour of quality time with my kids every day.

22 If that 15-minute talk had fizzled out, TED would have died, four years before ever putting a talk on the Internet. **(Para. 8)**

Paraphrase: If that 15-minute talk had failed, TED would have died, four years before its talks were ever put on the Internet.

23 I'll share why I think that talk ended up being effective, despite its evident awkwardness. It's an **insight** that can be applied to any talk. **(Para. 9)**

Paraphrase: I'll tell you my understanding of why my speech turned out to be successful although obviously I had done it in an awkward way. It is a thought that can be used for any talk.

insight: *n.* an understanding of what sth. is like 深刻见解

The financial data help gain **insight** into the current activities and developments of the company.

24 There were many things wrong with that talk, but it succeeded in one key **aspect**. **(Para. 10)**

Paraphrase: My talk had many drawbacks, but it was successful in handling one important thing.

aspect: *n.* one part of a situation, idea, plan, etc. 方面

Bruce says that planning is the most important **aspect** of his work.

25 TED's uniqueness **lay in** being a place where people from every discipline could come together and understand each other. **(Para. 10)**

Paraphrase: TED is special in that it provides a place for people from different fields to meet and learn about each other's experiences, values and beliefs.

lie in: exist or be found in sth. 在于

The secret of success **lies in** building the daily habits for high achievement.

26 This **cross-fertilization** really mattered for the world, and therefore the conference would be given **nonprofit** status and **held in trust for public good**. **(Para. 10)**

Paraphrase: That different people exchange their ideas, customs, methods, etc. is really important for the world. This is why we would make the conference a non-business organization and have another organization manage its finance for the interest of the public.

cross-fertilization: *n.* an exchange of ideas, customs, methods, etc. between different people or groups（思想、习惯、方法等的）交流

The role of the coordinator will be to encourage **cross-fertilization** of ideas among the people involved in the program.

nonprofit: *adj.* not seeking or producing a profit or profits 非营利性的，非谋利的

Starting a **nonprofit** organization can be an inspiring way to give back to your community and help those in need.

be held in trust: have sb.'s property or money legally held or managed by sb. else or by an organization 代管，托管

The money raised for school projects will **be held in trust** by the School Board.

for ... good/for the good of: in order to help sb. or improve a situation 为了……的利益/好处

He does many bold deeds **for the good of** his friends.

27 This idea changed the way the audience thought about the TED **transition**. (Para. 11)
Paraphrase: This idea made the audience think differently about the change TED was facing.

transition: *n.* the process of changing from one situation, form, or state to another 转变，过渡，变迁

The biggest problem will be making the **transition** from one operation system to the other.

PART IV Keys to Exercises

Reading to Learn

Reading Comprehension

I   1 He was an architect and the owner and host of TED.
  2 TED was undergoing the change of leadership: The owner and host of TED, Richard Saul Wurman, was leaving.
  3 TED probably couldn't survive after Wurman left.
  4 He stood up and began clapping.
  5 They seemed to have collectively decided to support the change of TED, and during the break that followed, some 200 people committed to buying passes for the following year's conference.

II   1 B   2 C   3 D   4 C   5 B

III **Text Organization**

  1 nervous   2 what I wanted to say

  3 my strong belief   4 sharing ideas from every discipline

| 5 clapped | 6 buying passes |
| 7 who took over from the founder | 8 should be preserved |

Language in Use

Words and Expressions

I
| 1 departed | 2 vision | 3 utter | 4 aspect |
| 5 collapse | 6 conviction | 7 survive | 8 desperate |

II
| 1 lies in | 2 sign up for | 3 taken over | 4 immersing yourself in |
| 5 after all | 6 reeling from | 7 been held in trust | 8 in any case |

III
| 1 vision | 2 attendees | 3 halfway | 4 come to | 5 resigned |
| 6 immersing | 7 insight | 8 turn things around | 9 summon | 10 massive |

Word Formation

| 1 juicy | 2 noisy | 3 messy | 4 foggy | 5 scary |
| 6 costly | 7 orderly | 8 timely | 9 manly | 10 brotherly |

Collocation

1 preserve the balance	2 preserve the memory
3 preserve their unique culture	4 preserve peace
5 preserve the way	6 preserve our environment
7 preserve the diversity	8 preserve its value

Grammar and Structure

1 If he had come to the Christmas party, I would have given him the gift.

2 If he had told us about his situation, we could have helped him.

3 I wish my father had been there for my wedding ceremony.

4 If she had woken up earlier this morning, Anna would have caught the first train.

5 I would rather she had asked me before watching that awful movie.

6 He talked as if he had had the firsthand knowledge of the grand project.

7 If there had not been a long queue, I would have bought the popular smartphone.

8 If I had known that you were sick, I would have come to help you.

Translation

I
1 避免失败的唯一希望就在于我们要成为一个团结的队伍。

2 一个成功的产品是巨大需求的结果：用户对你的产品需求越大，就越有可能购买它。

3 没受过教育的她很快发现，经营公司最困难的方面就是她必须处理一大堆的账簿。

4 妈妈是我最重要的人：无论我做什么，她总是在身边支持我。

5 老师的任务是帮助孩子们了解人类经验发展的一些基本方式。

II

1 At first, he just stood there and listened. Then, to my amazement, he said, "I think I agree with you."

2 I believe we're doing the right thing; it's for the good of the company.

3 The Xi'an City Wall represents one of the oldest, largest and best preserved city walls in China.

4 While developing itself, China commits to a win-win strategy of opening up, welcoming other countries to make joint efforts for common development.

5 Start of Autumn in the lunar calendar has always been considered a very important seasonal transition, marking the end of summer and the beginning of autumn.

III Before moveable-type printing was invented, the printing of every new book required the engraving of a full set of wooden boards. If one character was not correctly engraved, the whole board would become useless. Bi Sheng was a printing worker in the Song dynasty. He thought, "Wouldn't it be great to have a more convenient and efficient way to do it?" One day, he saw his two sons playing games by freely arranging pots, bowls, tables and chairs which were made of clay. He suddenly realized that if he engraved characters on clay stamps, he could also arrange them freely into passages. After repeated experiments, Bi Sheng invented the moveable-type printing technology, one of the four great inventions of ancient China.

Corpora in Language Learning

I (There can be more than one answer to some questions here, and to each question only one answer is provided for reference.)

dense/intense/ tense	Nouns that collocate with *dense/intense/tense*	Chinese translations of the collocations
dense	fog	浓雾
	object	高密度的物体
intense	criticism	猛烈的批评
	workout	剧烈的运动
	reaction	强烈的反应
	game	激烈的比赛
	exercise	剧烈的运动
	negotiation	紧张的磋商
tense	environment	紧张的环境
	situation	紧张的局面

II **1** tense   **2** intense   **3** dense   **4** intense   **5** intense

Writing

I **Problem:** Suffering from exam anxiety

Solutions:

1 Get a good night's sleep.

2 Change their poor study habits.

3 Think positive.

Conclusion: These are effective solutions to deal with exam anxiety.

Reading to Explore

Reading Comprehension

I	1 C	2 C	3 D	4 A	5 D
II	1 F	2 F	3 T	4 T	5 T
III	A 5	B 1	C 9	D 4	E 10
	F 6	G 7	H 11	I 8	J 2

Words and Expressions

I	1 breakthrough	2 passionate	3 deserve	4 assignment	5 complex
	6 genius	7 compelling	8 grabbed	9 underestimate	10 awful

II	1 there was something in/to	2 wrapped up in	3 in a very real sense
	4 come to a conclusion	5 searching for	6 conjured up
	7 draw a lesson from	8 is aware of	9 in any case	10 is capable of

PART V Text Translation

Text A

TED大会儿近夭折之日

克里斯·安德森

1 　2001年底我刚接任TED的领导位子时，我正为自己经营了15年的公司濒临倒闭而心烦意乱，害怕在公众面前再次失败。我一直在极力劝说TED社区支持我对TED的愿景，担心它会逐渐消亡。当时，TED还是在加州举办的一项年会，由一位充满魅力的名叫理查德·索尔·沃尔曼的建筑师发起和主办。

2   每年大约有800人参加年会，其中大部分人似乎认定一旦沃尔曼离开，TED就可能不复存在。2002年2月的TED年会是沃尔曼领导下的最后一次大会，而我有一次机会，仅此一次机会，来说服TED的参加者们大会将继续顺利举办。但是，我以前从没主办过大会，尽管我已历经数月努力推广，第二年的活动只有70个人报名。

3   在那届大会的最后一天上午，我有15分钟的时间来阐述我的理由。关于我本人，你要了解以下几点：我不是个天生的大演说家。我经常说太多的"嗯"和"你知道"。我会一句话讲到一半停下来，费力寻找合适的词儿再往下讲。我说话会过于直白，声音太柔和，或者讲得太笼统。我古怪的英式幽默也往往不被人接受。

4   我太害怕这一时刻，太担心自己会下不来台，连站都站不稳。于是我从后台推了一把椅子到台前坐下，开始讲话。

5   现在回头看那次演讲，我自觉难堪——十分难堪。如果把它放到今天来评判，会有太多地方需要改正，我身上那件皱巴巴的白色T恤就首当其冲。不过，演讲内容我已事先悉心准备。我知道至少有一部分观众热切盼望TED能坚持下去。假如我能给这些支持者们一个激动人心的理由，他们或许就能扭转局面。由于近期的互联网公司倒闭潮，许多观众跟我一样在业务上损失惨重。或许，我可以从这方面跟他们交交心？

6   我的演讲发自内心，尽量开诚布公、意志坚定。我告诉大家：我刚刚经历了一场生意上的大失败，我开始觉得自己是一个彻头彻尾的失败者。而让我避免精神崩溃的唯一方法就是让自己沉浸在思想世界里。TED就是我的一切，它是一个分享不同学科思想的独特之所。我将竭尽全力来捍卫它的卓越价值。不管怎样，TED大会给我们带来了如此丰富的启迪和知识，我们绝不能任其消亡……对不对？

7   我万万没想到，演讲结束后，杰夫·贝佐斯——坐在观众席正中央的亚马逊公司老板，起身鼓掌。全场观众也随之起立。似乎整个TED社区在片刻之间就一致决定支持TED开启新篇章。在随后的60分钟休息时间里，约200个人承诺购买下一年大会的入场票，从而确保了大会的成功。

8   假如那次为时15分钟的演讲毫无效果，那么在其演讲首次发布到网上的四年前，TED就已经夭折了。

9   我想分享一下，为什么在明摆着尴尬的情况下，那次演讲能够最终奏效。这其中的奥秘适用于任何演讲。

10   虽说那次演讲破绽百出，但是在一个关键的方面却成功了：我提出了这样的观点，即TED的真正特别之处并非仅仅是我接替的那位创立者。TED的特别之处在于，它是一个不同学科的人们能够相聚一堂、彼此了解的平台。这种跨学科的交流对世界极其重要，因此，为了公众的利益，TED大会具有非盈利性的性质，并由信托机构托管。它的未来属于我们所有人。

11   这一观点扭转了观众对TED转型的看法。创立者的离任已经不再重要。现在重要的是这样一种分享知识的特殊方式应该得到保留。自那以后，TED大会取得了惊人的成就。

Text B

始于想法

克里斯·安德森

1　本书的中心思想就是，任何人只要有值得分享的想法，就能做出精彩的演讲。公众演讲唯一真正重要的并不是自信满满、风度翩翩或口齿流利，而是要有值得讲的想法。

2　这里我所说的"想法"所指范畴较广。它不一定非得是科学突破、天才发明或者繁复的法律理论。它可以是一个简单的指南，或者是借助故事的力量传递的人生见解，一幅富有意义的美丽画面，你希望未来可能发生的一件事情，或者也许仅仅是提醒人们生活中最重要的是什么。

3　想法是能够改变人们世界观的任何事物。假如你能在人们头脑中营造某种令人激动的想法，那么你就做了很了不起的一件事。你给了他们一件无价的礼物。毫不夸张地说，你的一小部分已融入他们之中。

4　你有值得让更多观众倾听的想法吗？令人惊讶的是，我们在回答这一问题时判断力很差。许多演讲者似乎热衷于自己的声音，喜欢连讲几小时却不能分享任何有价值的内容。但是，也有许多人过度低估了自己在工作、学识和思想上的价值。

5　如果你拿起这本书仅仅因为你喜欢在台上神气活现地走来走去，喜欢成为TED演讲明星，喜欢靠你的个人魅力来激励听众，那么请你立即放下本书。相反，你要去寻找值得分享的东西。金玉其外败絮其中是很糟糕的。

6　然而，更可能的是，你拥有很多值得分享的东西却不自知。你不必发明"驱狮灯"。你过的是你自己的生活，而且是你独有的生活。你有自己独特的经历。有些经历可提炼出十分值得分享的见解。你只需找出是哪些见解就可以。

7　你是否对此感到有压力？也许你要完成作业；或者需要在小型会议上展示研究结果；或者你有机会向一家当地扶轮国际机构介绍你的组织，试图获得他们的支持。你可能觉得自己没有干过任何值得宣讲的事情。你没有什么发明。也不是特别有创意。你不觉得自己智力超群。对未来没有任何特别出色的想法。甚至不确定自己有什么特别热衷的爱好。

8　好吧，我承认，这是个困难的起步。为了对得起听众的时间，大多数演讲要求有一定深度的内容。理论上可以说，你目前能做的最好的事情就是继续你的人生旅程，寻找能真正让你兴奋、深入钻研的东西，然后在若干年后重拾本书。

9　但在得出上述结论之前，有必要再确认一下你的自我评估是准确的。也许你只是缺乏自信而已。这里存在着一个矛盾：一直以来你就是你，你只由内审视自己。别人从你身上发现的闪光点也许你自己完全看不到。要找到这些闪光点，你也许要跟那些最了解你的人进行真诚的对话。他们对你有些方面的了解比你自己更清楚。

10　无论如何，你有一样东西别人都没有：你的亲身经历。昨天你目睹了一系列事件，经历了一系列情感体验，这些都是实实在在的独特经历。70亿人中你是唯一拥有这一确切经历的人。所以……你能从中感悟出些什么吗？许多优秀演讲都就是以个人的故事为基础，讲述从中得出的简单道理。你是否有注意到任何令你惊讶的事物呢？也许你看到了几个孩子在公园里玩耍，或者与一个流浪汉交谈了几句。你的所见所闻里会不会有让别人感兴趣的东西呢？如果没有，你能不能设想一下，在随后几周里，四处走走，留心看看，关注这样的可能性，即你独特旅程的某一部分可能会引起别人的兴趣，并让他人受益呢？

11 人们喜欢听故事，而每个人都能学会讲一个好故事。即使你从故事中得出的道理众人熟知，那也没关系——我们都是凡人！我们需要被提醒！用鲜活的故事包装重要的想法，再用合适的方式讲述，就能成就一次精彩的演讲。

2 THE MAGIC OF LOVE

PART I Introduction

As the French novelist George Sand said, "there is only one happiness in this life, to love and to be loved." In this world, almost everybody is looking for their true love. Some believe they will naturally find their perfect match, their soulmate, once the two of them bump into each other. Others, however, believe true love comes from hard efforts and compromise from both sides. This unit deals with a question that many people are interested in: Should we believe in soulmates or in romantic growth? Text A is a love story of two figure skating champions, Sergei and Katia, who were the best possible example of soulmates. Text B presents a different perspective. By comparing the belief in "romantic destiny" (i.e. soulmates) with that in "romantic growth", the author suggests that we should be careful about soulmate mentality and work hard to accomplish and maintain a healthy and happy relationship through mutual growth. After learning the unit, you are encouraged to think about the following questions: Why is love the most important and powerful thing in human life? Why are factors such as commitment, responsibility, respect, compromise, and mutual growth important in developing and maintaining a good relationship? What can we do to extend our love for our lovers, family members, and friends to others and to our nation?

In this unit you will:

1 Read a story about a perfect couple;
2 Explore the advantages and disadvantages of believing in soulmates;
3 Reflect on the importance of commitment in building a healthy relationship;
4 Get familiar with the way of using the suffix *-ed* to form adjectives;
5 Learn to use proper collective nouns for different groups of people, animals, etc.;
6 Learn to create an inverted sentence using a specific adverb or adverb phrase, such as *neither, nor, not only ... but ...*, *in no way*, and *only after*;
7 Learn verbs ending with *-serve* by using CADEL;
8 Learn to write narratives in chronological order;
9 Learn to create your own Valentine's Day card.

PART II Teaching Suggestions

Sayings

Learning objectives:

- Get a general idea of the unit
- Get inspirations from the sayings
- Get useful advice and guidance from famous people or books
- Learn to develop a positive attitude toward life

Teaching steps:

1 Ask students to translate the two sayings into Chinese.
   Reference translations for the sayings:

   - 死生契阔，与子成说。执子之手，与子偕老。 ——《诗经》
   - 有个词让我们摆脱生活中所有的沉重和痛苦，那就是"爱"。 ——索福克勒斯

2 For the first saying, tell students that for a relationship to last, it's important to have commitment. The quote is excerpted from the poem "Drumbeats" (《击鼓》) in *The Book of Songs*. Some say the poem is about commitment to friendship among soldiers. Now it is constantly referred to as a quote on the commitment of love between lovers. A happy marriage requires full commitment, which involves mutual understanding, respect, honesty, and cooperation.

3 The second saying is a quote from Sophocles, a great tragic playwright of ancient Greek. For this quote, tell students that love is powerful. It gives us courage and hope. It brings happiness to us. Ask students to reflect on how powerful love is to them and the people around them.

Lead-in

Learning objectives:

- Get to know different views on the idea of soulmates
- Learn about some movie quotes about love

Teaching steps:

1 Make a brief introduction to the unit and explain its learning objectives.
2 Ask students to do Exercise I and find out how their partners view soulmates. The class can have a quick vote to see how many of them believe in soulmates.
3 Ask students to do Exercise II. Encourage them to provide their own favorite quotes about love.

Reading to Learn

Text A

Soulmates on Ice

Learning objectives:

- Learn the love story of Sergei and Katia and their life as soulmates
- Learn about the text organization pattern: writing in chronological order

Teaching steps:

1   Introduce the topic of Text A: Should we believe in soulmates? What does the life of a perfect match look like?
2   Ask students to go through the text and get some ideas about the timeline of the events mentioned in the text. Then ask them to confirm their understanding by referring to the Text Organization exercise.
3   Go to Part III Detailed Study of Text A. Help students understand difficult sentences in the text accurately. Introduce important new words and expressions with explanations and examples.
4   Ask students to do the exercises following the text.

Critical Thinking

Learning objectives:

- Reflect on the key factors that lead to a healthy and happy relationship
- Learn to balance academic study with the building of a relationship
- Learn the importance of mutual growth in maintaining a good relationship

Teaching steps:

1   Ask students to read the questions first and then give them some ideas on how to approach each question.
2   For Question 1, ask students to share what they think contributes to the wonderful relationship between Sergei and Katia. Sergei and Katia shared much in common: their passion for skating, their affection for each other, their love for their child, and their mutual trust. Encourage students to learn from this couple and value mutual trust in building a healthy relationship.
3   For Question 2, ask students to reflect on the importance of striking a balance between academic study and building a relationship. Ask students to discuss the advantages and disadvantages of having a romantic relationship in college. Encourage them to share why they should make study the top priority and how they can achieve academic excellence while developing a romantic relationship.
4   For Question 3, ask students to reflect on the factors that are important to a healthy and happy relationship. While love for each other is the basis of starting a romantic relationship, trust,

responsibility, compromise, and mutual growth are the key elements that help to maintain a wonderful relationship. As Pearl S. Buck（赛珍珠） said, "A good marriage is one which allows for change and growth in the individuals and in the way they express their love." Ask students how they are inspired by the quote. Emphasize the importance of responsibility and mutual growth in developing a happy relationship.

5   Ask students to work in pairs or small groups to share their opinions. Encourage each pair or group to present their favorite ideas in class.

Corpora in Language Learning

Learning objectives:

● Learn to search CADEL for verbs ending with "serve" with "*serve" as the search term, using the "Concordance" function of AntConc
● Learn to search CADEL for nouns that collocate with verbs ending with "serve", using the "Concordance" function of AntConc
● Learn to translate into Chinese the collocations of the verbs ending with "serve" with the retrieved nouns
● Learn to complete the given sentences with verbs ending with "serve" based on the contexts in which they appear

Teaching steps:

1   Demonstrate how to search CADEL for verbs ending with *-serve* with "*serve" as the search term, using the "Concordance" function of AntConc. Ask students to identify the verbs that begin with the given letters.

2   Ask students to search CADEL for nouns that collocate with these verbs, using the "Concordance" function of AntConc. Ask them to identify the nouns that begin with the given letters. Remind students that some collocating nouns may not come right next to the verbs, and that they should search the context for the collocating nouns.

3   Ask students to sort the search results by setting KWIC sort.

4   Discuss the use of the verbs ending with *-serve* and the collocations of these verbs with the retrieved nouns, and their Chinese translations.

Writing

Learning objectives:

● Learn to write a narrative passage in chronological order
● Practice writing a passage in chronological order with the use of signal words of time sequence

Teaching steps:

1   Introduce the writing pattern of chronological order and the related signal words of time

sequence.

2   Ask students to read the two examples and emphasize the two keys to writing chronologically.

3   Ask students to do Exercise I to reinforce the idea of writing chronologically.

4   Ask them to do Exercise II after class.

Language Functions

Learning objectives:

- Learn different ways of expressing love and affection
- Learn to use love quotes in writing
- Learn to create a special Valentine's Day card in English

Teaching steps:

1   Introduce Valentine's Day and the importance of writing a special Valentine's Day card.

2   Explain the different ways of expressing love and affection and show how the sample Valentine's Day card is used to express love.

3   Ask students to do Exercise I and ask them to recommend any quote they would like to add in their card.

4   Ask students to do Exercise II. Encourage students to share their own Valentine's Day card with their partner or even with the whole class. Students are allowed to use assumed names in creating their cards. Tell students that they may be excused if they would like to keep their card as a secret instead.

5   Offer some more expressions of love if necessary, e.g.:

- *You cast a spell on me; hold the key to my heart; make my heart skip a beat; lift me up; rock my world*
- *You are the best thing that ever happened to me, my perfect match.*
- *You are my heart's desire, one true love, and reason for living.*

Reading to Explore

Text B

Why You Shouldn't Believe in Soulmates

Learning objectives:

- Learn about different characteristics of believers of soulmates and believers of romantic growth
- Understand the importance of improving relationships over time through hard work and compromise
- Understand the use of new words and expressions based on the context and through related exercises
- Learn to collect the most important information in each paragraph

Teaching steps:

1. Ask students to read the text and finish the exercises following the text before class.
2. Check answers to the exercises.
3. Show students how to make a comparison between two different beliefs, i.e. the belief in romantic destiny and the belief in romantic growth.
4. Encourage students to give their own opinions on the two beliefs and talk about which belief they prefer to hold to.

Summary of Text B

This text makes a comparison of different characteristics between believers of "romantic destiny" (i.e. soulmates) and those of "relationship growth" (e.g. a belief that relationships are developed with work over time). Through comparison, the author suggests that believers of romantic destiny tend to have a short and intense relationship because they rely too much on compatibility at the very beginning and tend to leave the relationship when things do not work. Believers of romantic growth, however, tend to have a longer and happier relationship as they keep improving their relationship over time with commitment to each other. Therefore, believing in romantic growth is much more rewarding.

PART III Detailed Study of Text A

Soulmates on Ice

Background Information

1. **Sergei Mikhailovich Grinkov:** 谢尔盖·米哈伊洛维奇·格林科夫
   Sergei Grinkov (1967–1995) was a Russian pair skating athlete. Together with his partner and wife Ekaterina Gordeeva, he won Olympic Champions in 1988 and 1994 and World Champions in 1986, 1987, 1989, and 1990. He died from a heart attack in 1995 when practicing in the US.
2. **Ekaterina "Katia" Alexandrovna Gordeeva:** 叶卡捷琳娜（卡佳）·亚历山德罗夫娜·戈蒂耶娃
   Ekaterina Gordeeva (1971–　) is a Russian skating athlete. She won Olympic Champions in 1988 and 1994, and World Champions in 1986, 1987, 1989, and 1990 in pair skating with her partner and husband, the late Sergei Grinkov.
3. **Lake Placid:** 普莱西德湖
   Lake Placid is a village in Essex County, New York, US. Lake Placid, together with the nearby Saranac Lake and Tupper Lake, comprises the Tri-Lakes region. Lake Placid hosted the 1932 and 1980 Winter Olympics, the 1972 Winter Universiade, and the 2000 Goodwill Games.

4   Stars on Ice: "冰上之星"（花样滑冰巡演）

Stars on Ice is a touring figure skating show founded in the US in 1986. It tours the United States, Canada, Japan and China on an annual basis, and has also staged shows in Europe, Brazil, and Korea. It has become the most famous figure skating show in the world.

5   HBO: 美国家庭影院频道

HBO, abbreviated from Home Box Office, is an American premium cable and satellite TV channel owned by Warner Media. The program consists of theatrically released movies, original television shows, documentaries, boxing matches, and comedy shows and concerts. It is the oldest pay TV network in the US.

6   *Mr. Bean*:《憨豆先生》

Mr. Bean is a sitcom series produced by Tiger Aspect Productions (UK) with Rowan Atkinson starring as the title character. The series centers on Mr. Bean, "a child in a grown man's body", as he clumsily solves various everyday problems but often causes disruption in the process.

Understanding the Text

Part 1 (Para. 1)

Ask students to read Para. 1 and answer Questions 1 and 2 in Exercise II of Reading Comprehension:

1   Why did Katia prefer a bunch of fading flowers for her husband's funeral? (Because they had been given by her husband.)

2   What could we tell from the story of the bunch of fading flowers? (Katia and Sergei often expressed their love to each other.)

Part 2 (Paras. 2–10)

Paras. 2–4

Ask students to read Paras. 2–4 and have a general idea of the life of Sergei and Katia. Answer the following questions:

1   How did Sergei and Katia meet each other? (They were put together to practice professional figure skating when they were very young.)

2   What probably caused the death of Sergei? (Like his father, Sergei died of heart failure when he was practicing.)

Paras. 5–6

Ask students to read Paras. 5–6 and answer Question 3 in Exercise II of Reading Comprehension:

According to Zhulin, what happened after Sergei and Katia got married? (They understood life better and skated better.)

Paras. 7–8

Ask students to read Paras. 7–8 and talk about the romantic things Sergei and Katia did together. Then ask students to do Exercise I of Reading Comprehension.

Paras. 9–10

1   Ask students to read Paras. 9–10 and answer Question 4 in Exercise II of Reading Comprehension:

How did Katia behave at the gathering in New York 30 hours after Sergei's death? (She tried her best to stay strong.)

2   Encourage students to talk about how they were impressed and inspired by Katia's behavior.

Part 3 (Para. 11)

Ask students to read Para. 11 and answer Question 5 in Exercise II of Reading Comprehension:
According to Sumners, what seems to be a relief in spite of Sergei's death? (The last thing Sergei saw was Katia in her landing position and this was exactly what they had worked for since they were young.)

Language Points

1   As she prepared to travel to Moscow for her husband Sergei Grinkov's funeral on Nov. 25, 1995, Ekaterina Gordeeva (Katia) **clutched** a **bunch** of red and yellow flowers. **(Para. 1)**

clutch: *v.* hold sth. tightly 紧握，紧抓

Staring at the stranger, the girl **clutched** her purse, but she didn't back away.

bunch: *n.* a group of things that are fastened, held, or growing together 串，束

This painting is of a woman holding a **bunch** of roses.

2   Her close friend and fellow **figure skating** star Alexander Zhulin asked Katia why she had chosen them rather than one of the many **gorgeous condolence bouquets** she had received that week. **(Para. 1)**

Paraphrase: Alexander Zhulin, a good friend of Katia and a figure skating star too, asked her why she had selected the fading bunch of flowers instead of one of the many beautiful bunches of flowers given to her that week as a token of sympathy.

figure skating: skating in an attractive pattern 花样滑冰

During the new **figure skating** show, former **figure skating** champions will perform Disneyland classics on ice.

gorgeous: *adj.* extremely beautiful or attractive 极其漂亮的，极其吸引人的

It was a **gorgeous** day, not a cloud in sight.

condolence: *n.* sympathy 同情；吊唁

Please accept my deepest **condolences** for your family's loss.

bouquet: *n.* an arrangement of flowers 花束

Lisa received a beautiful **bouquet** of flowers from her boyfriend on her birthday.

3   He learned that the **fading** flowers had a special meaning: Sergei had given them to Katia the day before he died. **(Para. 1)**

Paraphrase: He was told that the flowers losing color and brightness meant something special, because they had been given by Sergei to Katia the day before he died.

fade: *v.* lose color and brightness （使）褪色，（使）失去光泽

When I washed the blue skirt, I found the color **faded**.

4 They were not to celebrate some victory or mark some **anniversary**. Nor were they from a fancy shop. **(Para. 1)**

Paraphrase: These fading flowers were not given for winning a game or marking an important event. Nor were they bought from an expensive shop.

anniversary: *n.* a date on which sth. special or important happened in a previous year 周年纪念（日）

Fireworks exploded on the night of the 20th **anniversary** of Hong Kong's return to the motherland on July 1, 2017.

Note: The author tries to show that sending flowers to each other was a very common thing in the life of Sergei and Katia, who were leading a truly romantic life.

5 **By all accounts**, Grinkov, 28, and Gordeeva, 24 — or G&G, as they were known in the world of professional figure skating — led a **storybook** life. **(Para. 2)**

Paraphrase: According to what a lot of people say, Grinkov, 28, and Gordeeva, 24 — they were known as G&G in the world of professional figure skating — led a perfectly happy life, like one in a storybook.

by all accounts: according to what a lot of people say 根据各方面所说

I've never been to Dali, Yunnan, but it's a lovely place, **by all accounts**.

storybook: *adj.* so happy or perfect that it is like one in a children's story 童话式的；像故事书中的

It was a **storybook** wedding that surpassed even the wildest dreams of most princesses.

6 A pair of **mismatched** children thrown together at age 15 and 11, respectively, and told to practice professional figure skating, they grew up to become the most **celebrated** pairs skaters ever — and, along the way, to **fall** madly **in love** with each other. **(Para. 2)**

Paraphrase: The two children, one 15 years old and the other 11 years old, had not looked suitable for each other, but they were put together and made to practice figure skating as professionals. As they grew up, they became the most famous pairs skaters ever — and during the time, they found themselves deeply in love with each other.

mismatched: *adj.* not working well together or not suitable for each other 不匹配的，不协调的

The game is not competitive with **mismatched** teams like these.

celebrated: *adj.* famous 著名的；驰名的

The owner of this restaurant is also a **celebrated** chef in France.

fall in love: feel a sudden strong attraction for sb. 爱上，坠入爱河

They **fell in love** at a party and got married two months later.

7 It was **as though** they had the whole world ... What happened to him was **heartbreaking**. **(Para. 2)**

Paraphrase: It seemed that they had everything in the world ... What happened to him made everyone feel extremely sad.

as though: as if; in a way that suggests sth. 好像

It seems **as though** he's got everything and knows everybody.

heartbreaking: *adj.* making you feel very sad or upset 令人心碎的

It was **heartbreaking** to see her beautiful house destroyed by the flood.

8   On Nov. 20, 1995, while training with Katia in Lake Placid, N. Y., for the Stars on Ice show tour, Sergei **complained of dizziness**. (**Para. 3**)

Paraphrase: On Nov. 20, 1995, while practicing with Katia in Lake Placid, N. Y. for the show tour called Stars on Ice, Sergei said that he felt that everything was spinning around and that he could not stand steadily.

complain of: report (a pain, etc.) 诉说（病痛等）；主诉

Some patients may **complain of** blurry vision or may simply **complain of** a headache after reading.

dizziness: *n.* the feeling of being unable to stand steadily 昏眩

Intense hunger can cause **dizziness**, increased heart rate, and shaking.

9   **Paramedics responded** in minutes, and doctors at the Adirondack Medical Center **worked on** Sergei, whose father had died of heart failure at 56 in 1990, for more than an hour, **to no avail**. (**Para. 4**)

Paraphrase: Emergency medical responders took action in a few minutes, and doctors at the Adirondack Medical Center gave treatments to Sergei for more than an hour but they failed. The cause of Sergei's father's death at the age of 56 in 1990 was heart disease.

paramedic: *n.* sb. who has been trained to help people who are hurt or to do medical work, but who is not a doctor or nurse（非医生或护士）护理人员，医务辅助人员

As a **paramedic**, she can legally offer advanced emergency medical care.

respond: *v.* act in answer to (sth.) 反应，回应，响应

I texted her requesting a meeting in person but she didn't **respond**.

work on: spend time working in order to produce or repair sth. 从事，致力于，忙于

The rock band is **working on** their new CD.

to no avail: not successful in getting what you want 没结果，无效果

I have been trying to contact him but **to no avail**.

10 "He was dead **the moment** he hit the ice — he felt no pain," says Dr. Josh Schwartzberg. (**Para. 4**)

Paraphrase: "He died as soon as he fell onto the ice — he did not feel any pain," says Dr. Josh Schwartzberg.

the moment (that) sb. does sth.: as soon as sb. does sth. 某人一做某事就……

The moment I walked in I was greeted like a star.

11 ... and **from** that point **on** they skated like no other pair had before. (**Para. 5**)

Paraphrase: Since then, they skated in a wonderful way beyond compare.

from ... on: starting at the specified time and continuing for an indefinite period 从……起

I am not satisfied with my works to date, and **from now on** I want to take a new path.

12 "They didn't become one person until Dasha was born," says **Olympic** champion Scott Hamilton. (**Para. 6**)

Paraphrase: "They finally were of one mind and performed in perfect unison（一致）after their daughter Dasha was born," says Scott Hamilton, an Olympic champion.

Olympic: *adj.* of or connected with the Olympic Games 奥林匹克运动会的

The Chinese women's diving team presented the audiences the most beautiful sights ever seen at any **Olympic** contest.

13 "They liked to do **romantic** things," says Elena Bechke, a friend and 1992 Olympic silver **medalist** in pairs skating. **(Para. 7)**

romantic: *adj.* making you have feelings of love and excitement 浪漫的

The new couple just returned to Britain from a **romantic** holiday on the island of Bali.

medalist: *n.* sb. who has won a medal in a competition 奖牌获得者

She is an Olympic gold **medalist** and world champion.

14 When asked for the Stars on Ice program **bio** what his favorite dinner was, Sergei responded, "Any dinner my wife made." **(Para. 7)**

Paraphrase: In preparing a biographical sketch about Sergei for the Stars on Ice program, someone asked Sergei what dinner he liked best, Sergei replied, "Any dinner my wife made."

bio: *n.* a biographical sketch or outline（尤指供公开发表的）个人介绍（biography的缩写）

When you read Wolfgang Amadeus Mozart's **bio**, you can find out more about his early symphonies.

15 He loved HBO's *Mr. Bean* and watching **hockey**, and old **musicals** too. **(Para. 8)**

hockey: *n.* 曲棍球

Hockey is a popular sport in the Netherlands.

musical: *n.* a play or film that includes singing and dancing 音乐剧；音乐片

The classic **musical** *The Sound of Music*, the oldest and mostly loved **musical**, celebrated its 60th birthday in 2019.

16 Sergei and Katia had a life that was so **genuine** in its values. **(Para. 8)**

Paraphrase: Sergei and Katia led a life that had true values.

genuine: *adj.* real, rather than pretended or false 真正的；真实的

This sofa is a bit expensive as it is made of **genuine** leather.

17 They had a real work **ethic** and an understanding of people that was so **down-to-earth** and pure. **(Para. 8)**

Paraphrase: They believed in the virtue of hard work and they understood people and treated them in a practical and genuine way.

ethic: *n.* a general idea or belief that influences people's behaviour and attitudes 道德准则；伦理标准

It's a lawyer's basic work **ethic** to protect the client's rights.

down-to-earth: *adj.* practical and sensible 实际的，脚踏实地的

She is a **down-to-earth** designer who puts her customers' needs and interests ahead of superficial decorations.

18 Thirty hours after Sergei's death, friends and fellow performers in Stars on Ice **bade farewell** to him at a Saranac Lake, N. Y. funeral home. **(Para. 9)**

Paraphrase: Thirty hours after Sergei's death, friends and other performers in the Stars on Ice show said goodbye to him at a funeral home in Saranac Lake, N. Y. **(Para. 9)**

bid: *v.* (**bade, bidden**) greet sb. 问候，打招呼

After the concert, he **bade** her goodnight and drove back home.

farewell: *n.* goodbye 再会；再见

The outgoing president received a painting as his **farewell** gift.

bid farewell to: the action of saying goodbye 告别

Let's **bid farewell to** unhealthy sweetened milk and enjoy natural dairy products from grass-fed cows.

19 She **stroked** Sergei's face and talked to him softly while he **lay in state**. (Para. 9)

Paraphrase: She moved her hand gently over Sergei's face and talked to him tenderly while he was put there for other people to pay their respects.

stroke: *v.* move your hand gently over sth. 轻抚，抚摸

The little girl quieted as the mother **stroked** her hair.

lie in state: (of the dead body of an important person) be placed on view in a public place before being buried（要人的遗体安葬前）受公众瞻仰

Hundreds of people lined up to pay their respects to the late mayor as he **lied in state** at the city hall.

20 After the **wake**, and before she left for Moscow and the **burial** in Vagankovskoye **Cemetery**, she joined her fellow skaters at the Lake Placid apartment where she and Sergei had been staying. **(Para. 10)**

Paraphrase: After the gathering to remember Sergei, and before she went to Moscow for the burial ceremony in Vagankovskoye Cemetery, she and her fellow skaters gathered at the apartment in Lake Placid, where she and Sergei had been staying.

wake: *n.* the time before or after a funeral when friends and relatives meet to remember the dead person 守灵

Traditionally, a **wake** takes place in the house of the deceased.

burial: *n.* the act or ceremony of putting a dead body into a grave 埋葬，葬礼

A sad song was sung by the mourners at the **burial** of the hero who sacrificed his life to save others.

cemetery: *n.* an area of land, not a churchyard, used for burying the dead 墓地，公墓

The **cemetery** in which Audrey Hepburn lies at rest in Tolochenaz, Switzerland, is small and simple.

21 Her friends wanted to **console** her, but she ended up consoling them. **(Para. 10)**

Paraphrase: Her friends wanted to comfort her, but in the end she was giving comfort to her friends instead.

console: *v.* give comfort or sympathy 安慰，慰问

With her loving words she **consoled** him and settled his mind.

22 They were the **epitome** of soulmates. **(Para. 11)**

Paraphrase: They were the best possible example to show what soulmates are.

epitome: *n.* the best possible example 典型，典范

George was truly an **epitome** of strength and confidence and we all admired him for that.

Reading to Learn

Reading Comprehension

I 1 having dinners with candles
   2 cakes
   3 a good book, watch a good movie
   4 *Mr. Bean*
   5 Daria
   6 an understanding of people

II 1 C   2 B   3 A   4 B   5 D

III **Text Organization**
   1 professional figure skating   2 married
   3 Paras. 3–4   4 heart failure
   5 Para. 5   6 bade farewell
   7 Para. 9   8 Moscow
   9 Para. 1

Language in Use

Words and Expressions

I 1 condolence   2 bunch   3 celebrated   4 genuine
   5 fade   6 anniversary   7 mismatched   8 respond

II 1 working on   2 died of   3 complaining of   4 from ... on
   5 bid farewell to   6 by all accounts   7 fell in love   8 to no avail

III 1 complaining of   2 gorgeous   3 responding   4 the moment   5 falling in love
   6 clutch   7 to no avail   8 consoled   9 burial   10 romantic

Word Formation

1 Left-handed   2 accustomed   3 classified   4 addicted   5 indebted
6 applied   7 well-informed   8 absent-minded   9 privileged   10 skilled

1 a swarm of   2 a fleet of   3 a herd of   4 A school of   5 a crew of
6 a pack of   7 a stack of   8 a flock of   9 a panel of   10 a staff of

Grammar and Structure

1 He hadn't done any homework. Neither/Nor had he brought any of his books to class.

2 We didn't get to see the art museum. Neither/Nor did we see the castle.

3 Not only did my friends enjoy the diet I gave them, but it certainly worked extremely well for those that followed it properly.

4 Not until the children start to grow plants for themselves may they see in which circumstances the plants grow better.

5 Only after the disaster is over can you know its lessons.

6 Hardly had he come out of the bus when the fire broke out.

7 Seldom did he challenge his parents or question their judgments or decisions.

8 In no way did I intend to say that they didn't work hard.

Translation

I   1 我们一致认为沟通上出现了问题，但是希望从现在开始，我们能够以开放和建设性的方式合作。

2 她是个真正关心顾客、非常脚踏实地的人。

3 大熊猫不喜欢像猫或狗一样被紧紧抱住或用力抚摸。

4 2008年5月12日汶川大地震后，中国中央政府的高层领导们飞赴当地慰问受灾家庭。

5 这要让他的医生来决定他的健康状况是否足以重返工作岗位。但是从各方面来说，种种迹象令人鼓舞。

II   1 This gorgeous Chinese painting is a watercolor hand painted on silk.

2 A 64-year-old man complained of poor memory and bad eyesight.

3 China is working on a manned lunar-landing project and has made remarkable progress so far.

4 The moment the alarm goes off, information is immediately sent to the center of the alarm system.

5 She looked so confident and relaxed as though she had already won the match.

III   Mutual respect plays an extremely important role in developing a healthy and happy relationship. It means that you and your partner are equal. When couples have mutual respect, they are able to be themselves, have their own interests, opinions, and feelings without fear of rejection from their partner. Couples with mutual respect often show appreciation, understanding, and care for each other. They try their best to support each other, but they also know how to give space to the other. They may disagree, but they do not mind if they win or lose, as they believe that there is no right or wrong in relationships.

Corpora in Language Learning

I (There can be more than one answer to some questions here, and to each question only one answer is provided for reference.)

Verbs ending with -*serve*	Nouns that collocate with the verbs	Chinese translations of the collocations
conserve	energy	节约能源
	farmland	保护耕地
	resources	节约资源
deserve	attention	值得关注
	respect	值得尊重
	protection	应得到保护
observe	brain areas	观察大脑区域
	rules	遵守规则
	development	观察发展
preserve	species	保护物种
	memories	保存记忆
	status quo	维持现状
reserve	procedures	保留程序

II 1 reserve   2 Conserving   3 deserve   4 observe   5 preserve

Writing

I **Passage 1**

Disneyland Park is the first of two theme parks built at the Disneyland Resort in Anaheim, California, opened on July 17, 1955. It is the only theme park designed and built to completion under the direct supervision of Walt Disney. Walt Disney came up with the concept of Disneyland after visiting various amusement parks with his daughters in the 1930s and 1940s. He initially envisioned building a tourist attraction adjacent to his studios in Burbank to entertain fans who wished to visit; however, he soon realized that the proposed site was too small. After hiring a consultant to help him determine an appropriate site for his project, Disney bought a 160-acre site near Anaheim in 1953. Construction began in 1954 and the park was unveiled during a special televised press event on July 17, 1955.

Passage 2

    I grew up in the suburbs of southeast Michigan in a middle-class family. I wanted to be a doctor <u>in fifth grade</u> based on my love of science and the idea of wanting to help others. Winning a science fair project about the circulatory system <u>in sixth grade</u> really aroused my interest in the field. <u>Throughout high school</u>, I took several science courses that again reinforced my interest in the field of medicine. I <u>then</u> enrolled at St. Louis University to advance my training for a total of eight years of intense education, including undergraduate and medical school. <u>After</u> graduation from medical school <u>at age 26</u>, I <u>then</u> pursued a three-year training program in internal medicine at the University of Michigan. I <u>then</u> went on to pursue an additional three years of specialty medical training in the field of gastroenterology. The completion of that program marked the end of 14 years of post-high school education. It was at that point, <u>at the age of 32</u> and searching for my first job, that I could say that my career in medicine began.

Reading to Explore

Reading Comprehension

I

1 initial	**2** compromise	**3** passionate	**4** satisfied
5 Unable	**6** committed	**7** short	**8** longer

II **1** T   **2** F   **3** F   **4** T   **5** T

III

A 6	**B** 2	**C** 12	**D** 5	**E** 11
F 8	**G** 3	**H** 12	**I** 10	**J** 7

Words and Expressions

I

1 continually	**2** indicate	**3** inevitably	**4** evaluation	**5** adopted
6 compatible	**7** response	**8** committed	**9** motivation	**10** dumped

II

1 move on	**2** work at	**3** as opposed to	**4** in the long run	**5** believe in
6 hold to	**7** was to blame	**8** work out	**9** prevented ... from	**10** are destined to

PART V   Text Translation

Text A

冰上的灵魂伴侣

威廉·普卢默

1   叶卡捷琳娜·戈蒂耶娃（卡佳）紧握着一捧红黄相间的花束，准备去莫斯科参加将于1995年11

月25日举行的丈夫谢尔盖·格林科夫的葬礼。花不是特别的夺目，甚至也不新鲜。她的好友、同样也是花样滑冰明星的亚历山大·茹林问卡佳，为什么她选了这些花，而没有从她那周收到的众多绚丽的吊唁花束中选一束。然后他得知，这些正凋谢的花有着特殊的意义：谢尔盖在去世前一天把它们送给了卡佳。这些花不是用来庆祝胜利或者某个纪念日，也并非来自哪家高级花店。"它们就是有生命的鲜花，"茹林说道，"送花是他们夫妇平时生活中的常态。"

2　众所周知，28岁的格林科夫和24岁的戈蒂耶娃，在职业花样滑冰世界中被称为G&G，过着传奇故事般的生活。当年两个看着并不搭的孩子，一个15岁，一个11岁，被阴差阳错地安排在一起练职业花样滑冰，结果成长为最著名的双人滑运动员——而且，与此同时，疯狂地爱上了彼此。确实，前滑冰冠军迪克·巴顿曾说，"他们好像拥有了整个世界。谢尔盖是完美的双人滑选手、完美的丈夫、完美的父亲（他们有个3岁的女儿达丽雅）。发生在他身上的事令人心碎。"

3　1995年11月20日，当谢尔盖与卡佳在纽约州普莱西德湖为准备"冰上之星"巡回演出一起训练时，谢尔盖说感到头晕。这时夫妇两人刚完成一次托举动作，卡佳扶着他坐到冰上。他随即仰头倒下，不省人事。

4　卡佳开始尖叫。急救人员几分钟就赶到，阿迪朗达克医学中心的医生对谢尔盖实施抢救，谢尔盖的父亲在1990年56岁时也死于心脏病。抢救进行了一个多小时但是无济于事。"他倒在冰上的那一刻就去世了——没有任何痛苦。"乔希·施瓦兹伯格医生说道。

5　谢尔盖和卡佳于1991年4月21日在莫斯科结婚，从那一刻起他们的滑冰水平就超越了所有双人滑组合。"他们没结婚之前滑冰时，"茹林说，"滑得是很漂亮。但是像两个还没有理解生命的意义的孩子。而在过去的几年中，他们滑得越来越好。我想这是因为一切都完美了：他们彼此相爱，都爱着达丽雅。"

6　达丽雅，他们又叫她"达莎"，她的到来极大地改变了他们的生活。"直到达莎出生后，他俩才完全步调一致，表演时如同一人，"奥运会冠军斯考特·汉密尔顿如是说。

7　"他们喜欢做浪漫的事，"叶连娜·别契克说道，她是他们的好友，也是1992年奥运会双人滑的银牌得主，"比如私下的烛光晚餐。卡佳喜欢做饭给谢尔盖吃。她个子娇小，自己吃不了多少，但是她喜欢给他做蛋糕。"在准备"冰上之星"演出选手简介时，谢尔盖被问到最喜欢吃的主餐是什么，谢尔盖回答说，"太太做的都是我的最爱。"

8　对于谢尔盖而言，幸福是读一本好书或者看一部电影。"谢尔盖兴趣广泛，"汉密尔顿说，"他也看很多电视节目。他喜欢美国家庭影院频道放映的《憨豆先生》，也爱看曲棍球和老的音乐剧。他会为了有了新车兴奋不已。谢尔盖和卡佳的生活过得很真实。他们有着真正的职业道德，善解人意，为人踏实而又纯真。我感到跟他们度过的每一天都是值得的。"

9　谢尔盖去世30个小时后，好友们和"冰上之星"表演团的伙伴们在纽约州萨拉纳克湖的殡仪馆跟他告别。卡佳手上戴着达丽雅出生时他送给她的手表，脖子上戴着一条串着谢尔盖婚戒的项链。瞻仰遗容时，她抚摸着谢尔盖的脸，轻声跟他说话。

10　守灵仪式过后，在回莫斯科去瓦岗科夫斯卡娅公墓举行葬礼之前，她跟滑冰伙伴们在普莱西德湖的公寓相聚，她跟谢尔盖曾住在这里。朋友们试图安慰她，但是结果她反过来安慰他们。"她在哭泣，但是她抓着我的衣领，"前美国冠军罗莎琳·萨姆纳斯说，"她说，'罗丝，开心点。要天天开心。谢尔盖懂得怎么生活。他会每天对我说，卡佳，开心点。'"

11　在回忆那晚卡佳强作坚强的情景时，萨姆纳斯的眼里充满了泪花。"我为她痛失爱人而伤心，"她说，"他俩是灵魂伴侣的典范。你怎么能与你的伴侣——你心心相印的伴侣告别？不过，你知道吗，谢尔盖看到的最后一幕是卡佳平稳落地的动作，而从在莫斯科两人还是孩子时候起，这就是他们一直努力在完成的最重要的事。"

Text B

为什么不要相信"灵魂伴侣"的说法

杰里米·尼克尔森

1　你相信灵魂伴侣吗？你坚信会有某个人（或几个人）是你的绝配吗？你是否认为遇到对的人，就能轻松地爱上真实的彼此，"顺理成章修成正果"？

2　如果你这样想，你肯定不是唯一的一个。事实上，根据马里斯特民调中心2011年1月的调查，73%的美国人相信他们注定会找到属于自己的那个独一无二的、真正的灵魂伴侣。其中男性的比例（74%）略高于女性（71%）。而在年轻人中这种想法更普遍，其中45岁以下的人中有79%相信有灵魂伴侣（相比之下，45岁以上的人中只有69%）。

3　很显然，人们普遍相信有灵魂伴侣。大多数人坚信爱情是命中注定的。然而，问题是，这种信念最终能否修得正果。那些寻找灵魂伴侣的人如愿以偿了吗？灵魂伴侣是否更容易"从此过上了幸福的生活"呢？

4　幸运的是，有研究提供了答案。

5　尼（1998）的研究评估了"爱情注定说"（即灵魂伴侣说）对实际爱情关系质量的影响。具体来说，他把相信灵魂伴侣说的人群（如，相信人们的缘分是命中注定的）和相信"爱情成长说"（如，相信爱情是通过一段时间慢慢努力培养起来的）的人群的爱情生活作了比较。他的评估结果显示：

6　那些相信爱情注定说（灵魂伴侣说）的人，倾向于在伴侣身上寻求积极的情感响应，而且希求一上来就投缘。他们相信两人要么"一见如故"，注定在一起，要么无缘，应该另寻他人。结果，这种思想容易让追求灵魂伴侣的人一上来对对方激情满满、百看不厌，当诸事和谐时尤其如此。但是，当问题不可避免地产生时，灵魂伴侣的坚信者往往不能很好处理，转而甩手离去。换言之，人们若抱有灵魂伴侣应该如天造地设般和谐的这种想法，在面对并非十全十美的爱情时，就只会轻言放弃，转而到别处另寻"真爱"伴侣。结果，其爱情往往轰轰烈烈却难以持久。

7　那些相信爱情成长说的人，注重寻找能够和自己一起努力和成长的伴侣，当矛盾产生时也能化解冲突。他们相信，哪怕困难重重，爱情也可以通过努力和忍让而开花结果。结果是，他们在跟伴侣相处的初期往往没有那么激情澎湃、称心如意。秉持爱情成长说的人，他们对爱情关系的反应没那么强烈和欣喜。然而困难出现时，他们会主动解决，不离不弃。结果是，随着时间的推移，他们的爱情往往更长久、更令人满意。他们不会为一丁点儿不和就抛弃对方，而是一起努力、成长，培养一段令人满意的爱情关系。

8　这项研究还显示，假如一个人追求短暂而热烈的爱情，那么相信灵魂伴侣说对其十分有用。最初的那种融洽感会如同魔法般神奇。这是一种美妙的情感高潮，至少在十全十美的幻想破灭之前如此。

9 然而，在所有的关系中，终会有意见相左、冲突矛盾和格格不入的情况发生。说到底，没有人是十全十美的——或者说没有人是十全十美的伴侣。要通过努力、进步和改变才能让爱情保持长久和令人满意。而在这种情形下，相信灵魂伴侣说的人往往会心灰意冷，失望沮丧，无法坚持。

10 所以，假如有人发现自己一而再、再而三地爱上"完美"的伴侣，而最终只是很快感到失望并抛弃对方，那么问题可能出在他们对灵魂伴侣的笃信上。这会让他们在事情不那么完美（但可能还不错或很棒）的时候轻言放弃。当对方无法百分之百地爱上完完全全的自己时，他们不愿妥协、努力或者改变。最终，他们还是会认为，换一个人，生活就会更令人满意，于是不断地寻找更般配的伴侣，而不去努力适应和认可已经很好的眼前人。

11 最后，这成了一个有些残酷的玩笑，相信灵魂伴侣，反而可能会妨碍你找到自认为命中注定的真爱。

12 总之，显而易见，追求完美的般配和灵魂伴侣会扼杀你跟好伴侣努力营造成功爱情的积极性。长远来看，笃信爱情成长说更为有益，特别是对追求爱情天长地久的人而言。不过，与追求灵魂伴侣不同，相信爱情成长说确实意味着要花更多的努力，做更多的尝试，和愿意做出改变。因此，要真正收获满意的爱情，一个人不仅必须抛弃追求"完美"伴侣的想法，而且要愿意承认对方并非总是"本来就那么完美"。只有那样，两个人才能携手共进、同德同心，直至天长地久。

3 BE SMART WITH YOUR SMARTPHONE

In the past, when we didn't have a smartphone, we had many problems. We got lost easily, paid too much for a thing for lack of price comparison information, and failed to remember things. With a smartphone and its various apps, we have all these problems solved. Text A in this unit explains why the author is free of all these worries. However, things are not so rosy for some other people. For example, the author of Text B found her life a mess as she was addicted to the smartphone. She felt lucky and happy to get back to the real world by quitting such an addiction. These two stories make us rethink the proper use of the smartphone. While enjoying the benefits brought by advanced technologies, we should not forget that anything could become negative if it is used in an inappropriate way. You are welcome to examine your own smartphone habits and think about how you are going to avoid the negative impacts while making full use of the smartphone and other technologies.

In this unit you will:
1   Read two different stories about the use of the smartphone;
2   Learn to describe the advantages and disadvantages of the smartphone;
3   Reflect on the importance of using the smartphone and other technologies in a wise way;
4   Learn how the prefix re- combines with verbs and their related nouns to form new verbs and nouns;
5   Learn nouns that collocate with "restore" or "ruin";
6   Learn to write inverted sentences;
7   Learn verb phrases of "come + preposition/adverb" by using CADEL;
8   Learn to write useful reviews online;
9   Learn to use text and chat abbreviations.

PART II

Teaching Suggestions

Sayings

Learning objectives:

- Get a general idea of the unit
- Get inspirations from the sayings
- Get useful advice and guidance from famous people or books
- Learn to develop a positive attitude toward life

Teaching steps:

1   Ask students to translate the two sayings into Chinese.
    Reference translations for the sayings:
    - 欲思其利，必虑其害；欲思其成，必虑其败。 ——诸葛亮
    - 技术固然重要，但是真正重要的是我们用技术做什么。 ——穆罕默德·尤努斯

2   The first saying is a quote from Zhuge Liang, a famous ancient Chinese statesman and military strategist. For this quote, tell students that it is important to weigh the advantages and disadvantages before taking actions. Everything is a double-edged sword. While it brings happiness to you, it may have some negative impacts on you as well. So, when you are considering the benefits of a thing, you should also think about what harm it may bring. When you think about gaining success, you have to think about what kind of failure you may possibly face. Only through carefully weighing the gains against the losses can one make a well-thought decision and overcome difficulties in achieving the goal. Similarly, we should use the smartphone and other technologies properly by weighing their advantages and disadvantages.

3   The second saying is a quote from Muhammad Yunus, a Bangladeshi social entrepreneur, banker, and economist who was awarded the Nobel Peace Prize in 2006. While new technologies have brought wonderful changes to our life, they have also given rise to such problems as technology addiction. Muhammad Yunus' words tell us that it is important to develop a right attitude to the use of technologies. While we enjoy the benefits of technologies, we should be aware that the proper use of technologies is more important than technologies themselves. Encourage students to reflect on how this quote changes their way of viewing the use of the smartphone and other technologies.

Lead-in

Learning objectives:

- Find out some problems with the use of the smartphone
- Discuss how the smartphone is affecting different aspects of our life

Teaching steps:

1 Make a brief introduction to the unit and explain its learning objectives.

2 Ask students to listen to a dialogue about the use of the smartphone and pay attention to the questions of the male speaker and the answers of the female speaker. Ask students to do Exercise I.

3 Ask students to listen to the dialogue again and do Exercise II.

4 After the pair work, ask some students to present to the class their ideas about how the use of the smartphone affects human life.

Reading to Learn

Text A

How I Learned to Stop Worrying by Loving the Smartphone

Learning objectives:

● Learn new words and expressions and use them to talk about the advantages and disadvantages of the smartphone

● Learn how to express one's changing attitude towards the smartphone through detailed descriptions

Teaching steps:

1 Introduce the topic of Text A: How the use of the smartphone has changed the author's life for the better.

2 Ask students to read Para. 1, Para. 4 and Para. 7 and guess what the text is most probably about. (What I was like without a smartphone, and what I have become after using a smartphone.) Ask students to identify the words that support their guess. ("think back to" vs. "now"; "a quivering ball of anxiety" vs. "sunny and carefree"; "will change ... for the better. The little improvements in life will matter. How? Don't get me started.")

3 Ask students to go through the whole passage and divide it into two parts. After that, ask them to look at the Text Organization exercise to check if they have made the same division. The passage can be divided as follows: Part 1 (Paras. 1–3), Part 2 (Paras. 4–15).

4 Go to Part III Detailed Study of Text A. Help students understand difficult sentences in this text accurately. Introduce important new words and expressions with explanations and examples.

5 Ask students to do the exercises following the text.

Critical Thinking

Learning objectives:

● Share positive experiences of using the smartphone

- Reflect on the possible risks of using the smartphone
- Discuss how to avoid the risks caused by the overuse of the smartphone
- Learn the importance of self-discipline in preventing distraction by or addiction to technologies

Teaching steps:

1 Ask students to read the questions first and then give them some ideas on how to approach each question.

2 For Question 1, ask students to share the benefits the smartphone has brought to them. Encourage them to discuss how important technologies are in our daily life. You may encourage students to talk about how Chinese people benefit from the advancement of technologies in terms of communication, transportation, education, security, entertainment, and so on.

3 For Question 2, ask students to reflect on the risks of overusing the smartphone and other technologies. Ask students to share if the use of the smartphone affects their memory and how to avoid the risk. Encourage them to discuss other potential risks of overusing the smartphone and effective ways to reduce these risks.

4 For Question 3, tell students the importance of practicing self-discipline to prevent addiction to the use of the smartphone and other technologies. Technologies by themselves are no evil. It's all about how we choose to use them. It is important to build a healthy relationship between human beings and new technologies, as Albert Einstein said, "The human spirit must prevail over technology." The overuse of the smartphone may seriously affect our work, life and relationships with our family and friends. Self-discipline is the key to reducing the harm. Self-discipline is about breaking a habit and getting focused on your goals. It is about making wise choices. For example, you may start by setting technology-free time in your life and paying attention to what is happening in real time. Self-discipline becomes very powerful when combined with goal-setting, passion, and planning. Ask students to share how they regulate their use of the smartphone through self-discipline.

5 Ask students to work in pairs or small groups to share their opinions. Encourage each pair or group to present their favorite ideas in class.

Corpora in Language Learning

Learning objectives:

- Learn to search CADEL for verb phrases of "come + preposition/adverb" according to their definitions with "come *" as the search term, using the "Concordance" function of AntConc
- Learn to complete the given sentences with verb phrases of "come + preposition/adverb" based on the contexts in which they appear

Teaching steps:

1 Ask students to search CADEL for verb phrases of "come + preposition/adverb" according to their definitions with "come *" as the search term, using the "Concordance" function of AntConc.

2 Ask students to sort the search results by setting KWIC sort.

3 Discuss the use of the verb phrases of "come +preposition/adverb".

Writing

Learning objectives:

- Learn to write genuinely useful reviews online
- Get familiar with the writing pattern of a good online review

Teaching steps:

1 Ask students to read the introduction about how to write genuinely useful reviews online and pay special attention to the four basic parts that comprise a review.

2 Ask students to read the sample review in Exercise I and analyze its organization in terms of the four basic parts.

3 Ask students to learn from the sample and write a review on their own.

Language Functions

Learning objectives:

- Learn about the importance of using text and chat abbreviations
- Get familiar with some popular text and chat abbreviations
- Learn to understand a text message conversation with text and chat abbreviations
- Learn to construct a text message conversation using text and chat abbreviations

Teaching steps:

1 Ask students to provide some text and chat abbreviations they know before reading the list given in the introduction.

2 Ask students to read the list of popular text and chat abbreviations given in the introduction and check the ones they didn't know.

3 After students get familiar with the given list of text and chat abbreviations, ask them to do Exercise I. Ask them to read the text message conversation and try to figure out its actual meaning. Refer to the list when necessary.

4 Ask students to study closely the sample text message conversation and write one as a group, using the text and chat abbreviations they have just learned.

5 Ask students to present the conversation to the class and ask them to work out its meaning.

Reading to Explore

Text B

How I Quit My Smartphone Addiction and Really Started Living

Learning objectives:

- Extract the main idea of each paragraph
- Learn the words and expressions to describe the addiction to the smartphone
- Learn how one can get rid of the addiction to the smartphone
- Learn the importance of getting back to the real world

Teaching steps:

1   Ask students to read the text and finish the exercises following the text before class.
2   Check answers to the exercises.
3   Ask students to read the text and examine how the author's life has changed after stopping the use of the smartphone.
4   Encourage students to share their own experience of using the smartphone and suggest ways on how to use the smartphone wisely.

Summary of Text B

The author was once addicted to the use of the smartphone. She slept with her phone by her side and texted at any time, even while she was driving. She couldn't stand leaving her smartphone behind for 30 seconds. Determined to change this terrible situation, she gave up her smartphone completely. To her amazement, she finds her life not affected but improved. As her business and social life remain active and connected, she is glad to be back in the real world again.

PART III   Detailed Study of Text A

How I Learned to Stop Worrying by Loving the Smartphone

Background Information

1   **Longfellow tavern:** 朗费罗客栈
    Henry Wadsworth Longfellow and his publisher visited the old Howe Tavern in 1862 and made it the gathering place for his characters in *Tales of a Wayside Inn*. Purchased by Henry Ford in 1923, the Longfellow's Wayside Inn is now the oldest inn still operating in the United States.

2   **Longfellow:** 朗费罗 (1807–1882)

Henry Wadsworth Longfellow, American poet and educator. He was heavily influenced by Romanticism and wrote many lyric poems known for their musicality. Longfellow was regarded as the most popular American poet of his day. His works include *The Song of Hiawatha* and *Evangeline*.

3   **Henry Ford:** 亨利·福特 (1863–1947)

American automobile manufacturer and the founder of the Ford Motor Company. He created the Model T and developed the assembly line mode of production, which revolutionized transportation and American industry.

4   **Jaron Lanier:** 加隆·雷尼尔 (1960–)

American computer philosophy writer, computer scientist, composer, and visual artist. Often regarded as the person who coined the term Virtual Reality (VR), Lanier is considered a founding father of the VR field. In 1984, he founded VPL Research, one of the first companies to sell VR products in the world.

5   **Nicholas Carr:** 尼古拉斯·卡尔 (1959–)

American writer who writes about technology, business, and culture. He is the author of the 2011 Pulitzer Prize finalist *The Shallows: What the Internet Is Doing to Our Brains*. He has also written for many newspapers, magazines, and journals, including *The New York Times*, *The Wall Street Journal*, *Wired*, etc.

Understanding the Text

Part 1 (Paras. 1–3)

1   Ask students to read Paras. 1–3 and answer the following questions:

   1)   How did the author feel before using the smartphone? (He felt very worried.)

   2)   What problem might the author have when he went for an appointment? (He might get lost and couldn't get the right direction from the ruined public map.)

   3)   What was wrong with the author's memory? (He could no longer remember important facts.)

2   Ask students to explain how they were impressed with the examples of "You Are Here" and "Longfellow tavern". (The first one is familiar to many people and one can well understand the awkward situation of getting lost. The second one is about some facts that one finds difficult to remember unless they get help from something like a smartphone. They are all good examples.)

Part 2 (Paras. 4–15)

Paras. 4–7

Ask students to read Paras. 4–7 and answer the following questions:

1   What's the difference between the smartphone and other inventions such as the elevator, air-conditioner and automobile in changing our lives? (Other inventions such as the elevator, air-conditioner and automobile have changed our external lives while the smartphone has changed our internal lives.)

2   What are the two different views towards those inventions? (Some people think they are making our world better while others think they are changing our lives for the worse.)

3   What is the author's attitude towards those inventions? (The inventions, including the smartphone, are most likely to make our life better and he could make a long list of the little improvements they have brought about.)

Paras. 8–10

Ask students to read Paras. 8–10 and find out what benefits the author gains from using the smartphone. (He can use the maps on a smartphone to get the right direction and the translation software to communicate in a foreign country, and read almost any menu in different languages.)

Para. 11

Ask students to read Para. 11 and identify the example to show the benefit of the smartphone. Do Exercise I of Reading Comprehension. (He can use apps like SnapTell and Hipmunk to get price comparison information.)

Paras. 12–13

Ask students to read Paras. 12–13 and identify the example to show the benefit of the smartphone. Do Exercise I of Reading Comprehension. (He can use Instapaper to automatically download articles to read.)

Paras. 14–15

1   Ask students to read Paras. 14–15 and identify the example to show the benefit of the smartphone. Do Exercise I of Reading Comprehension. (He can use Evernote to record details and help with the memory.)

2   Ask students to discuss what the author implies by saying "Now what was my next point?" (The author implies that after he has listed so many improvements brought about by the smartphone, he could still go on listing more.)

Language Points

1   When I **think back to** what I was like before the **advent** of the smartphone, I realize I must have been a **quivering** ball of anxiety. (**Para. 1**)
Paraphrase: When I think about what I was like before the coming of the smartphone, I realize that at that time I must have been a nervous person full of worry and anxiety.
think back to (sth.): think about things that happened in the past 回想起，追忆
Thinking back to my childhood, I remember summers at the beach.
advent: *n.* (**the advent of**) the coming of an important event, person, invention, etc. （重要事件、人物、发明等的）出现，到来
The **advent** of the Internet may be one of the most important technological developments in the last century.
quiver: *v.* shake slightly 颤抖，发抖
Seeing the snake, her eyes widened and her hands **quivered** in fear.
Note: There is a fixed phrase, "a ball of fire", which means "a person full of energy and enthusiasm（生龙活虎的人）". Similarly, "a ball of anxiety" means "a person full of anxiety".

2 I'd come out of a subway and walk for blocks in the wrong direction, searching as my appointment neared for a public map only to find the "You Are Here" X **blotted out** by the thousands of lost souls before me who pressed their fingers to the same spot **in hopes of somehow** getting **reoriented**. **(Para. 2)**

Paraphrase: I would get out of a subway and walk as far as several blocks in the wrong way. As my time of appointment was approaching, I was looking for a public map, but then I just found that the sign X showing my current position had faded away completely. This was because thousands of people who lost their way before me had pressed their fingers on the same place to look for the correct directions and had ruined the sign.

blot: *v.* make a blot or blots on (paper); stain (with ink) 在（纸）上留下污点；弄脏

The city has removed all the rooftop advertisement boards as they **blot** the beautiful skyline of the city.

blot out: cover or hide sth. completely 遮盖，涂去，隐藏

During a partial solar eclipse, only part of the sun is **blotted out**.

in hopes of: because of the wish for sth. 怀着……的希望

Mike dropped out of high school **in hopes of** becoming a rock star.

somehow: *adv.* in some way, or by some means 用某种方法（或方式）

Somehow I managed to fit a third couch into the living room, so we should have plenty of seating for tomorrow's party!

reorient: *v.* find one's position again in relation to one's surroundings 重定方向；重定方位

China is committed to **reorienting** its economy on a more sustainable, more equitable and more balanced path.

3 I'd begin worrying about memory loss when I could no longer remember important facts like what Longfellow **tavern** Henry Ford had bought and **restored**. **(Para. 3)**

Paraphrase: I would start to fear that I was losing my memory when I could not remember important facts such as what Longfellow tavern Henry Ford had bought and repaired.

tavern: *n.* a pub where you can also stay the night 小旅店，客栈

We spent a very pleasant afternoon in the **tavern** in the village and enjoyed delicious local food and wine.

restore: *v.* rebuild or repair (a ruined building, work of art, etc.) 重建或修复

It is truly wonderful to see a historical building coming back to life and being **restored** and conserved.

4 Now I'm sunny and carefree. It's all because of a **bundle** of plastic, glass, **microchips** and **loads of software**: my smartphone. **(Para. 4)**

Paraphrase: Now I am positive and free of worries. This is all because I have my smartphone, a collection of plastic, glass, microchips and plenty of software.

bundle: *n.* a collection of things fastened or wrapped together 捆，把，束

There was a **bundle** of branches in a corner of the cave, and I lit a fire.

microchip: *n.* 芯片

Many owners turn to **microchip** technology to help their pets return home if they're ever lost.

loads of: plenty of sth. 大量，许多

With the advent of mobile payment, Chinese people don't need to carry **loads of** cash any more today.

software: *n.* [计算机]软件

Language learning **software** has made learning and maintaining foreign language skills easier than ever before.

5   It should **come as no surprise** to anyone that the device is changing our lives. **(Para. 5)**

Paraphrase: It should be naturally expected that the smartphone is changing our lives.

come as no surprise: be expected to happen 意料之中

Mike is an excellent student and studied hard for the final exam, so it **came as no surprise** to me that he passed it.

6   Historians will remember the advent of the smartphone as something as important as the **elevator**, air-conditioner and **automobile**. **(Para. 5)**

Paraphrase: Historians will note that the appearance of the smartphone is as important as the invention of the lift, air-conditioner and car.

elevator: *n.* [美]电梯

Walking up a flight of stairs is better for you, physically speaking, than taking an **elevator**.

automobile: *n.* a car 汽车

Automobiles are one of the greatest contributors to air pollution.

7   Those inventions **reshaped** our **external** lives with tall buildings in spreading cities in previously **inhospitable** places. The smartphone has changed our **internal** lives. **(Para. 5)**

Paraphrase: The invention of these things changed the outer part of our lives: in the places where people found it difficult to live in the past, tall buildings have been put up and the cities are getting bigger. The invention of the smartphone has changed the mental side of our lives.

reshape: *v.* change the way that sth. operates or develops 重组；重塑

My high school teacher created a positive impact on my life that **reshaped** my vision and purpose.

external: *adj.* relating to the outside of sth. or of a person's body 外部的，外面的

Poor nutrition is one of the **external** factors that can affect wound healing.

inhospitable: *adj.* difficult to live or stay in 不适合居住的

Mars is an **inhospitable** place for the human body.

internal: *adj.* existing in your mind 内心的

Motivation is one of the various **internal** factors that may influence language learning.

8   Some people see those inventions as **ruining** our world. According to some social **critics**, like Jaron Lanier or Nicholas Carr, who wrote whole books on the subject, the smartphone is changing their world **for the worse**. **(Para. 6)**

Paraphrase: Some people think those inventions are destroying our world. Some social reviewers such as Jaron Lanier or Nicholas Carr wrote whole books dealing with this topic. As they point out, the smartphone is making the world become worse.

ruin: *v.* spoil or destroy sth. completely（完全地）毁坏，毁掉，糟蹋

I did love the food in that restaurant, but my mood was totally **ruined** by one fly!

critic: *n.* sb. who expresses opinions about the good and bad qualities of books, music, etc. 批评家；评论员

Albert was a chef before becoming a famous food **critic**.

for the worse: in a way that makes a situation worse 变得更差

When things take a turn **for the worse**, you've got to act fast.

9   … a smartphone will change their lives and most likely **for the better**. The little improvements in life will matter. How? Don't get me started. **(Para. 7)**

Paraphrase: … a smartphone will change their lives and most probably change them in a better way. The small progress in life will be important. In what way? Don't make me talk about it, because I can do it without stopping.

for the better: in a way that improves the situation 有所好转

May we use our anger in a productive way to try and change things **for the better**.

Note: By saying "Don't get me started", the author means he has a lot to talk about the benefits of the smartphone. "Start (on) sth.; start sb. on sth." means "(cause sb. to) make a beginning on sth.; (cause sb. to) begin doing (a job, an activity, a piece of work, etc.)（使某人）开始进行某事；（使某人）着手做（某事）". For example:

"I'm very disappointed with Jim's laziness," said Melisa. "Don't get me started!" replied Charlie. (Implied meaning: If I want to complain about Jim's laziness, I can talk a lot.)

10 First, I'm never lost. It is more than the maps on a smartphone that **keep** me **from** going in the wrong direction. **(Para. 8)**

Paraphrase: First, I have never lost my way with the help of the smartphone. It is not just about using the maps on a smartphone to avoid going in the wrong way.

keep sb. from doing: prevent sb. from doing sth. 不让（某人）做（某事）

Every little noise **keeps** me **from** falling asleep.

11 The translation software on a smartphone with its ability to "hear" foreign languages is good enough that I could ask a stranger in a strange land how to find a bathroom without **resorting** to the desperate use of gestures. **(Para. 8)**

Paraphrase: The translation app on a smartphone is able to "hear" foreign languages. With the help of this translation app, I could ask a stranger in a foreign country for the direction to a bathroom and don't have to move my hands or arms hopelessly to make myself understood.

resort: (resort to) do sth. extreme or unpleasant in order to solve a problem 采取，诉诸（不好的事物）

One should try eating healthily to lose weight instead of **resorting to** fad diets and pills.

12 I can also **navigate** nearly any menu — although I am still waiting for an **app** that can read **handwritten** Chinese characters on a menu. **(Para. 9)**

Paraphrase: I can also manage to understand almost all the menus — although I am still waiting for the development of an app which can help me understand the Chinese characters written by hand on a menu.

navigate: *v.* understand or deal with sth. complicated 理解，应付（困难复杂的情况）

With my years of experience, I have confidence to **navigate** any job to a successful completion.

app: *n.* a computer application 应用（程序）

Price comparison **apps** can comb through millions of goods to help you find the best price.

handwritten: *adj.* written by hand, not printed 手写的

Nowadays **handwritten** letters are a lost art as too many people text and email.

13 Best of all, I never look like a tourist anymore because instead of a map signaling "**Fleece** me," I am just one more person staring into the phone. (**Para. 10**)

Paraphrase: The best thing is that, as I do not have to hold a map looking for directions, I no longer look like a traveller and nobody would try to trick me and take money from me. Instead, as I am looking for directions on the phone, I just look like one of those ordinary people using a smartphone.

fleece: *v.* take (a lot of money) from sb., esp. by tricking him 诈取，敲竹杠

These tourists were **fleeced** of almost $800 when taking a taxi from the airport to their hotel.

14 Speaking of getting fleeced, the phone relieves the anxiety of thinking — no, knowing — that somewhere you could have bought it for less. (**Para. 11**)

Paraphrase: Talking about being tricked, the phone makes us less worried when you think — no, when you know — that you could have bought something for a lower price somewhere else.

15 There are apps like SnapTell, which gives you the price of books online when you **snap** a picture of the cover, and Hipmunk for **airfares**. (**Para. 11**)

Paraphrase: There are apps like SnapTell, which tells you the online price of a book when you take a picture of its cover, and Hipmunk, which helps you compare the price of airplane tickets.

snap: *v.* take a photograph 给……拍照，摄影

Many people like to **snap** pictures for souvenirs as they travel around the world.

airfare: *n.* the price of a journey by plane 飞机票价

Check out this website for the cheapest **airfare** to New York.

16 Going to price **comparison** sites is nothing new, but having them available in the store is. (**Para. 11**)

Paraphrase: It's not unusual to go to websites that allow you to compare prices, but it's a new thing to be able to go to these websites when you are shopping in the store.

comparison: *n.* the process of comparing two or more people or things 比较

A **comparison** of the two films shows surprising similarities between the main characters.

17 The slow checkout line? The delayed flight? These are no longer sources of **distress**. (**Para. 12**)

Paraphrase: Things such as waiting in a slow checkout line or waiting for a flight that has been postponed won't make you upset any more.

distress: *n.* a feeling of extreme unhappiness 忧虑，苦恼，悲伤

The recent serious flooding has caused great **distress** to the life of the local families.

18 They are opportunities to relax by playing games, listening to the **soundtrack** of your life that is always with you or reading. (**Para. 12**)

Paraphrase: The apps on a smartphone turns the waiting time into a chance to relax by playing games, listening to your personal collection of music that brings you good memories, or reading.

soundtrack: *n.* the recorded music from a film 电影配乐

The **soundtrack** captures the mood of the film with some exciting music.

Note: "The soundtrack of your life" is a personal collection of music that gives you that flashback（往事重现）feeling whenever you hear them.

19 It gives me a chance to **catch up on** all the online articles that I saved using Instapaper, which **automatically** downloads them to my phone in **readable format**. **(Para. 13)**

Paraphrase: The smartphone gives me the opportunity to read all the online articles that I've saved using Instapaper. I don't need to do anything and Instapaper will download the articles for me to my phone in a style that is easy to read.

catch up on: do what needs to be done because you have not been able to do it until now 赶做，补做

I stayed up all night to **catch up on** my chemistry assignments.

automatically: *adv.* by the action of a machine, without a person making it work（机器）自动地

Once the app is updated, it will be **automatically** downloaded to your device within 24 hours.

readable: *adj.* writing or print that is readable is clear and easy to read 清晰的，易读的

When making a presentation, remember to choose a font size that will make the text **readable** to the audience.

format: *n.* 格式

PDF is a file **format** designed to present documents consistently across multiple devices and platforms.

20 I've started buying books and magazine **subscriptions** because it is so handy to carry my **bookshelf** with me on the phone. **(Para. 13)**

Paraphrase: I've started buying books and subscribing to magazines because it is so convenient to have all my books on the phone that it's like carrying my whole bookshelf with me.

subscription: *n.* 订阅；订购

The newspaper has seen **subscription** sales jump 200 percent in the last year.

bookshelf: *n.* a shelf that you keep books on 书架

My students need a new **bookshelf** to organize their new classroom library books.

21 Most importantly, I never forget anything. Well, hardly anything. O.K., not as much as I used to. **(Para. 14)**

Paraphrase: The most important thing is that with the help of the smartphone, I never forget anything. Well, I should say I almost never forget anything. Alright, what I actually want to say is I don't forget things as much as I used to.

Note: By saying "Well, hardly anything. O.K., not as much as I used to", the author is implying that he admits that he still forgets things even with the help of his smartphone. He doesn't want to sound too assertive though he says "I never forget anything".

22 Of course, search engines begin to **substitute** for my memory of those useless details. That may be changing our inner lives by making us all a little bit **dumber**. **(Para. 14)**

Paraphrase: Of course, I start to use search engines instead of my memory to remember those unimportant details. That may be changing our mental lives by making us all a little more stupid.

substitute: *v.* take the place of sb./sth. else; use sb./sth. instead of sb./sth. else 替代，顶替，替换

Regarding the new project, I don't think I'll be able to continue so Elwin will **substitute** for me.

dumb: *adj.* stupid 愚蠢的

I can't believe I was so **dumb**. I spilled the milk on the carpet again this morning.

23 But if the smartphone can help us **recall** events in our own lives, it has yet another purpose that makes us, if not smarter, at least wiser. **(Para. 14)**

Paraphrase: But if the smartphone can help us remember things that happened in our own lives, then it has another goal, which is to make us at least wiser if not smarter.

recall: *v.* remember sth. 回想，回忆起

It took me a while to **recall** where I parked my car.

24 The smartphone gives me the ability to record my life and becomes an **auxiliary** memory of everything I do. **(Para. 14)**

Paraphrase: The smartphone enables me to keep track of my life and becomes an additional memory of everything I do.

auxiliary: *adj.* giving help or support; additional 辅助的；附加的

The ice cream plant has an **auxiliary** power system in case of a power failure to keep the products frozen.

25 Granted, most of it is **trivial**. **(Para. 14)**

Paraphrase: Of course, most of the things it records are unimportant.

trivial: *adj.* that has little importance 不重要的；琐碎的

I hate cheating and I can't believe he thinks cheating is a **trivial** thing!

26 It **captures** and organizes all my business cards. But it also holds **snatches** of conversation, ideas for articles and things I research. **(Para. 14)**

Paraphrase: Evernote records and organizes all my business cards in the digital form. It also records short parts of conversation, ideas for articles and things I research.

capture: *v.* put sth. in a form that a computer can use 采集；记录

Photographs and documents can be scanned or **captured** using a camera or an image capture board.

snatch: *n.* a short part of a conversation, song, etc. 谈话、歌曲等的片段

When I was outside the door of my boss' office, I overheard a **snatch** of conversation that I couldn't ignore.

27 So I'd like to think that it frees my mind for more important things and helps me make connections. Now what was my next point? **(Para. 15)**

Paraphrase: So I'd like to think that the smartphone allows me to pay greater attention to more important things and helps me build connections with other people. Now what should I talk about next?

Note: "Now what was my next point?" echoes the words "Don't get me started" in Para. 7. The author implies that he has lots to talk about and after he has listed so many improvements in life, he could still go on listing more. Here the past tense "was" is used to show that the author has lots of ideas in his mind and could not remember what he wanted to say next.

Lead-in

I 1 About 18 or 19 hours.
2 Fear of Missing Out. (In order to catch up with what is going on, I have to keep checking the phone to make sure I do not miss out on anything.)
3 Yes.
4 I cannot leave the smartphone for more than one minute.

Script

Rob:	Hello, welcome to 6 Minute English. I'm Rob.
Catherine:	And I'm Catherine.
Rob:	So Catherine, how long do you spend on your smartphone?
Catherine:	My smartphone … hmm … Not that long really, about 18 or 19 hours.
Rob:	No, sorry, I meant in a day, not in a week.
Catherine:	Er, that's what I meant too, Rob — a day.
Rob:	Oh wow, so you've even got it right here …
Catherine:	… Yep, got it now, Rob. Yes, I should tell you that I suffer from FOMO.
Rob:	FOMO?
Catherine:	FOMO — Fear of Missing Out. Something cool or interesting might be happening somewhere, Rob, and I want to be sure I catch it, so I have to keep checking my phone, to make sure, you know, I don't miss out on anything.
Rob:	So we could call you a phubber … Hello … I said, so you're a phubber? Someone who ignores other people because you'd rather look at your phone.
Catherine:	Oh yeah, that's right.
Rob:	It sounds like you have a bit of a problem there, Catherine. But you're not the only one. According to one recent survey, half of teenagers in the USA feel like they are addicted to their mobile phones. If you are addicted to something, you have a physical or mental need to keep on doing it. You can't stop doing it. You often hear about people being addicted to drugs or alcohol, but you can be addicted to other things too, like mobile phones. So, Catherine, do you think you are addicted to your phone? How long could you go without it? Catherine? Catherine!
Catherine:	Oh sorry, Rob, yes, well … I think if I went more than a minute, I'd probably get sort of sweaty palms and I think I'd start feeling a bit panicky.
Rob:	Oh dear! Well, if I can distract you just for a few minutes, can we look at this topic in more detail please? Let's start with a quiz question first though. In what year did the term "smartphone" first appear in print? Was

it: a) 1995, b) 2000, or c) 2005? What do you think?

Catherine: Okay, you've got my full attention now, Rob, and I think it's 2000 but actually can I just have a quick look on my phone to check the answer?

Rob: No, no, that would be cheating for you — maybe not for the listeners.

Catherine: Spoilsport.

Reading to Learn

Reading Comprehension

I 1 b   2 d   3 a   4 c

II 1 B   2 C   3 C   4 D   5 D

III Text Organization

1 find directions
2 no longer remembered
3 get lost
4 almost gone
5 buy something for less
6 play games
7 read online articles
8 recall events in our own lives
9 more important things

Language in Use

Words and Expressions

I 1 quivered   2 internal   3 format   4 comparison
   5 recall   6 trivial   7 capturing   8 navigate

II 1 blotted out   2 came as no surprise   3 Thinking back   4 in hopes of
   5 resorting to   6 keeps ... from   7 substitute for   8 for the worse

III 1 external   2 ruining   3 dumb   4 for the better   5 blots out
   6 loads of   7 restore   8 distress   9 resort to   10 advent

Word Formation

1 reappearance   2 Reanalyze   3 reunited   4 reconstruction   5 regain
6 reordered   7 reproduced   8 replace   9 re-collect   10 redefine

Collocation

1 ruined the southern tower   2 restore this building   3 ruin the relationship
4 restored the painting   5 restore the vision   6 ruined the quietness
7 ruins the ending   8 restore his confidence

1   In the center of the stage were a black grand piano and a microphone.

2   Inside the cardboard box were some unlabeled bottles in different colors.

3   So grateful was the town for the heroic actions of the little boy that they showered him with all kinds of gifts and flowers.

4   So popular is the game of table tennis that it is played everywhere in the country.

5   Were there a better solution to this problem, it would already have been put forward.

6   I couldn't have planned my wedding had it not been for my mom, my mother-in-law and a few close family friends.

7   Should you have any further questions regarding our service, please do not hesitate to contact us.

8   My visit to Vancouver might have been warmer and sunnier had I been there during the summer months.

Translation

I 1 从小我就一直喜爱数字。一上学，果不其然，我的数学和科学都很优秀。

   2 该心理学家认为，花个晚上享受一下歌舞，确实能够让人们变得更好。"听音乐剧会让人精神振作，"他说。

   3 伊丽莎白觉得她那篇关于拯救世界的文章有机会得奖，奖品是订阅一年她最喜爱的杂志。

   4 在我开始撰写自传的过程中，我不断回忆起自己的童年经历。

   5 许多人搭起露营设施，睡在售票处附近的马路上，以期买到观看演出的最佳位子。

II 1 If you're too tired to think clearly and write productively, try to force yourself to catch up on some sleep.

   2 We can all recall the time when we were young and our mothers asked us not to speak to strangers.

   3 Try to substitute brown rice for white rice if possible because brown rice is more nutritious.

   4 The game of Go, originated in China, is the earliest form of chess in the world. Players have to resort to all sorts of tactics in order to win.

   5 China's market-oriented reforms have reshaped the economic landscape, allowing private companies to compete with state-owned enterprises on a fair basis.

III While smartphones and the Internet have brought convenience to many people's life, they have also brought challenges to senior people. Thus, China is launching a nation-wide campaign to help senior people cross the digital gap and enjoy benefits of digital technology. In many cities, local volunteers teach seniors to use smartphones and apps in classrooms located in residential areas. "Now I can do many things with my phone like the young people, such as shopping, scanning codes, taking photos, and chatting with my children," said one senior student proudly.

Corpora in Language Learning

Verb phrases of "come + preposition/adverb"	Definitions
come about	to happen
come across	to find or meet sb./sth. by chance
come off	to stop being fixed to sth.; to achieve a particular result in an activity
come up	to be mentioned or to be discussed
come up with	to think of an idea or a plan and propose it

II   **1** come up   **2** comes about   **3** come across   **4** come up with   **5** come off

Writing

I   **1** Introduction:

Happy with the phone and the deal

2 Pros:

A good smartphone

Helpful service team

Got exactly what I wanted

3 Cons:

Had to separately claim for the offered cash back deal

This information not stated

4 Suggestion:

Optimize the cash back deal process

Language Functions

I   Sam: Free tomorrow?

Jen: Yeah. Why?

Sam: Great. Because I want you to be my girlfriend. I like you.

Jen: Too much information. Let's talk face to face tomorrow.

Sam: I've never felt like this before.

Jen: Please call me now.

Sam: Haha just kidding. You believed me?

Jen: You are definitely not funny!

Sam: Laughing out loud. See you tomorrow. Estimated time of arrival?

Jen: Don't know. 9 I guess.

Sam: Let me know.

Jen: Got to go. Talk later.

Sam: Bye. Hugs and kisses.

Reading to Explore

Reading Comprehension

I   **1** D   **2** C   **3** B   **4** D   **5** B

II   **1** F   **2** F   **3** F   **4** T   **5** T

III   **A** 5   **B** 2   **C** 10   **D** 6   **E** 2   **F** 8   **G** 12   **H** 1   **I** 11   **J** 8

Words and Expressions

I   **1** trusty   **2** obligated   **3** connectivity   **4** alert   **5** downgraded

   6 vacation   **7** simplified   **8** feature   **9** idleness   **10** overnight

II   **1** was ... hooked   **2** miss out   **3** write off   **4** on her terms   **5** getting rid of

   6 hang up   **7** be obligated to   **8** revert ... to   **9** opt out   **10** pick ... up

PART V   Text Translation

Text A

我是如何通过爱上智能手机而学会不再发愁的

达蒙·达林

1   回想起智能手机尚未面世时的自己，我意识到自己那时一定属于战战兢兢的焦虑一族。

2   从地铁出来，我会奔着错误的方向一走走出好几个街区，随着约会时间的逼近，我寻找着公共地图，却只发现图上标记"你在此处"的大叉已被戳得模糊不清——在我之前有成千上万的迷路者抱着好歹能找到方向的希望，用手指头按在了同一位置。

3   当我再也记不起重要的事，比如记不得亨利·福特购买并修缮的朗费罗客栈是哪一家之类的事，我就开始担心自己记忆丧失。

4   而现在，我心情开朗，无忧无虑。这全仰仗一个东西，这个东西由一堆塑料、玻璃、芯片和大量软件组成：我的智能手机。

5   这款设备正在改变我们的生活，对此任何人都不会感到意外。在历史学家的记载中，智能手机的出现，会同电梯、空调和汽车之类一样重要。那些发明重塑了我们的外部生活，我们在原本的荒凉之地，建造起了不断扩张的城市和高楼。而智能手机则改变了我们的内在人生。

6   有人认为，这些发明毁坏了我们的世界。一些社会批评家，如加隆·雷尼尔或者尼古拉斯·卡

尔，以此为主题写了大量著作，认为智能手机正让他们的世界每况愈下。

7　但是对大多数人而言——随着技术变得更加便宜，数十亿人将成为这一设备的新用户——一部智能手机将改变他们的生活，而且更可能是改善他们的生活。生活中的点滴改善真的重要。怎样重要？那我可要打开话匣子了。

8　首先，我再也不会迷路了。有了智能手机上的地图，我不再走错方向，但远不止这些。智能手机上，能够"听懂"外语的翻译软件很给力，让我能在陌生的地方问一个陌生人厕所在哪里，而不必拼命比划手势。

9　我也能浏览几乎各种菜单——尽管我还缺一款应用软件，来读懂菜单上手写的汉字。

10　我旅行时曾有的忐忑也基本烟消云散。最大的好处是，我再也不会看上去像一个游客，因为我不会端着地图，提示别人"来敲我竹杠呀"，我只是跟众人一样，目不转睛地盯着手机而已。

11　说到被敲竹杠，手机帮我们缓解了这样的焦虑，就是意识到——应该说发现——在别的地方你花更少的钱就能买到东西。有了诸如SnapTell这种应用软件，你拍一张书的封面照片，它就能给出网上的售价，还有像Hipmunk这种买机票软件。虽说在网上比价早已屡见不鲜，但是能够在门店当场用上还是挺新鲜的。

12　排队付账太慢？航班晚点？这些已不再令人痛苦不安，反而让我们有机会放松下来玩玩游戏，听听带着美好回忆的个人精选音乐，或者看看书。

13　它让我有机会读完所有我用Instapaper保存的网上文章，这个软件能自动下载文章，并用易于阅读的格式存到我手机上。我也开始买书和订阅杂志，因为有了手机就可以很方便地携带我的"书架"。

14　最重要的是，我不再忘记任何事。好吧，我几乎不再忘记任何事。这么说吧，没有像以前那么健忘了。当然，搜索引擎开始代替我去记住那些无关紧要的琐碎小事。这也许会让我们变得愚钝些，从而改变我们的内在人生。可如果智能手机能帮我们回忆起自己生活中的点点滴滴，那也起到了另一个作用，即哪怕没让我们变得更聪明，也至少更明智。智能手机赋予我记录人生的能力，成为我一切所作所为的辅助存储器。当然，我承认，记的大多数都是琐碎的小事。我用Evernote软件记录我喝的葡萄酒或者饭店的名字——因为我对这些事的记忆力极差。它拍摄和管理我所有的名片。同时它还保存对话的片段、文章的想法和我研究的内容。

15　所以我觉得，智能手机解放了我的头脑，让它去做更重要的事，而且还帮我与人沟通。说到这儿，我下面该讲啥了？

Text B

我是如何戒掉智能手机并真正开始生活的

詹娜·沃金瑞奇

1　电话铃响了：是我朋友来电，问我能否在去晚宴的路上顺道接上她。我问她在哪里。在她解释时，我尽力伸手越过料理台去拿笔。我快速地把地址记在了我那本可靠的笔记簿上，这个笔记簿我一直放在后裤兜里。我告诉她我大约过20分钟到她那儿。然后，我挂掉了电话。是真的把听筒挂掉。

2　我拿出笔记本电脑，搜索地址，把最佳行车路线记在我的笔记簿上，出门走向我那辆1989年的皮卡车（该车最新的技术卖点是带磁带播放机），然后开车过去。假如我在路上迷路，我就得向人打听路线。假如朋友改变了她的计划，那她也无法很快地通知我或取消约定。假如我路上撞了车，我也无法拨打911。

3 这些我都不介意。正如你现在已经猜到的，我已经超过18个月没用手机了。

4 我并非仅仅取消手机运营商服务而保留智能手机在无线网络环境下使用，我也不是降级到使用翻盖手机实现"简约化"；我是完完全全地放弃。我的生活里没有手机，无论何种形式，彻底没有。

5 也许，我应该用手机。我是一个自由作家和平面设计师。我有众多的理由在口袋里揣上一部小电脑，但我并不怀念它。在电子邮件和社交媒体之外还有不少方法能联系到我。我根据自己的意愿去接收信息。没人能在我五音不全地大唱《魂牵梦萦》时发短消息来打断我。这种感觉就像度假的第一天晚上那样，自由自在。

6 "我的电话"变成了"那部电话"。它不再是我的私人助理；它变回了一件居家用品——就像"冰箱"或"沙发"一样，后两样你也不可能挂在屁股后面。

7 我摆脱手机并不是要追求某个反技术潮流的理想，也不是因为我买不起，而是因为手机曾使我上瘾。我会不停地查收电子邮件和社交媒体信息，或者玩游戏。当我发现我可以下载有声书后，耳塞就再没有离开过我的耳朵。我曾是个铁杆用户。我曾喜爱使用手机的分分秒秒。

8 甚至睡觉时，我也把手机放在旁边。手机是我入睡前看的东西，也是唤醒我的闹钟。我永不关机。我敢肯定，我曾在开车时、在漆黑的电影院里、在跟朋友外出围坐在饭店的桌子旁时都在发短信。事情变得如此糟糕，以致我只要手里空闲30秒就会不舒服。我觉得必须回复每一封邮件、每一条短信、推特信息和游戏邀请。

9 作为一个作家，我把这一切看作是进行读者互动、免费提高公众知名度、开展重要的底层推广所必须付出的代价。其实这些只是一个瘾君子的自我辩解而已。

10 我现在已经脱瘾一年半了，一切良好。我接到足够的活儿，我不会错过邀请，我也不再害怕自己的想法。在一个即时通信不仅是一种便捷附件——而是人的第二张皮的世界中，这些胜利可不是小胜利。

11 我安装了一部固定电话，有了更多的睡眠。我看着别人的时候直视他们的眼睛。我吃食物，而不是拍食物，也不会一边驾驶半吨重的钢铁大家伙汇入车流，一边低头看小小的屏幕了。我的业务、社交生活和自身安全也没有在一夜之间消散。原来，一条基本的互联网线路，加上笔记本电脑，就足够维系跟朋友们的联络，维持周末的开心活动和保证火车不误点。虽说我也许无法随时随地拨打911报警电话，但是这点牺牲对我是值得的。酒鬼也可以用烈酒来给伤口消毒，但这并不意味着他们应该在后裤兜里带上一瓶以备不时之需。

12 我很高兴又回到了真实世界。相比以前要靠手机信息提醒自己存在，现在的感觉好多了。

4 SPACE ODYSSEY

PART I

Introduction

The first people going into space only went up for short trips to see what it was like. Today, astronauts can spend weeks or even months living and working in space. What is their life like in space? What do they do every day? How do they get their food supplies? This unit aims to increase our understanding of life in space. Text A talks about what a typical day of an astronaut is like on the ISS (the International Space Station); that is, what the astronaut does in the morning, during the day, and at the end of the day while in space. Text B informs us about how astronauts on the ISS capture *Dragon*, a special cargo ship devoted to carrying supplies and material for new experiments from the Earth to the ISS. In spite of our enduring fascination with space, out there in the universe there is still so much left to be discovered. Do you aspire to be one of the persons who can explore the space and touch the stars?

In this unit you will:

1 Learn what a day's life is like for an astronaut on board the ISS;
2 Learn how astronauts on board the ISS work together with teams on the ground to capture *Dragon*, a special cargo ship;
3 Reflect on the importance of space exploration to China and to human beings;
4 Learn how the suffix *-ity* or *-ness* combines with an adjective to form a noun;
5 Learn how the verbs *earn, take, assemble,* and *maintain* collocate with other words;
6 Learn to use linking words of contrast: *though, although, despite, in spite of, while,* and *whereas*;
7 Learn nouns that collocate with *earn/gain/obtain/win* by using CADEL;
8 Learn to write a process essay;
9 Learn to use English for air travel.

PART II | Teaching Suggestions

Sayings

Learning objectives:

- Get a general idea of the unit
- Get inspirations from the sayings
- Get useful advice and guidance from famous people or books
- Learn to develop a positive attitude toward life

Teaching steps:

1 Ask students to translate the two sayings into Chinese.
   Reference translations for the sayings:

   - 攻城不怕坚，攻书莫畏难。科学有险阻，苦战能过关。   ——叶剑英
   - 人类必须冲出地球——冲出大气层或更远——因为只有这样，他才能完全了解他所生活的世界。   ——苏格拉底

2 For the first saying, tell students that there can be great difficulties and challenges on the road of scientific research, but as long as we are determined and work hard, we will finally achieve our goals. As is written by Chairman Mao in his poem: "Nothing is hard under the sky if we but dare to climb up high（世上无难事，只要肯登攀）." You can also introduce to students one similar quote from John Heywood (English writer, c. 1497–c. 1580): "Nothing is impossible to a willing heart（心之所愿，无事不成）."

3 The second saying is a quote from Socrates, an ancient Greek philosopher. For this saying, tell students the significance of space exploration. Space exploration allows scientists to prove or disprove scientific theories developed on Earth. It also helps us human beings better understand our planet and our place in the universe.

Lead-in

Learning objectives:

- Learn some basic information about the ISS
- Learn some interesting facts about living in space

Teaching steps:

1 Make a brief introduction to the unit and explain its learning objectives.
2 Ask students to do Exercises I and II. Encourage students to engage in the pair work actively after they watch the video for Exercise II.

Reading to Learn

Text A

A Day in Space: Explore Life on the ISS

Learning objectives:

- Learn what a day's life is like for an astronaut on board the ISS
- Learn about the text organization pattern: following a chronological order to record a day's life

Teaching steps:

1   Introduce the topic of Text A: What is a day's life like in space? Is it boring or exciting? Do you want to know some detailed facts about it?

2   Ask students to go through the whole text and answer the question "What is the text mainly about?" in Exercise I of Reading Comprehension. (The text is mainly about a typical day of an ISS astronaut in space; that is, what she does in the morning, during the day, and at the end of the day.)

3   Ask students to divide the text into three parts. After that, ask them to look at the Text Organization exercise to check if they have made the same division. The text can be divided as follows: Part 1 (Paras. 1–3), Part 2 (Paras. 4–13) and Part 3 (Para. 14).

4   Help students recognize the writing pattern of the text by reminding them of the features of chronological order introduced in Unit 2, Book 2.

5   Go to Part III Detailed Study of Text A. Help students understand difficult sentences in the text accurately. Introduce important new words and expressions with explanations and examples.

6   Ask students to do the exercises following the text.

Critical Thinking

Learning objectives:

- Develop interest in space exploration
- Understand the significance of space exploration to China and to the whole world
- Learn some important qualities from China's pioneering astronauts

Teaching steps:

1   Ask students to read the questions first and then give them some ideas on how to approach each question.

2   For Question 1, ask students to discuss the exciting part of space life. While we know it is challenging to live in space, there can be a lot of excitement living there too. Ask students to imagine they are about to make a space travel and will stay in a space station for two weeks. Encourage them to describe what interesting things they expect to experience there, what different views they expect to see, and what insights they want to share with others.

3   For Question 2, ask students to discuss the significance of space exploration to China and to the whole world. You can guide students through the following questions: How can space exploration drive the development of various technologies? How can space technologies such as navigation, communication and remote sensing capabilities improve our lives on the Earth as well? What potential benefits can space exploration bring in terms of discovery and use of natural resources? How can space exploration lift our national spirit? How can it help us better understand our own place in the universe and make us do more to protect the Earth?

4   For Question 3, ask students to talk about what qualities they can learn from the pioneering astronauts of our country. You may provide some useful vocabulary such as *persevering, dedicated, innovative, determined, unyielding,* etc.

5   Ask students to work in pairs or small groups to share their opinions. Encourage each pair or group to present their favorite ideas in class.

Corpora in Language Learning

Learning objectives:

- Learn to search CADEL for nouns that collocate with *earn/gain/obtain/win* with "earn/gain/ obtain/win *" as the search terms, using the "Concordance" function of AntConc
- Learn to translate into Chinese the collocations of "earn/gain/obtain/win + noun"
- Learn to complete the given sentences with *earn/gain/obtain/win* based on the contexts in which they appear

Teaching steps:

1   Ask students to search CADEL for nouns that collocate with *earn/gain/obtain/win* with "earn/ gain/obtain/win *" as the search terms, using the "Concordance" function of AntConc. Ask students to identify the nouns that begin with the given letters. Remind students that some collocating nouns may not come right next to the verbs, and that they should search the context for the collocating nouns.

2   Ask students to sort the search results by setting KWIC sort.

3   Discuss the use of the collocations "earn/gain/obtain/win + noun" and their Chinese translations.

Writing

Learning objectives:

- Learn to write a process essay in chronological order
- Practice writing a process essay in chronological order with the tips introduced in this part

Teaching steps:

1   Introduce the concept of process essay and the two types of process essay.

2 Introduce the structure of a process essay and some tips for writing it.

3 Ask students to read the passage in Exercise I and analyze how the tips introduced to them are used.

4 Ask students to do Exercise II after class.

Language Functions

Learning objectives:

- Get familiar with some important words and expressions related to air travel
- Learn to use some of the words and expressions listed in this part for real situations

Teaching steps:

1 Explain the need to get familiar with the English vocabulary related to air travel.

2 Ask students to read the list of words and expressions in the table. Explain some of them if necessary.

3 Ask students to do the exercises by using some of the words and expressions they have learned.

Reading to Explore

Text B
Space Odyssey

Learning objectives:

- Increase knowledge about space exploration
- Learn how astronauts on board the ISS capture *Dragon*, a special cargo ship
- Learn more about how to describe a process of doing something
- Learn to use new words and expressions correctly

Teaching steps:

1 Ask students to read the text and finish the exercises following the text before class.

2 Check answers to the exercises.

3 Ask students to describe briefly the process of capturing the cargo ship *Dragon*.

4 Ask students to discuss what is the most important while working in space.

> **Summary of Text B**
>
> This text describes how Samantha Cristoforetti and other crew members on board the ISS work together with ground workers to capture the *Dragon*, a special cargo ship used to carry supplies and material for new experiments to the ISS. Samantha Cristoforetti plays a key role, operating the robot arm from the robotics workstation in the Cupola of the ISS. She is aided by two other astronauts, Terry Virts and the author himself. They need to move very slowly and carefully during the capture process, as the closer the *Dragon* gets to the ISS, the bigger threat it brings to it. At the same time, workers on the ground join the capture process in a supportive way. With Samantha's extraordinary skills and other people's support, the *Dragon* is successfully captured.

A Day in Space: Explore Life on the ISS

Background Information

1   **ISS: International Space Station**，国际空间站

The ISS is currently the largest habitable human-made body in low Earth orbit. It serves as a microgravity and space environment research laboratory in which crew members conduct various scientific experiments. The programme is a joint project involving five participating space agencies: NASA (United States), Roscosmos (Russia), JAXA (Japan), ESA (Europe), and CSA (Canada). Its first component was launched into orbit in Nov., 1998. The station is expected to operate until 2028.

2   **Samantha Cristoforetti:** 萨曼莎·克里斯托弗雷蒂

Samantha Cristoforetti is an Italian European Space Agency astronaut, former Italian Air Force pilot and engineer. She is also the first Italian woman in space. Born in Milan in 1977, she was officially selected as an astronaut in 2009 by the European Space Agency, and began her first space travel in 2014.

3   **European Space Agency (ESA):** 欧洲航天局

European Space Agency is an intergovernmental organisation of more than 20 member states dedicated to the exploration of space. It was established in 1975, and is headquartered in Paris, France.

4   ***Dragon:*** "龙"飞船

Dragon is a cargo spacecraft developed by SpaceX, an American private space transportation company, with the capability to deliver cargo to the ISS. The spacecraft can return to Earth and be reused. It began its regular cargo flights in Oct., 2012.

Understanding the Text

Part 1 (Paras. 1–3)

Ask students to read Paras. 1–3 and answer the following questions:

1   Who is Samantha Cristoforetti? Where is she? (She is an Italian astronaut with the European Space Agency. She is now on the ISS orbiting 250 miles above Earth.)

2   What is her "bed"? (Her "bed" is actually a sleeping bag.)

3   What is the very first thing Samantha Cristoforetti does after waking up in the morning? (She reaches for her laptop to check her schedule for the day.)

Part 2 (Paras. 4–13)

Paras. 4–5

Ask students to read Paras. 4–5 and answer the following questions:

1   What does Cristoforetti do first after getting up? (She goes to the gym to exercise.)

2   Why does Cristoforetti have to spend a long time exercising every day? (Question 2 in Exercise I of Reading Comprehension) (Because she needs to prevent her bone density and muscle mass loss in a weightless environment.)

Paras. 6–7

Ask students to read Paras. 6–7 and answer the following questions:

1   What does Cristoforetti use to take a shower? (She uses a small soapy towel and water squirted from a foil packet.)

2   Why is an ISS astronaut's productivity very valuable? (Question 3 in Exercise I of Reading Comprehension) (A huge amount of money has been invested for the work of the ISS, which means that the astronauts' work is very important and that they have to work hard to make sure the money spent is worthwhile.)

Para. 8

Ask students to read Para. 8 and answer the following question:

1   What is *Dragon*? (*Dragon* is a special cargo ship loaded with supplies and material for new experiments.)

Paras. 9–10

Ask students to read Paras. 9–10 and answer the following questions:

1   What are these two paragraphs mainly about? (These two paragraphs are mainly about using toilet in space.)

2   What does the word "product" in Para. 9 refer to? (It refers to the astronauts' liquid waste.)

3   How is an astronaut's liquid waste disposed of in space? (Question 4 in Exercise I of Reading Comprehension) (It is converted back into water for reuse.)

Paras. 11–12

Ask students to read Paras. 11–12 and answer the following questions:

1   What food could astronauts only have in the past? (They could only have mushy tube food in the past.)

2   How has astronaut food changed now? (Astronaut food is much better now. There are many more choices like tomatoes, mushrooms, and chicken that an astronaut can assemble into a full meal.)

Para. 13

Ask students to read Para. 13 and answer the following question:

1   What does Cristoforetti do to relax at the end of the day? (She would update her online logbook, enjoy a view of Earth from the Cupola, or take pictures of Earth.)

Part 3 (Para. 14)

Ask students to read Para. 14 and answer the following questions:

1   What record did Cristoforetti earn after 199 days' working on the ISS? (She earned the record for longest uninterrupted spaceflight by a woman.)

2   What does the last sentence mean? (It means although she wants to go back to space, she really enjoys the fresh fruit on Earth.)

Language Points

1   A night owl, Samantha Cristoforetti starts her day by sleepily **reaching for** her laptop. **(Para. 1)**
Paraphrase: Samantha Cristoforetti stays up late at night. She starts her day by stretching out her hand to get her laptop computer before she fully wakes up from her sleep in the morning.
reach for: stretch out (one's hand) in order to touch or take sth. 伸手去拿
After washing her hands, she **reached for** the coffee on the table and sipped it slowly.

2   Unlike **approximately** all of us, Cristoforetti's "bed" is a green sleeping bag on the International Space Station, and that laptop links Cristoforetti to Earth as she **orbits** 250 miles above the planet's surface. **(Para. 2)**
Paraphrase: Different from nearly all of us, Cristoforetti's "bed" is actually a green sleeping bag on the International Space Station, and her laptop computer connects her to Earth as she travels around Earth at a distance of 250 miles above its surface.
approximately: *adv.* 近似地，大约地
Despite treatment with penicillin, the child remained ill for **approximately** one week.
orbit: *v.* move around a large object in space such as a planet（绕……）作轨道运行
The astronaut said when he **orbited** Earth in the spaceship, he saw for the first time how beautiful our planet was.

3   **In case** you didn't already guess, Cristoforetti is an Italian astronaut with the European Space **Agency**. **(Para. 3)**
Paraphrase: If you still didn't guess who she is, (let me tell you that) Cristoforetti is an Italian astronaut working with the European Space Agency.
in case: if 如果，假使
In case you missed it, you can watch the complete news conference on our website.
agency: *n.* an organization or department, esp. within a government, that does a specific job 机构，（政府内的）局，部，处
A travel **agency** can often help you plan the best vacation destinations anywhere you desire.

4   After waking up in her phone booth-sized room, checking the day's schedule on her computer, and floating out of her sleeping bag, Cristoforetti begins her day. For Cristoforetti, this means by **hitting up** the gym — every day. **(Para. 4)**
Paraphrase: After she wakes up in her room, which is as small as a phone booth, checks the tasks she needs to do during the day from her computer, and floats out of her sleeping bag, Cristoforetti begins her day. For Cristoforetti, this means she will go to the gym to exercise first — it's her daily routine.
hit up: go somewhere or do sth. 去某处或做某事
Instead of **hitting up** the gym, running in the sun or eating three balanced meals will make you feel better too.

5   In order to prevent bone **density** and **muscle** mass loss while in orbit, Cristoforetti and other astronauts spend at least an hour and a half in the gym each day, where they use specialized weightlift **simulation** equipment such as the Advanced **Resistive** Exercise Device, as lifting regular weights in a **weightless** environment just isn't effective. **(Para. 5)**

Paraphrase: In order to prevent the loss of bone density and muscle mass while traveling in space, Cristoforetti and other astronauts exercise at least an hour and a half in the gym every day. There they can exercise by using special weightlift equipment such as the Advance Resistive Exercise Device. These types of special weightlift equipment function like normal ones, since lifting weights normally used on Earth in a weightless environment is simply of no use.

density: *n.* the relationship between the mass of sth. and its size（物质的）密度

This graph shows the population **density** of the province from 1970 to 2020.

muscle: *n.* 肌肉

Healthy **muscles** let you move freely and keep your body strong.

simulation: *n.* the activity of producing conditions which are similar to real ones, esp. in order to test sth. 仿真，模拟

The airport is developing a computer **simulation** of air-traffic control that handles events such as landings and takeoffs.

resistive: *adj.* 电阻的

These $99 and $199 devices use cheaper **resistive** touchscreens which can be a real pain to use.

weightless: *adj.* having no weight, esp. when it is floating in space or water（尤指在太空或水中）失重的；无重量的

In a **weightless** environment, we can't use muscles and bones to support our body weight.

6   In space, the cheat day simply does not exist. **(Para. 5)**

Paraphrase: Being in space doesn't allow a day's break from the exercise schedule.

Note: "A cheat day" is a scheduled break in a diet. It is believed that when people are going on a diet, they can "cheat" for one day a week as long as they eat to their diet plan for the remaining six days. In this text, it means "having a break from the exercise schedule". The sentence implies that if you don't exercise as much as required in space, you will have to suffer the consequences (that is, the loss of bone density and muscle mass).

7   After a long **workout**, many of us would **head to** the bathroom for a cool shower. **(Para. 6)**

Paraphrase: After a long time of physical exercise, many of us would go to the bathroom to take a cool shower.

workout: *n.* a period of physical exercise, esp. as training for a sport（尤指体育）锻炼，训练

Starting the day with a good **workout** can give you more energy to work during the day.

head to: go towards 朝……行进，向……去

When he got home, he **headed to** the second floor and took a shower.

8   Cristoforetti does more or less the same, but in her case, instead of running water, she must **make do with** a small, **soapy** towel and water **squirted** from a **foil** packet. **(Para. 6)**

Paraphrase: Cristoforetti does nearly the same thing, but since she is in space, instead of using the running water like we do on Earth, she has to take the shower by using a small towel that contains soap in it and water that comes out thinly and quickly from a foil packet.

make do with sth.: manage with sth. that is not really adequate or satisfactory 用某物勉强应付；将就；凑合

For the first two years of his marriage, he had to **make do with** used furniture, most of which he had got from his friends.

soapy: *adj.* containing soap 含有肥皂的

She wiped her **soapy** hands on a dishcloth after she went into the kitchen.

squirt: *v.* come out of a narrow opening in a thin fast stream 喷出

Water suddenly **squirted** out from a hole in the pipe.

foil: *n.* 箔，锡纸

We'd better not use aluminum **foil** to wrap foods for any long-term storage.

9 Water **sticks to** her skin and floats through the air in **drinkable** bubbles due to surface tension — but Cristoforetti rarely has time to **dawdle** in the shower. **(Para. 6)**

Paraphrase: Because of surface tension, water stays on her skin and floats through the air in the form of bubbles that are safe to drink. But Cristoforetti can seldom afford to spend much time on the shower.

stick to sth.: become attached to sth. 粘住

Due to electrostatic force, the balloon will **stick to** the wall for some time.

drinkable: *adj.* suitable or safe for drinking 可饮用的；适合饮用的

Seventy percent of the Earth is covered by water, but 97% of that water is salt water and not **drinkable**.

dawdle: *v.* be slow; waste time 磨蹭，拖延；浪费时间

We **dawdled** about on our way back to the town, trying new roads and seeing changing sceneries.

10 Since the beginning of its use in 1998, the International Space Station has cost over one hundred billion dollars, meaning that an astronaut's productivity is very valuable. **(Para. 7)**

Paraphrase: Since it was first put to use in 1998, the International Space Station has cost more than one hundred billion dollars, which means an astronaut's work efficiency is very valuable.

11 The European Space Agency makes Cristoforetti's schedule and task list from the ground each day, so once she's **suitably** clean, it's time to get to work. **(Para. 7)**

Paraphrase: Every day from the Earth, the European Space Agency makes the list of tasks for Cristoforetti to do in space, so once she feels she is clean enough in the shower, she will go to work immediately.

suitably: *adv.* in a way that is right for a particular purpose or situation 合适地，得体地

In the tech sector, the demand for **suitably** skilled candidates has always been high.

12 As Flight Engineer, Cristoforetti played a key role in **docking** the *Dragon*, a special **cargo** ship loaded with supplies and material for new experiments — such as an **espresso** machine. **(Para. 8)**

Paraphrase: As Flight Engineer, Cristoforetti worked as the most important person in joining the *Dragon*, a special cargo ship, with the International Space Station. The *Dragon* carries essential life necessities for the astronauts and material for new experiments in the space station — such as an espresso machine.

dock: *v.* join (two spacecraft) together in space （使两架航天器）对接

Shenzhou-12 manned spaceship successfully **docked** with *Tianhe*, the Chinese space station core module, on Thursday, June 17, 2021, about 6 hours and a half after lifting off.

cargo: *n.* the goods that are being carried in a ship or plane（船或飞机运输的）货物

The **cargo** container will be designed so that it can be smoothly loaded onto trucks and other vehicles.

espresso: *n.* strong black Italian coffee 蒸馏咖啡，（意式）浓咖啡

The main differences between **espresso** coffee and drip coffee are the fineness of the grind and the brewing time.

13 After it docked, Cristoforetti **brewed** herself a strong cup of space coffee, which she **sipped** while dressed in a *Star Trek* uniform. **(Para. 8)**

Paraphrase: After the *Dragon* and the International Space Station were successfully joined, Cristoforetti made herself a strong cup of space coffee. Then she enjoyed the coffee slowly while wearing a *Star Trek* uniform.

brew: *v.* make a drink of tea or coffee 泡（茶）；煮（咖啡）

The most important factor in **brewing** a good cup of tea is to start with quality leaves.

sip: *v.* drink sth. slowly, taking very small mouthfuls 小口喝; 抿

He smiled and **sipped** his beer, clearly very happy with himself.

trek: *n.* a long and difficult journey, made esp. on foot as an adventure（尤指徒步的）艰苦长途旅行

I was feeling pretty great for completing a long **trek** through the jungle.

14 Don't worry: the Italian Space Agency **assures** us that the coffee-brewing adventure was "a very serious study into **fluid** physics" in a near-weightless environment. **(Para. 8)**

Paraphrase: You don't have to worry: the Italian Space Agency has informed us with certainty that the adventure of making coffee in space was "a very serious research project in fluid physics" in a nearly weightless environment.

assure: *v.* tell sb. that sth. will definitely happen or is definitely true so that they are less worried 使确信，使放心

She **assured** him that further inquiries into the matter would be conducted.

fluid: *n.* a liquid 流体，液体

You should be able to hear normally once the **fluid** has been cleared from behind your ear drum.

15 When she's not **maintaining** her muscle mass at the gym, communicating with on-ground ESA employees, or brewing the world's first cup of space espresso, Cristoforetti has to take a few minutes of the day to, well, **replenish** the station's water supply. **(Para. 9)**

Paraphrase: When she is not exercising at the gym to keep her muscle mass, talking with the ESA employees working on the Earth, or making the world's first strong cup of space coffee, Cristoforetti has to spend a few minutes of the day to use the toilet, as a way, say, to restore the water supply of the space station.

maintain: *v.* make sth. continue in the same way or at the same standard as before 保持，维持

These benefits will allow individuals to **maintain** their standard of living even after they are retired.

replenish: *v.* get a further supply of sth. 补充

Food stocks in the grocery store are constantly **replenished** with fresh supplies from the local farms.

16 When astronauts use the restroom, the product gets **converted** back **into** water for reuse. The

same thing happens here on Earth, just **on a** longer time **scale**. (**Para. 9**)

Paraphrase: When astronauts use the toilet in space, the liquid waste they produce is changed back into water to be used again. The same thing happens here on Earth as well, simply over a longer period of time.

convert: *v.* change sth. into a different form of thing 使改变，使转换

By **converting** the attic, they were able to have two extra bedrooms.

convert sth. to/into sth.: 把……改变为……

The old cinema **has** now **been converted into** a modern study center.

scale: *n.* the size or level of sth., or the amount that sth. is happening 规模；程度；范围

The **scale** of the fighting is almost unimaginable.

on a … scale: 在……规模（范围、程度）上

Everybody would like clean and chemical-free food produced locally **on a small scale**.

17 "In the end," Cristoforetti points out in one of her **logbook** entries, "there're two things that you really want to be very familiar with when you**'re about to launch** to space: your spaceship and everything that has to do with using the toilet!" (**Para. 10**)

Paraphrase: "Finally", Cristoforetti says in one of her logbook records, "there're two things that you really want to know very well about when it's time for you to be launched to space: your spaceship and everything about how to use the toilet!"

logbook: *n.* an official record of events, esp. on a journey in a ship or plane（事件的）正式记录；（尤指）航海日志，飞行日志

Students should keep a **logbook** that consists of notes, homework items, quizzes, lab writings, chapter reviews, etc.

be about to do sth.: intend to do sth. immediately; be on the point of doing sth. 即将；正要

She had a sad face, like she **was about to** cry.

launch: *v.* send a weapon or spacecraft into the sky or into space 发射

The *Chang'e-5* lunar probe was **launched** on Nov. 24, 2020, and its lander-ascender combination（着陆器和上升器组合体）touched down on the moon on Dec. 1.

18 Of course, what goes out must have gone in **at one point**. (**Para. 11**)

Paraphrase: Certainly, what comes out of the body of the astronauts must have been taken in at another time.

Note: The sentence means that the human waste the astronauts produce comes from the food that they ate earlier.

at one point: at a particular time or instant 曾经；一度

The man has been put in a mental hospital **at one point** in his life.

19 Although astronaut food used to be **notoriously** bad — think **mushy tube** food that you wouldn't even want to feed to a baby — flight **fare** is much better these days. (**Para. 11**)

Paraphrase: Although astronaut food has been known to be very bad — just imagine the kind of tube food, unpleasantly soft and wet, that you wouldn't even want to use to feed a baby — food that is supplied for spaceships today is much better.

notoriously: *adv.* famous or well-known for sth. bad 臭名昭著地；声名狼藉地

This train company is overstaffed and **notoriously** inefficient.

mushy: *adj.* soft, wet, and unpleasant 粘稠的，糊状的

Some babies prefer **mushy** food because it needs less chewing.

tube: *n.* （装有柔软物质的）软管

The patient had to receive **tube** feeding 24 hours a day.

fare: *n.* food, esp. when offered at a meal 食物，饭菜

On the corner of the street, there is a restaurant that serves traditional Scottish **fare**.

20 Cristoforetti does have some small bags of premade food, but other bags feature **yummy ingredients** like tomatoes, mushrooms, and chicken that she can **assemble** into a meal. **(Para. 12)**
Paraphrase: Cristoforetti does have some small bags of food that are readily made for her, but other bags usually contain things that are tastier, like tomatoes, mushrooms, and chicken that she can put together to make a full meal by herself.

yummy: *adj.* tasting very good 美味的；好吃的

The chocolate cake smelled so **yummy** that I couldn't wait to eat it.

ingredient: *n.* any of the foods that are combined to make a particular dish（烹调用的）材料，原料，成分

There are a couple of key **ingredients** for our homemade cheesecake.

assemble: *v.* come together; collect 集合；聚集；收集

The greatest challenge for him was to **assemble** a team in three hours for the trip to town.

21 As she points out, though, assembling a full meal can be "quite a challenge in **weightlessness**." **(Para. 12)**
Paraphrase: But, as she says in her logbook, putting things together to make a full meal can be "a quite difficult task in a weightless environment."

weightlessness: *n.* 失重状态；无重状态

While walking on the moon, the astronaut experienced **weightlessness**.

22 As she **winds down** for the day, Cristoforetti may take a few minutes to **update** her online logbook or enjoy a view of Earth from the **Cupola**, the window-filled observation room in the International Space Station. **(Para. 13)**
Paraphrase: When she tries to slow down and relax at the end of the day, Cristoforetti may take a few minutes to add some newest information to her online logbook, or enjoy a view of Earth from the observatory module named "**Cupola**", which is an observation room with many windows.

wind down: relax, esp. after a period of stress or excitement（紧张工作或兴奋之后）平静下来，放松

After we finished moving the furniture to the new office, we went to a tea house to **wind down**.

update: *v.* add the most recent information to sth. 更新

He hasn't **updated** his blog for a whole month.

cupola: *n.* a round structure on the top of a building 穹顶，圆屋顶

The wooden building has a **cupola** at the top of it.

23 After 199 days on the *Futura* mission, Cristoforetti earned the **current** record for longest **uninterrupted spaceflight** by a woman. **(Para. 14)**
Paraphrase: After working on the *Futura* mission for 199 days in the International Space

Station, Cristoforetti created the present record of a woman traveling in space for the longest time without interruption.

current: *adj.* happening or existing now 当前的；现在的

By **current** standards, they were very young when they got married.

uninterrupted: *adj.* continuous 连续的；不间断的

Pedestrian overpasses and underpasses allow for the **uninterrupted** flow of pedestrian movement separate from vehicle traffic.

spaceflight: *n.* a trip into space 航天，宇宙飞行

China has achieved a series of innovative developments in recent years, from deep-sea exploration to manned **spaceflights**.

24 She arrived safely back to Earth in June, 2015, with her sense of humor **intact**, it seems. **(Para. 14)**

Paraphrase: She returned safely to Earth in June, 2015, and it seemed that her sense of humor remained unchanged at all.

intact: *adj.* undamaged; complete 无损伤的；完整的

Fortunately, most of the cargo on the ship was left **intact** after the explosion.

25 But she might be back soon: Cristoforetti has already noted that she misses space and would definitely go back if given the opportunity. Still, fresh fruit there has got to taste pretty good. **(Para. 14)**

Paraphrase: But she might go back to the International Space Station soon: Cristoforetti has already mentioned that she misses space and would certainly go back if she is given the chance. But, fresh fruit there has to taste very good.

Note: The last sentence implies that although she would like to go back to the International Space Station, she really enjoys the taste of the fresh fruit on the Earth.

PART IV   Keys to Exercises

Lead-in

I   **1** A   **2** B   **3** C   **4** A   **5** B   **6** C   **7** B   **8** A

> **Script**
>
> Hello I'm Sonny Williams. I'm up here on the International Space Station so this is Node 2 — this is a really cool module. Of course, most of these modules you'll see they have four sides. And they're put together that way we could sort of walk, work on a flat plane — either a wall, a floor, another wall, or the ceiling. But you know again all you have to do is turn yourself and your reference changes.
>
> The reason I'm bringing that up is because this is where four out of six of us sleep. And so, people always ask about sleeping in space. Do you lie down? Or are you in a

bed? Not really. Because it doesn't matter. You don't really have the sensation of lying down. You just sit in your sleeping bag. So here's one sleep station right here. I'm going in right now. You can follow me if you want. So I'm inside. It's sort of like a little phone booth but it's pretty comfy. I've got a sleeping bag right here that we sleep in. So we don't have … sort of like a little bit of a cover … so we don't fly all over the place. But you know you can sleep in any orientation. I have it sleeping feeling like I'm standing up right now. But like you saw I'm on the floor. But it doesn't matter if I turn over and I sleep upside down. I can't have it. I don't have any sensation in my head that tells me that I'm upside down. So it really doesn't matter.

The sleep station is also like a little office. We've got a computer in here. As you can see, we've got a couple little toys. I've got some books. I've got some clothes and other things that make it sort of like home. I'm coming out. And just for reference, that's one sleep station. This one's another right here. There's one on the ceiling if you want to call it. Right here, and then there's a fourth on the other wall over here. So, all of us sleep in a little bit of a circle.

All right, come on back. There's more to show you. I know that there're some questions about how to use the bathroom and how do you actually live in space like normal … like at home. I mentioned real quickly about getting up in the morning and brushing your teeth and washing your face. Well, how do you do that?

Well here is the bathroom essentially. You get up in the morning and we have a little kit. And it has all the essential things that you need, like your toothbrush and toothpaste and brush. See how… see how much better the brush makes my hair look? I'm just joking. It still stands up straight. It doesn't matter where you are. It's always going to stand up straight while you're up in space. A lot of people ask about toothbrush and toothpaste. So luckily enough, toothpaste, you can do it upside right this way. It's sticky and so it sticks to your toothbrush. No problem. Another cool thing is that water sticks to your toothbrush too. You can see it. I'll have some water come out. Water is pretty neat up in space. It'll stick to your toothbrush, and it will make a bubble … A big bubble! And that's just by surface tension. And then you can drink it. So a lot of people ask about what you'll do with the toothpaste after you brush your teeth? Two options: swallow it and it's sort of like mouthwash. But it tastes a little gross. Or, you can just spit it out in a paper towel and then you don't have to worry about it. The swallowing thing I wouldn't recommend at home. I'm only up here for four months. So it's not that bad.

One of the most pressing questions about using … living in space … of course is the bathroom. So let's take a look at that little piece of work. Come on in. Here we are at the throne. This is awesome. You might see the little … um … you might have noticed a little moon on the outside. This is our orbital outhouse right here. And of course, it serves for two functions: Number two, right here. I'll show you. But you see it's pretty small. So, you have to have pretty good aim and you'll be ready to make sure things get let go the right direction. And it smells a little bit so I'm closing it up. And that's of course for number two. And this guy right here is for number one. So there're sort of two slightly separate functions. But you can do a little essentially both by hanging on right here and doing number one and number two. I might add it's color coded so you really don't get it mixed up which is nice. This is yellow it's for number one.

And, also there's a selection of paper. People always ask about toilet paper. What do you do of toilet paper? What kind of toilet paper do you have? We have gloves just because sometimes it does get messy. We have some Russian wipes which are a little bit coarse if you like the coarse type of toilet paper. We have some nice tissues which are nice and soft if you like soft toilet paper. We have Huggies just for any cleanup. You know we're all babies once and this sort of helps. And then if things get really out of control, we have disinfectant wipes just to make sure we clean up here. Because you know just like the water I showed you, the number one stuff can sort of go all over the place if you don't aim correctly. And did I mention both of these have a little bit of suction so they should keep things going in the right direction. But like I said sometimes things get a little out of control if you are out of control yourself flying around. So we have lots of protective stuff. And of course, you do have your privacy. There's a little door. So other people know that you're in there.

Here's a pretty cool place. This is sort of like in your house where everybody meets in the morning after you wash your face, brush your teeth. You want to find something for breakfast. And this is our kitchen you might notice there're all sorts of foods here. It's like opening the refrigerator. You got all your different stuff that you want to have — drinks, meats, eggs, vegetables, cereals, bread, snacks (and that's a good place. That's where you find all the candy), side dishes, and then some little power bars just in case.

So we have all this type of food … some of it is dehydrated. And so we have to hydrate it. Fill it up with water. Some of it is already made and then all we have to do is heat it up. So something like this I'm pulling out — barbecued beef brisket. Pretty yummy! Not only is this food made in the US, but we also have food here from Japan. We've got Russian food, as you can see all these red containers are filled with food that's from Russia. And then we get some of our specialty stuff, some things that we like, some of our favorite stuff that your family can send up. In fact, I like fluffernutter's and so I got sent up some fluffs so I could make my fluffernutter with peanut butter. So you have a lot of food up here. No problems.

Reading to Learn

Reading Comprehension

1 The text is mainly about a typical day of an ISS astronaut in space; that is, what she does in the morning, during the day, and at the end of the day.

2 Because she needs to prevent her bone density and muscle mass loss in a weightless environment.

3 A huge amount of money has been invested for the work of the ISS, which means that the astronauts' work is very important and that they have to work hard to make sure the money spent is worthwhile.

4 It is converted back into water for reuse.

5 Astronaut food used to be very limited in choice, only mushy tube food. But it now has more choices, such as tomatoes, mushrooms, and chicken that can be assembled into a full meal, and is tastier too.

II   **1** B   **2** D   **3** A   **4** C   **5** C

III   **Text Organization**

     1 Italian astronaut   **2** the International Space Station

     3 reaching for her laptop   **4** go to the gym

     5 prevent bone density and muscle mass loss   **6** go to take a quick shower

     7 begin her work   **8** docking the *Dragon*

     9 herself a strong cup of space coffee   **10** converted back into water for reuse

     11 assembling different ingredients together   **12** update her online logbook

     13 a view of Earth   **14** longest uninterrupted spaceflight by a woman

Language in Use

Words and Expressions

I   **1** brewed   **2** current   **3** intact   **4** notoriously

     5 density   **6** ingredient   **7** approximately   **8** simulation

II   **1** make do with   **2** had stuck to   **3** on a ... scale   **4** wind down

     5 convert ... into   **6** at one point   **7** headed to   **8** reached for

III   **1** launched   **2** assembling   **3** orbit   **4** workout   **5** maintain

     6 dock   **7** approximately   **8** missions   **9** are about to   **10** simulation

Word Formation

1 complexity   **2** attractiveness   **3** popularity   **4** rudeness   **5** loneliness

6 curiosity   **7** productivity   **8** cleverness   **9** sensitivity   **10** emptiness

Collocation

1 earn the respect   **2** assemble a car   **3** take a stand   **4** earned the title

5 maintain high standards   **6** earn the opportunity   **7** take a break   **8** assemble a group

9 maintain market share   **10** take a breath

1 whereas/while
2 despite/in spite of
3 though/although
4 Whereas/While
5 While/Whereas
6 Though/Although
7 though
8 In spite of/Despite/Though/Although

Translation

I 1 他伸手想再拿点咖啡，结果发现壶里最后一点他都已经喝掉了。

2 这座岛上断电的时候比通电的时候多，断电时亚历山大通常就用蜡烛来对付一下。

3 这些办法保证会让你整个白天保持机敏，晚上又能及时放松下来睡个好觉。

4 社区学院在给大量低收入家庭的学生提供教育方面发挥着关键作用。

5 如果你对我正在谈论的人物不熟悉，这里有一些背景知识。

II 1 The company hopes to update the system and make the information available to anyone who needs it.

2 His colleague assured him that he was just having a small problem, not in big trouble, for losing the file.

3 Although the jigsaw puzzle was difficult, the boy succeeded in assembling all the parts without anybody's help.

4 In the past 2G, 3G, and 4G eras, most of the key chips used in China were imported from other countries, but in the 5G era, it is likely that China's self-developed chips will be applied on a large scale.

5 China will take a series of measures to maintain stable employment in the years to come.

III In 1992, China started the manned space program with a three-step strategy. The first step was to send astronauts into space and return them safely. The launches of *Shenzhou-5* in 2003 and *Shenzhou-6* in 2005 completed the mission. The second step was to test key technologies needed for a permanent space station. This phase included the launch of *Tiangong-1* in 2011, and the launch of *Tiangong-2* space lab in 2016. We are now in the third step: to assemble and operate a permanently manned space station. In the future, China will launch manned and cargo spaceships regularly to make sure that the space station is always manned for the in-orbit research and services.

Corpora in Language Learning

I (There can be more than one answer to some questions here, and to each question only one answer is provided for reference.)

earn/gain/obtain/ win	Nouns that collocate with the verbs	Chinese translations of the collocations
earn	bonus	获得奖金
	degree	获得学位
	money	挣钱
	promotion	获得晋升
	respect	赢得尊重
	living	谋生
gain	access	获准进入
	confidence	获得信心
	control	取得控制权
	experience	获得经验
	recognition	获得认可
	support	获得支持
obtain	revenue	赚取收入
	warrant	得到授权
	information	得到信息
	permission	得到允许
	recommendation	获得推荐
win	business	赢得业务
	medal	获得奖牌
	victory	赢得胜利
	prize	获得奖项
	confidence	赢得信任
	support	赢得支持

II
1 earn/gain   2 gain/obtain   3 win
4 obtain/gain   5 earn   6 gain/obtain/win

Writing

I   Paragraph 1 is the introduction. It hooks the reader by asking a question, and presents the thesis statement clearly with the last sentence.

Paragraphs 2–5 are the body paragraphs, each focusing on one specific part of the ivy-growing process. Paragraph 2 discusses the materials needed. Then the next paragraphs spell out the steps of the process. Each step has plenty of details so the reader can form a picture of what is happening in his or her mind. The language in this part is precise, and details are clear and not overly given. Transitions, such as "first", "when …", and "next", are used to guide the audience through the steps.

Paragraph 6 is the conclusion. It starts by restating the thesis sentence and ends with a closing remark, which signals the writing is finished.

Language Functions

1 book a flight, airline
2 boarding pass
3 Boarding time
4 seatbelt, turbulence
5 pick up their luggage
6 business class, economy class
7 Customs Declaration Form
8 checked luggage
9 arrivals lounge
10 stopover

Reading to Explore

Reading Comprehension

I   1 C   2 C   3 B   4 D   5 D
II 1 T   2 F   3 T   4 F   5 F
III A 2   B 4   C 6   D 3
    E 5   F 9   G 8   H 1

Words and Expressions

I   1 authority   2 imaginary   3 consistently   4 respectful   5 procedures
    6 attributes   7 competent   8 deliberately   9 fatal   10 inhibit

II 1 reaching out   2 line up   3 be open to   4 in reality
    5 move on to   6 helped out   7 be respectful of   8 serve as
    9 took control of   10 off course

Text A

太空中的一天：探索国际空间站上的生活

All That's Interesting 网

1 萨曼莎·克里斯托弗雷蒂是个夜猫子，她总是睡眼惺忪地伸手把笔记本电脑拿过来，开始一天的生活。和我们许多人一样，她把电脑就放在手边——确切地说，是离她的脸大约四英寸的地方——还没下床就在工作了。

2 与几乎所有人不同的是，克里斯托弗雷蒂的"床"是国际空间站上的一个绿色睡袋。当她在距地球表面上方250英里的轨道上飞行时，那台笔记本电脑将她与地球连接起来。

3 要是你还没猜出来，（那我来告诉你，）克里斯托弗雷蒂是欧洲航天局的一名意大利籍宇航员。

4 克里斯托弗雷蒂在电话亭大小的房间里醒来，在电脑上查看了当天的日程安排后，从睡袋中漂浮出来。之后，一天就开始了。对她来说，这意味着要先去健身房——天天如此。

5 为了防止在太空飞行时骨密度和肌肉量降低，克里斯托弗雷蒂和其他宇航员每天在健身房至少要锻炼一个半小时。在那里，他们使用高级阻力健身器之类的特制的举重模拟设备。在失重环境中使用常规的举重器械是无效的。在太空，是没有"放纵日"的。

6 长时间锻炼后，我们许多人都会去浴室冲个凉爽的澡。克里斯托弗雷蒂差不多也是这样。但就她而言，她用的不是自来水，而是必须靠一块涂上肥皂的小毛巾和从铝箔袋中喷出的水来将就完成。由于表面张力，水会粘在她的皮肤上并形成可饮用的水泡漂浮在空中——不过克里斯托弗雷蒂没什么时间在淋浴中磨蹭。

7 自1998年启用以来，国际空间站已耗资超一千亿美元，这意味着宇航员的工作效率非常宝贵。欧洲航天局每天都会从地面上给克里斯托弗雷蒂制定时间表和任务清单，所以一旦洗得差不多干净了，她就该去工作了。

8 作为飞行工程师，克里斯托弗雷蒂在对接"龙"飞船这一特殊货运飞船方面发挥了关键作用。该飞船装载了生活补给物资及用于新实验的材料，比如浓缩咖啡机。完成飞船对接后，克里斯托弗雷蒂给自己冲调了一杯太空浓咖啡。她穿着同《星际迷航》电影里一样的制服，啜饮着咖啡。你可别担心：意大利航天局向我们保证，在近乎失重的环境中探索咖啡冲调是"对流体物理学的一项非常严肃的研究"。

9 当克里斯托弗雷蒂没在健身房锻炼肌肉，没在与欧洲航天局地面工作人员联系，也没在冲调世界上第一杯太空浓咖啡时，她每天必须花几分钟时间，嗯，来给空间站补充供水。当宇航员使用洗手间时，排泄物会被转换成水循环使用。地球上也是这样一个过程，只是时间跨度更长。

10 克里斯托弗雷蒂在她的一条日志记录中写道，"最后，当你即将要被发射到太空时，有两件事你真的要烂熟于心：你的飞船以及跟上厕所相关的一切事项！"

11 当然，排出去的东西一定是一度吃进来的转化而成。尽管过去宇航员的食物是出了名的糟糕——想想那些你连婴儿都不想喂的糊状管装食物——飞行伙食现在有了明显改善。

12 克里斯托弗雷蒂确实有一些现成的小袋装食品，但其他一些袋里则装有美味的原料，比如西红柿、蘑菇和鸡肉。她可以把这些原料组合起来做成一顿饭。然而，正如她所指出的那样，要做一顿完整的大餐"在失重状态下会相当有挑战性"。

13 当她放慢节奏准备结束一天的工作时，克里斯托弗雷蒂会花几分钟更新她的网上日志，或者从国际空间站满是舷窗的观察室即"穹顶舱"内欣赏地球的景色。从那里，宇航员可以在地球经过飞船下面时拍下照片。

14 在执行"Futura"任务199天后，克里斯托弗雷蒂创造了当时女性在太空不间断飞行的最长时间记录。2015年6月，她安全返回地球，她的幽默感似乎丝毫没变。但她可能很快又会回到太空：克里斯托弗雷蒂提到她很想念太空，如果有机会的话，她一定会回去。不过，那儿的新鲜水果必须美味。

Text B

太空漫游

斯科特·凯利

1　"龙"飞船现在距离我们10公里远的轨道上，以每小时17,500英里的速度与我们相匹配。我们可以从外部摄像头上看到它的灯在闪烁。很快，位于加利福尼亚州霍桑市的美国太空探索技术公司 (SpaceX) 地面控制系统就将把它移动到距离我们2.5公里，然后1.2公里、250米、30米，然后10米的位置。在每个停顿点，地面上的团队都要先检查"龙"飞船的系统并评测其位置，再发出"继续"或"停止"的指令，进入下一阶段。在进入到250米以内时，我们将参与监控"龙"飞船的靠近，确保其处在安全的轨道，并按预期运行——如果必要的话，我们随时可以中止对接。一旦它离我们足够近，我的站内同事萨曼莎·克里斯托弗雷蒂就用空间站的机器人手臂抓住它。这是一个极其缓慢而小心的过程，也是电影与现实众多不同的地方之一。在电影《地心引力》和《2001太空漫游》中，一艘来访的太空船轻巧地靠上空间站并与其锁定，而后一扇舱门弹开，人通过舱门，整个过程用时约90秒。而在现实中我们操作时清楚，一艘太空船对另一艘太空船总是存在潜在的致命威胁——靠得越近威胁越大——因此，我们操作都缓慢而谨慎。

2　萨曼莎借助于穹顶舱的机器人工作站操作机器人手臂。空间站的另外一位美国人特里·弗茨将做她的替补，我则帮助操作飞船靠近和会合的程序。特里和我会和萨曼莎一起挤在穹顶舱里，注视着她肩膀上方显示"龙"飞船速度和位置的数据屏幕。

3　和我一样，特里在加入美国国家航空航天局之前也是一名试飞员——不过他是在空军。他的呼号是"弗兰德斯"，这是随《辛普森一家》中那个可爱又古板的人物内德·弗兰德斯而起的。特里拥有内德·弗兰德斯的优点——乐观、热情、友善——而内德·弗兰德斯的缺点他则一点也没有。我发现他一直很能干，也很欣赏他是一位注重寻求共识的领导者。自从我来到这里，他一直很尊重我以往的经验，总是乐于接受如何把事情做得更好的建议，而不是心怀戒备或要压人一头。

4　萨曼莎是为数不多的在意大利空军担任过战斗机飞行员的女性之一。她在所有技术方面始终表现出色。她也很友好，很爱笑。她拥有适合太空飞行方面的许多资质，其中一项便是她罕见的语言天赋。她的英语、俄语（国际空间站的两种官方语言）以及法语、德语都具有母语的流利程度，母语是意大利语，同时她还在学习中文。

5　休斯顿任务控制中心的加拿大籍宇航员大卫·圣亚克将在捕获"龙"飞船的过程中与我们保持通话，通报"龙"飞船移动时的位置。"龙"飞船的移动是从地面通过每个预先计划的停顿点加以控制的。

6　"'龙'飞船抵达200米禁区内，"大卫说。禁区是空间站周围假想的半径边界，旨在保护我们免受意外碰撞。"空间站工作人员现在有权发布中止令。"这意味着如果我们与休斯顿失去联系，或者"龙"飞船偏离了轨道，我们就可以自行中止这个过程。

7　"休斯顿，捕获条件已确认。我们已做好捕获'龙'飞船的准备，"特里回答道。

8　在距离10米远的地方，我们停用了空间站的推进器以防止任何意外的晃动。萨曼莎负责控制机器人手臂，她左手控制机器人手臂的平移（进、出、上、下、左、右），右手控制其旋转。

9　萨曼莎伸出机器人手臂，注视着显示器上由一部安装在机器人"手"部或者说手臂末端执行器上的摄像头所拍摄的画面，以及另外两个显示"龙"飞船位置和速度数据的视频监视器。她也可以从大窗户往外看自己的操作。她把机器人手臂从空间站移出——非常缓慢和小心。萨曼莎一英寸一英寸地缩小两个航天器之间的距离，没有丝毫摇晃或偏移。在中央屏幕上，"龙"飞船上的抓钩装置变得越来越大。她做了精确的调整，以保持飞船和机器人手臂完全对准。

10　机器人手臂慢慢地、慢慢地伸出来，几乎触到了"龙"飞船。

11　萨曼莎扣动开关。"捕获，"她说。

12　完美。

5 BUILDING STRENGTH

PART I   Introduction

As an ordinary college student, you may constantly feel overwhelmed by various assignments and exams, and you may wonder what career to take after graduation. As a student athlete, life can be even more challenging. In this unit, we will look at how student athletes juggle sport and study and overcome the challenges they face after ending their sporting career. Text A lists the strengths student athletes have such as being organized and disciplined, high efficiency, good teamwork, leadership, and effective communication. It illustrates how these qualities help student athletes improve their academic and sporting performance and boost their job prospect. Text B is an account of an athlete's transition from a professional athlete to a student athlete and then to a sports anchor. The writer's story tells us that "Once an athlete, always an athlete" — with all of the skills developed as an athlete, one can move on to the next phase of life successfully. After learning the unit, you will be encouraged to reflect on the benefits of doing sports, the importance of integrating physical education and intellectual education, and the significant role of developing an unyielding spirit in overcoming difficulties and achieving your goals.

In this unit you will:

1   Read a report on how student athletes balance their sporting career and academic study;
2   Read a story about how a professional athlete tried hard to accomplish her transition to a different career;
3   Reflect on the importance of developing an unyielding spirit;
4   Learn English vocabulary with the root "spect" or "spic";
5   Learn collocations of the verbs "boost", "balance", "develop", "maintain", "enhance" and "stimulate";
6   Learn to avoid dangling modifiers;
7   Learn nouns that collocate with *keep* and verb phrases of "keep + preposition/adverb" by using CADEL;
8   Learn to use reporting verbs and sentence structures to introduce information from other sources and express your attitude toward the information quoted;
9   Learn different words for body parts and body movements and learn to use them to describe yoga poses.

Sayings

Learning objectives:

- Get a general idea of the unit
- Get inspirations from the sayings
- Get useful advice and guidance from famous people or books
- Learn to develop a positive attitude toward life

Teaching steps:

1   Ask students to translate the two sayings into Chinese.
    Reference translations for the sayings:
    - 伟大的事业基于高深的学问，坚强的意志在于强健的体魄。　　　　　　　——孙中山
    - 宝剑锋从磨砺出，梅花香自苦寒来。　　　　　　　　　　　　　　　——《增广贤文》

2   The first saying is a quote from Sun Yat-sen, a Chinese statesman who was a forerunner of China's democratic revolution to end the Qing dynasty. For this quote, tell students the important role knowledge and physical health play in the growth of individuals and society. With profound knowledge, we know how we can pursue and achieve our life goals, and with a healthy body, we can keep moving on with perseverance. Encourage students to study hard and exercise hard to stay healthy and strong-willed so as to contribute more to the development of China.

3   For the second saying, tell students the importance of being hardworking and persistent. The saying is quoted from *The Wisdom of Ancient Aphorisms*. It suggests that just as persistent honing makes a sharp sword edge and bitter cold produces fragrant plum blossoms, working diligently and persistently helps turn one into a well-rounded person. Encourage students to list some essential qualities one must have to succeed in work and life. These qualities may include commitment, perseverance, patience, optimism, and self-discipline.

Lead-in

Learning objectives:

- Learn about how Yao Ming handled his study in the university
- Find out how playing sports can benefit academic study

Teaching steps:

1   Make a brief introduction to the unit and explain its learning objectives.
2   Ask students to do Exercise I. Ask them to listen to a news report about Yao Ming and pay attention to the details. Play the recording twice if necessary.
3   Ask students to do Exercise II. Ask students to think about the skills they can learn by doing sports and how these skills can be used to boost their academic study.

Reading to Learn

Text A

Do Athletes Make Better Students?

Learning objectives:

- Use new words and expressions to describe the skills student athletes have gained by doing sports
- Learn how one can cope with challenges in different phases of life using the skills gained by doing sports
- Learn to use reporting words and sentence structures to introduce information from other sources

Teaching steps:

1   Introduce the topic of Text A: How student athletes balance sport and study.
2   Ask students to read the first sentence of each paragraph and try to tell what skills student athletes gain by doing sports mentioned in the text. Refer to the Text Organization exercise to learn the structure of the text.
3   Ask students to do Exercise I in the Reading Comprehension section by scanning through the text for the names of the people included in the exercise and match them with the ideas these people have provided respectively.
4   Go to Part III Detailed Study of Text A. Help students understand difficult sentences in the text accurately. Introduce important new words and expressions with explanations and examples.
5   Ask students to do the exercises following the text.

Critical Thinking

Learning objectives:

- Discuss the benefits of doing sports and share plans to engage in sports
- Discuss some important elements in sports training
- Discuss the significance of developing an unyielding spirit

Teaching steps:

1   Ask students to read the questions first and then give them some ideas on how to approach each question.
2   For Question 1, ask students to discuss the benefits of playing sports and share their plans to do more sports. Encourage students to reflect on the advantages discussed in the text and think of more advantages of doing sports. Exercise not only changes our body, but also changes our mind, our attitude and our mood. Remind students that they should learn to strike a balance between exercise and study.

3 For Question 2, ask students to reflect on the important elements that are critical to sports training. Ask them to think about the following questions: What role does each of the five S's play in sports training? Which of these five elements is the most important to you? What kind of spirit is sports training advocating and cultivating? Why do you think Ken Doherty thinks spirit is the greatest among the five S's? Encourage students to think about how important these elements are to their study and work. You may also ask them to come up with more S's of sports training, such as *suppleness* (柔韧性), *schooling*, and *social skills*.

4 For Question 3, ask students to talk about how they are impressed and inspired by the Chinese women's volleyball team. Over the past decades, the women's volleyball team has brought glory to our nation by winning world championships many times. Their victories have deepened our love for our country and enhanced national confidence. We admire them not only because of their remarkable achievements, but also for the unyielding spirit the team has demonstrated. Their unyielding spirit inspires us to make greater efforts in our study and work, and to work even harder for the realization of the Chinese Dream. Only through unyielding efforts can we overcome challenges and difficulties and succeed eventually. You can also help students by providing some useful vocabulary, such as *perseverance*, *determination*, *adhere to sth. unremittingly*, *never give up*, *regardless of any odds or obstacles*, and *be persistent*.

5 Ask students to work in pairs or small groups to share their opinions. Encourage each pair or group to present their favorite ideas in class.

Corpora in Language Learning

Learning objectives:

- Learn to search CADEL for nouns that collocate with *keep* with "keep *" as the search term, using the "Concordance" function of AntConc
- Learn to search CADEL for verb phrases of "keep + preposition/adverb" with "keep *" as the search term, using the "Concordance" function of AntConc
- Learn to complete the given sentences with the verb phrases of "keep + preposition/adverb" based on the contexts in which they appear

Teaching steps:

1 Demonstrate how to search CADEL for nouns that collocate with *keep* with "keep *" as the search term, using the "Concordance" function of AntConc. Ask students to identify the nouns that begin with the given letters.

2 Explain how to search CADEL for verb phrases of "keep + preposition/adverb" with "keep *" as the search term, using the "Concordance" function of AntConc. Ask students to identify the verb phrases that match the given definitions.

3 Discuss the use of the collocations "keep + noun/noun phrase" and the verb phrases of "keep + preposition/adverb".

Writing

Learning objectives:

- Learn to use reporting verbs and sentence structures to introduce the ideas and findings of others
- Learn to tell the writer's attitude towards the quoted material by identifying the strength of the reporting verbs used
- Learn to indicate your attitude towards the material you have quoted by using reporting verbs of proper strength

Teaching steps:

1   Introduce the reporting verbs and sentence structures with specific examples.
2   Demonstrate how reporting verbs of different strength are used to show the writer's attitude toward the information quoted from others.
3   Ask students to do Exercise I and further explain how to use reporting verbs and sentence structures in a proper way.
4   Ask students to do Exercise II and ask them to look for sound sources to support their argument.

Language Functions

Learning objectives:

- Learn about names of body parts and expressions for yoga movements
- Learn to understand and describe yoga poses with proper words and expressions

Teaching steps:

1   Ask students to read the instructions for Bridge Pose and do Exercise I. Ask students to pay special attention to the names of different body parts and expressions for body movements. To get them better prepared for the exercise, ask students to search online for related instructions for yoga practice.
2   Before asking students to do Exercise II, introduce or ask students to suggest more words for body parts and body movements, such as: *joint, waist, palm, ankle, wrist, spine, elbow, in line, release, stretch, spread, hug, straighten*, etc.
3   Then ask students to do Exercise II. Ask them to work in pairs. One describes a yoga pose while the other guesses which one is being described. To make the task more interesting, the student instructor may ask the partner to act out the pose based on the instructions.
4   If students find Exercise II too difficult for them, the teacher can read the descriptions first to students and ask them to guess which posture is being described. After that, ask students to do Exercise II.

Reading to Explore

Text B

Moving on from Sports: A College Athlete's Greatest Challenge

Learning objectives:

- Learn new words and expressions used to describe a critical transition in life
- Identify the most important information in each paragraph
- Learn how to adapt to the working world with skills gained by doing sports

Teaching steps:

1 Ask students to read the text and finish the exercises following the text before class.
2 Check answers to the exercises.
3 Ask students to talk about what challenges student athletes may face when they switch from their sporting career to a new one.
4 Encourage students to discuss the significance of gaining important skills, such as commitment, perseverance, effective communication, and teamwork, to overcome the challenges in life.

Summary of Text B

This text is about how student athletes can use the qualities developed when doing sports to overcome the challenges in their academic studies and career development. As an outstanding athlete, the author takes herself as an example and describes her own experience transforming from a tennis player to a student athlete and then to a sports anchor. Tennis has been a very important part of the author's life since she was young. After becoming a student tennis player, she tried hard to balance tennis and study at university. After graduation, the author struggled a lot because she had to retire from the game she loved and face the challenge of becoming a sports anchor. Finally, the author figured out that she could use the skills she had learned as an athlete to deal with the challenges and move on to the next phase of her life.

PART III Detailed Study of Text A

Do Athletes Make Better Students?

Background Information

1 the British Universities and Colleges Sport (BUCS): 英国大学体育协会

Formed in 2008, BUCS is a university sport organization in the UK. It offers membership to more than 170 universities and colleges and organizes over 50 inter-university sports games within the UK. Sports in the BUCS competition include boxing, karate, rugby union, etc.

2 **Commonwealth Games:** 英联邦运动会

First held in 1930, the Commonwealth Games is an international multi-sport event that takes place every four years. Athletes who participate in this event are all from the Commonwealth of Nations.

3 **rugby sevens:** 七人制橄榄球

Rugby sevens, also known as sevens or seven-a-side rugby, is a variant of rugby union. Each team is formed by seven players instead of the usual fifteen players. The game is also shorter in duration, with each half lasting seven minutes instead of forty minutes.

Understanding the Text

Part 1 (Paras. 1–2)

1 Ask students to read Paras. 1–2 and answer the following questions:

    1) What could be the most demanding tasks for average students? (Trying hard to meet deadlines and attend lectures on time.)

    2) How would some students feel when they think of doing sports while studying? (They would be frightened.)

    3) What are the benefits of having two careers at the same time? (It makes people more motivated for training and prepared for games, more interested in study and less stressed.)

2 Ask students to identify what words related to sports are used and what might be the reason for the author to use them. (Please see Language Points 2 for reference.)

Part 2 (Paras. 3–17)

Paras. 3–5

1 Before reading, ask students if they do sports and if they can balance sport and study.

2 Ask students to read Paras. 3–5 and answer the following questions:

    1) According to Professor Ian Henry at Loughborough University, how can taking interest in another area help athletes with their sport? (It can help them to view their training and performance in a sensible way, and handle more effectively the challenges of sport, including setbacks and injury.)

    2) In what way does Loughborough University stand out among the British universities? (Question 2 in Exercise II of Reading Comprehension) (It ranks the top in terms of sporting achievements.)

Paras. 6–10

3 Ask students to read Paras. 6–10 and answer the following questions:

    1) What qualities can an athlete develop through doing sports? (Being organized, disciplined, efficient and focused.)

    2) What does Baddeley mean by "a very transferable skill"? (He means self-discipline, a skill developed through sporting, can be applied to academic study as well.)

3) In the case of Luke Belton, how did pushing himself to the physical limit benefit his study? (It boosted his academic commitment and perseverance.)

Paras. 11–12

Ask students to read Paras. 11–12 and answer the following questions:

1) How is physical exercise related to mental health? (Physical exercise can make one mentally healthier.)

2) Is there evidence for the saying that "a healthy body equals a healthy mind"? (Yes. According to the director of the counselling service at Durham University, their students are mentally healthy because they are physically active.)

Paras. 13–16

1   Before reading, ask students to discuss what other skills can be gained from sport to help them find a job.

2   Ask students to read Paras. 13–16 and answer the following questions:

1) What specific traits are employers looking for? (The ability to balance study and other commitments, such as training for competitions, teamwork, and decision-making.)

2) What skills can be developed through volunteering on a committee or coaching? (Leadership skills.)

Para. 17

Ask students to read Para. 17 and answer the following question:

1   What does Luke Treharne's experience with rugby sevens tell us? (Athletes may be better at communicating and working with other team members.)

Part 3 (Paras. 18–19)

1   Ask students to read Paras. 18–19 and answer the following questions:

1) According to Keith Fleming, what is the most important part of juggling two careers for student athletes? (They graduate with the best degree possible and not to sacrifice one for the other.)

2) What can we learn from the experiences of the two student athletes, Belton and Treharne? (With commitment and the right attitude, we can excel in both sporting and academic performance.)

2   After the whole text is finished, ask students to do Exercise III in the Reading Comprehension section and check if they have got all the main points mentioned in the text.

Language Points

1   Do Athletes Make Better Students? **(Title)**
    Paraphrase: Are students with a sporting career better in academic performance?
    Note: Here the verb "make" means "be or become (sth.) through development (演变成)". For example:
    If you practise hard, you'll **make** a good dancer.

2 **Chasing** deadlines and running late to lectures are the most demanding forms of exercise many students **engage in**. (**Para. 1**)

Paraphrase: Meeting deadlines and rushing to attend lectures are the most challenging types of exercise many students take.

Note: Since this text is about sport and study, the author deliberately uses the words that are related to physical activities, such as "chase", "run", "exercise" in this sentence, and "sweat" in another sentence. These words help to link the two activities and at the same time create a sense of humor.

chase: *v.* run after in order to capture or overtake sb./sth. 追赶；追捕

The tiger **chased** the deer, and soon both disappeared into the woods.

engage: *v.* be doing or become involved in an activity 参加，参与活动

People **engage** in business for several reasons, but the most compelling reason for many is to earn a large income.

engage (sb.) in: (cause sb. to) take part in or be occupied in sth.（使某人）参加或从事某事

She tried desperately to **engage** him **in** conversation.

3 But evidence suggests that **juggling** the two can benefit both academic and sporting performance. (**Para. 2**)

Paraphrase: But evidence shows that trying to balance a sporting career with a university degree can improve the performances in both areas.

juggle: *v.* try to fit two or more jobs, activities, etc. into your life 同时应付（几份工作或多项活动等）

I also work full time as a consultant outside of photography, so **juggling** both can sometimes be a challenge.

4 Research has found that having "**dual** careers" provides motivation for training and preparation, **stimulates** athletes **intellectually** and relieves stress. (**Para. 2**)

Paraphrase: Research has found that having "two careers" (i.e. being an athlete and a university student at the same time) makes athletes more enthusiastic about training and better prepared for matches, more interested in academic studies and less stressed.

dual: *adj.* having two of sth. or two parts 双的，双重的，两部分的

A **dual**-purpose vehicle is designed to carry both goods and passengers.

stimulate: *v.* encourage sb. by making them excited about and interested in sth. 激发，激励

Peter's early love of books was **stimulated** by his mother's reading habits.

intellectually: *adv.* 智力上

Mike volunteers at a special care center for physically and **intellectually**-challenged children.

5 According to Professor Ian Henry at Loughborough University, having an **outlet** of interest other than sport helps athletes "to **put** their training and performance **into perspective**, allowing them to **deal** more effectively **with** the challenges of sport, including **setbacks** and injury". (**Para. 4**)

Paraphrase: According to Professor Ian Henry at Loughborough University, taking interest in another area aside from sport helps athletes view their training and performance in a sensible way, and cope with the difficulties in doing sports, including barriers and injury, in a more effective way.

outlet: *n.* a means of expressing one's talents, energy, or emotions（才能、精力、感情的）发挥或宣泄的途径（或手段）

Painting, drawing, sculpture, and even crafts can provide an **outlet** for anxiety and sadness.

perspective: *n.* a sensible way of judging and comparing situations（对事物的）合理判断，正确认识

To keep things in **perspective**, it is important to live in the present moment and avoid being overwhelmed by fears about the future.

put sth. into perspective: judge the real importance of sth. by considering it in relation to everything else 进行合理判断，正确看待

The college tutor is great about **putting** everything **into perspective**, offering helpful suggestions and tips to students.

deal with: take the necessary action, esp. in order to solve a problem 对付，应付，处理

To me, deadlines and **dealing with** difficult people are the biggest causes of work-related stress.

setback: *n.* a problem that delays or stops progress or makes a situation worse 阻碍，挫折

It is through dealing with **setbacks** and obstacles that we discover ourselves — our strengths as well as our weaknesses.

6 Opportunities to get involved in sport at university are plentiful and the UK has some world-class sporting **institutions**. **(Para. 5)**
Paraphrase: There are plenty of opportunities to engage in sport at university and the UK has some top sporting organizations in the world.
institution: *n.* 机构，团体
University, as a higher education **institution**, also operates in the areas of scientific research and professional activities.

7 Loughborough University has **dominated** the British Universities and Colleges Sport (BUCS) table, which ranks institutions **based on** sporting achievements, for the last decade. **(Para. 5)**
Paraphrase: For the past ten years, Loughborough University has been ranked as one of the top institutions in the British Universities and Colleges Sport (BUCS) table, which grades educational institutions in terms of their sporting performance.
dominate: *v.* have control of or a very strong influence on sb./sth. 支配，控制，主宰
No language in history has **dominated** international trade quite like English does today.
based on: 以……为基础，以……为根据
The movie, *The Captain*, is **based on** the true story of a Chinese pilot who brought 119 passengers and nine crew members home safely after his plane's windshield shattered.

8 It has **boasted** 25 student competitors in last week's Commonwealth Games. **(Para. 5)**
Paraphrase: Loughborough University is proud to have 25 student athletes participating in the Commonwealth Games held last week.
boast: *v.* possess sth. to be proud of 自豪地拥有
Known to be one of the most spectacular skylines in the world, Hong Kong **boasts** an impressive display of skyscrapers.

9 "Their weeks are highly **stressful**, so top sportspeople are extremely organised, disciplined and **efficient** with their time, which are useful skills in the academic side of their lives," says Stephen

Baddeley … (**Para. 6**)

Paraphrase: "The weeks of athletes are full of pressure, so top athletes are particularly good at planning, behave in a very controlled way, and work well without wasting time. These are all useful skills when they are studying as students," says Stephen Baddeley …

stressful: *adj.* involving or causing a lot of pressure or worry 充满压力的，紧张的

Any major life change can be **stressful** — even a happy event like a wedding.

efficient: *adj.* working well without wasting time, money, or energy 有效率的，高效能的

As you grow older, your body isn't so **efficient** at processing the food you take in, so you may need to take supplementary vitamins.

10 Self-discipline **lends itself** well **to** academic focus, helping to get rid of procrastination. (**Para. 7**)

Paraphrase: Self-discipline is very useful for making one focused on studying, which helps to stop delaying important tasks.

lend itself to sth.: be suitable or useful for sth. 适合于；适用于

This is an interesting and inspiring novel that **lends itself** well **to** book discussion.

11 "The mind **wanders** when doing essays, but if you develop a focus and know you have to use your time efficiently, then it's a very **transferable** skill," says Baddeley. (**Para. 7**)

Paraphrase: "When you write essays your thoughts may not always be focused on the writing. However, if you learn to be highly focused and know you need to use your time in an efficient way, then it's a useful skill that can be applied to studying as well," says Baddeley.

wander: *v.* no longer pay attention to sth. 走神；（思想）开小差

I'm always distracted and my mind is always **wandering**.

transferable: *adj.* that can be moved from one place, person or use to another 可转移的；可转让的

Transferable skills are a core set of skills and abilities that are helpful across different areas of life.

12 Luke Belton, a geology student at Durham University who **smashed** two island **records** swimming for Guernsey at the Commonwealth Games, says he is a better student because of his sport. (**Para. 8**)

Paraphrase: Luke Belton is a geology student at Durham University who broke two island records when he swam for Guernsey at the Commonwealth Games. He says that he is better at studying because he is doing sports.

smash a record: do sth. much faster, better, etc. than anyone has done before 打破纪录

A group of 63 female skydivers **smashed a** world **record** at the end of 2013.

13 I don't do much less than your average person because I still get it done and so far my results haven't suffered. (**Para. 9**)

Paraphrase: I don't study less compared to the usual type of student because I still finish every task on time and so far my academic results remain good.

Note: Here "suffer" means "become worse; lose quality (变坏；变差；变糟)". For example: Your studies will **suffer** if you spend too much time playing video games.

14 Pushing himself to the limit physically has also **boosted** his academic **commitment** and **perseverance**. (**Para. 10**)

Paraphrase: Forcing himself to do his best physically has also made him more devoted to studying as well as more determined.

boost: *v.* increase or improve sth. and make it more successful 促进，推动，使兴旺

Exercising regularly and getting sufficient sleep can help **boost** your energy levels.

commitment: *n.* the hard work and loyalty that sb. gives to an organization, activity, etc. 投入，忠诚，奉献

In 2019, 58 people were honored as China's national ethical role models, who were recognized for their outstanding contributions and **commitment** to society.

perseverance: *n.* continued steady effort to achieve an aim 坚持不懈；不屈不挠

It takes motivation, dedication and **perseverance** to exercise regularly, but the reward is a better quality of life.

15 If I'm not enjoying the work, it helps to be able to just **get through** and finish it. **(Para. 10)**

Paraphrase: If I'm not enjoying the work I'm doing, I'm able to just pass the difficult period and complete the work because I'm committed and perseverant.

get through: (manage to) do or complete sth., esp. when it is difficult （设法）做或完成某事

We have **got through** a lot of work, but there is even more to come.

16 Students are often advised to exercise because of its **mood**-enhancing **properties**. **(Para. 11)**

Paraphrase: Students are often encouraged to do exercise because physical activity can improve emotional health.

mood: *n.* the way you feel at a particular time 心情，心境，情绪

I skipped my gym class yesterday because I was not in the **mood** for exercise.

property: *n.* special quality or characteristic of a substance, etc. 特性，性质

One of the **properties** of X-rays is that they travel in straight lines.

17 "The saying that a healthy body equals a healthy mind is absolutely true," says Quentin Sloper, head of sport, music and **drama** at Durham University. **(Para. 11)**

Paraphrase: "The saying that if you are physically healthy then you will also be mentally healthy is completely true," says Quentin Sloper, who is the head of sport, music and drama at Durham University.

drama: *n.* a play for the theatre, radio or TV 戏；剧；戏剧艺术

Cao Yu is regarded as a great playwright of modern Chinese **drama**.

18 Four of its students competed in last week's Commonwealth Games and 90% of students **participate in** sport. **(Para. 12)**

Paraphrase: Four students from Durham University took part in last week's Commonwealth Games, and 90% of its students are involved in sport activities.

participate in: take part or become involved in an activity 参加，参与

All children in this school are encouraged to **participate in** as many extracurricular activities as they wish.

19 If we've been on a run, we feel better for the rest of the day. **(Para. 12)**

Paraphrase: If we've done some exercise such as running on a day, we will feel better for the rest of that day.

20 Research by British Universities and Colleges Sport (BUCS) last year suggested that **involvement** in university sport can also boost students' employment **prospects**. **(Para. 13)**

Paraphrase: Research by British Universities and Colleges Sport (BUCS) last year suggested that taking part in university sport can also increase students' chances of getting jobs.

involvement: *n.* the act of taking part in an activity or event 参与，加入；卷入

In the early years, parental **involvement** has a significant impact on children's cognitive development.

prospect: *n.* chances of future success 成功的机会；前景；前程

I was both anxious and excited by the **prospect** of going to college.

21 Even involvement in the non-physical side of sport — from volunteering on a **committee** to coaching — provides opportunities to develop leadership skills. **(Para. 15)**

Paraphrase: Even doing something just related to sport, other than actually doing the sport, such as volunteering on a committee and offering help as a coach, can provide chances to develop leadership skills.

committee: *n.* a group of people chosen to do a particular job, make decisions, etc. 委员会

The **committee** includes representatives from both management and workers.

22 Student athletes may also be better **communicators** and team players. **(Para. 17)**

Paraphrase: Student athletes may also be better at exchanging their ideas with other people and working in a team.

communicator: *n.* sb. who is able to express ideas or their feelings clearly to other people 交际者，交流者

One of the quickest ways to become an effective **communicator** is to learn to listen.

23 "In **rugby** sevens you're often meeting new team members, so you have to **work out** how to **get on with** them to play the best rugby on the field," ... **(Para. 17)**

Paraphrase: "In the English football game rugby sevens you often get to know new team members, so you have to understand how to maintain a friendly relationship with them in order to play the best rugby on the field," ...

rugby: *n.*（英式）橄榄球

The main difference between **rugby** and football is that the former is played by hands and the latter is played by feet.

work out: think about sth. and manage to understand it 设法弄懂某事

Before applying for a mortgage, you need to **work out** how much you can afford to borrow.

get on with sb.: have a friendly relationship with each other 友好相处

It's easy for me to **get on with** my parents because they always listen to my opinions.

24 While deciding to juggle a sporting and academic career may **elicit concern** from worried **tutors**, the examples provided by Commonwealth Games-standard athletes like Belton and Treharne show that, with commitment and the right attitude, it is possible to maintain **stellar** quality in both. **(Para. 19)**

Paraphrase: Although deciding to balance a sporting career with a university degree may cause their supervising teachers anxiety, the examples provided by athletes who compete at the level of Commonwealth Games, such as Belton and Treharne, show that it is possible to have excellent performance in both if you have strong determination and the right attitude.

elicit: *v.* draw (facts, a response, etc.) from sb. 引出，诱出

Teachers are encouraged to **elicit** student thinking by using open-ended questions.

concern: *n.* worry; anxiety 担心；忧虑；关切

My grandmother is always full of **concern**, compassion and care for others.

tutor: *n.* a university or college teacher responsible for the teaching and supervision of assigned students 大学导师

You will be allocated a **tutor** who will provide you with support and guidance throughout your time at this college.

stellar: *adj.* extremely good 非常出色的，优秀的

This photo recovery software is a **stellar** tool to recover video files lost due to deletion.

PART IV Keys to Exercises

Lead-in

I 1 When he was 17 years old.

2 In 2011.

3 38.

4 Because he wanted to fulfill his promise to his parents that he would finish university study after ending his athletic career.

5 Advanced math.

6 Seven years.

7 His promise to his parents.

8 To connect their own future with the future of the whole society. / To shoulder responsibilities beyond those for individuals.

> **Script**
>
> Yao Ming, the former basketball player and current head of the Chinese Basketball Association, graduated from Shanghai Jiao Tong University on July 8, 2018, together with another 3,300 some graduates at the university.
>
> Yao, 38, started his study at Antai College of Economics and Management in 2011.
>
> In an academic robe, Yao delivered a speech at the graduation ceremony on Sunday on behalf of this year's graduates of bachelor degrees.
>
> "I would like to thank my parents first as the reason that I decided to study at university was to fulfill my promise to them," he said.
>
> Yao said when he became a professional basketball player at 17, his parents asked him to promise that he would return to campus and finish university study after ending

his athletic career.

"I may not graduate today if I had not made the promise," he said. "I had thought about quitting several times, especially on advanced math classes. It was the promise that kept me going on."

He said he could not understand anything at all on the first advanced math class, but had emotionally prepared for the challenge and he could eventually do it with improvement day by day. It took him seven years to finish all the courses.

Yao encouraged the schoolmates to connect their own future with the future of the whole society so as to have more room to explore.

"The society could be as small as a family, or as big as a group," he said. "No matter how, we will learn to shoulder responsibilities beyond those for individuals."

Reading to Learn

Reading Comprehension

I   **1** C   **2** D   **3** A   **4** E   **5** B

II   **1** D   **2** A   **3** B   **4** C   **5** A

III **Text Organization**
- **1** academic and sporting performance
- **2** their training and performance
- **3** the challenges of sport
- **4** organized, disciplined and efficient
- **5** commitment and perseverance
- **6** employment prospects
- **7** teamwork, decision-making
- **8** be better communicators
- **9** commitment and the right attitude

Language in Use

Words and Expressions

I   **1** outlet   **2** wandering   **3** dual   **4** elicit
    5 chasing   **6** involvement   **7** efficiently   **8** setbacks

II **1** smashing a record **2** put … into perspective **3** based on **4** work out
    5 get through   **6** lend itself … to   **7** get on with   **8** participated in

III **1** engaging in **2** concern **3** stressful **4** properties **5** stimulate
    6 intellectually **7** commitment **8** work things out **9** deal with **10** prospect

Word Formation

I 1 H   2 C   3 F   4 I   5 D   6 G   7 J   8 A   9 E   10 B

II 1 spectrum   2 aspects   3 retrospect   4 spectacle   5 introspect
  6 suspect   7 inspect   8 suspicious   9 conspicuous   10 spectacular

Collocation

1 balance study and work   2 develop communication skills
3 boost production   4 maintain a good relationship
5 balance the past and present   6 stimulated economic growth
7 developed a habit of   8 enhance the quality
9 boost the prospect   10 stimulate his interest

Grammar and Structure

2 **Problem:** It is not clear who read the novel.
  Correction: After reading the amazing new novel, Jackie believed that the movie based on it was sure to be exciting.

3 **Problem:** It is not clear who did not know her name.
  Correction: Without knowing her name, I found it difficult to introduce her. / Since I did not know her name, it was difficult to introduce her.

4 **Problem:** It is the house, not "I", that was newly painted.
  Correction: Newly painted, the house where my grandmother had been living for many years could hardly be recognized.

5 **Problem:** "She", instead of "the words", was waiting for class to start.
  Correction: While she was waiting for class to start, the words on the chalkboard caught her attention.

6 **Problem:** "As a baby" cannot modify "my mother", as "my mother" is not a baby.
  Correction: When I was a baby, my mother would often rock me to sleep in her arms.

7 **Problem:** It is the experimenter, not Group A, that separated the participants into three groups.
  Correction: After separating the participants into three groups, I tested Group A first. / After I separated the participants into three groups (or: After the participants were separated into three groups), Group A was tested first.

8 **Problem:** The writer of the report, not the report itself, had been working through the night.
  Correction: Working through the night, I finished the report on student athletes in time for class.

Translation

I 1 学校应该鼓励老师们让学生参与关于防止网络欺凌、创建健康网络环境的课堂讨论。
  2 当羡慕之心激励你挑战自己、突破自己的极限时，它就成为一种正能量。
  3 摩根太太对工作的尽职尽责与全心投入令周围的人钦佩和赞赏。
  4 在进行小组活动时，会出现一些问题，如有些孩子独霸对话或不让其他人发言。
  5 想搞清如何给一家公司估价，就要在网上搜索在售的类似公司，熟悉一下市场。

II **1** There's been concern over water pollution in this area for several years and related measures are being taken to deal with it.

2 An easy way to boost patient satisfaction in medical care is to keep patient rooms clean.

3 My experience of severe illness has put everything into perspective for me, and I now pay more attention to the things that really matter to me, such as family.

4 Shanghai boasts the longest and the most developed subway system with the highest density in China.

5 Nearly 1,000 musicians from Beijing put on a show together in Tianjin and smashed the record for the largest performing rock band.

III China has always stressed the importance of student health and asks that families, schools and society should create conditions for students to improve their health. The health of students in China has further improved in recent years, and physical education at school played a significant role in that process. But the situation can be better if more resources from government departments and society are integrated and made full use of. To make it happen, China's Ministry of Education is working with other government departments to introduce new measures to advocate the idea of "Health Comes First". The aim is to boost the development of physical education and students' health, and cultivate more well-rounded talented people for the country.

Corpora in Language Learning

I (There can be more than one answer to some questions here, and to each question only one answer is provided for reference.)

Verb	Nouns or noun phrases	Chinese translations
keep	a digital <u>record</u>	保留电子记录
	a good <u>atmosphere</u>	保持良好氛围
	a very low <u>profile</u>	为人低调
	accurate <u>time</u>	准确计时
	<u>pace</u> with	跟上，赶上
	an <u>eye</u> on	注意，照看
	<u>balance</u>	保持平衡
	<u>commitments</u>	兑现承诺
	healthy <u>habits</u>	保持健康习惯
	<u>receipts</u>	保留收据
	the <u>goal</u>	保持目标不变

II

1

Verb phrases of "keep + preposition/adverb"	Definitions
keep at sth.	continue working at sth.
keep sth. down	not to let sth. get bigger or go higher
keep sb. from doing sth.	prevent sb. from doing sth.
keep up with	move or progress at the same rate as sb./sth.
keep on doing sth.	continue doing sth.

2 1) Keep at   2) keep on   3) keep … down
   4) keep on   5) keep up with   6) keep … from

Writing

I A number of studies <u>support the claim</u> that sports and other physical activities can contribute to the development of self-esteem. For example, Canadian scientists <u>found</u> that sixth grade students who were more physically active had considerably higher levels of self-esteem. A study in Switzerland <u>showed</u> that adolescents who participated in sports clubs had greater well-being, including being better socially adjusted, feeling less anxious, and generally being happier about their lives. Similar findings <u>were reported</u> in a study of Latino students, where participation in school sport <u>was found to</u> be significantly associated with self-esteem.

From the reporting verbs, we can see that the writer is mainly describing what other researchers have done and have found out. The first reporting word "support", however, shows that the writer has a strong belief in the claim that sports and other physical activities can contribute to the development of self-esteem.

Language Functions

I **Words for body parts:** back, face, <u>knees, feet, heels, sitting bones, inner feet, arms, tailbone, buttocks, thighs, hands, pelvis, shoulders, hips, chin, sternum, etc.</u>

Verbs for body movements: lie, bend, <u>exhale, press, push, lift, keep, clasp, extend, lengthen, etc.</u>

II **1** **Standing Forward Bend**

Stand straight, hands on hips. Exhale and bend forward from the hip joints. With your knees straight, bring your palms to the backs of your ankles. Press the heels firmly into the floor and lift the sitting bones toward the ceiling.

2 **Cat Pose**

Start on your hands and knees in a "tabletop" position. Center your head in a neutral position, eyes looking at the floor. As you exhale, round your spine toward the ceiling, making sure to keep your shoulders and knees in position. Release your head toward the floor, but don't force your chin to your chest. Then, inhale, coming back to neutral "tabletop" position on your hands and knees.

3 Cobra Pose

Lie on the floor, face downwards. Stretch your legs back, tops of the feet on the floor. Spread your hands on the floor under your shoulders. Hug the elbows back into your body. Begin to straighten the arms to lift the chest off the floor. Press the tailbone toward the pubis and lift the pubis toward the navel. Narrow the hip points. Firm but don't harden the buttocks. Firm the shoulder blades against the back, puffing the side ribs forward.

Reading to Explore

Reading Comprehension

I	**1** B	**2** D	**3** C	**4** D	**5** C				
II	**1** F	**2** T	**3** T	**4** F	**5** F				
III	**A** 15	**B** 7	**C** 17	**D** 10	**E** 6				
	F 3	**G** 11	**H** 16	**I** 1	**J** 12				

Words and Expressions

I **1** pursue **2** tackle **3** self-esteem **4** agony **5** retired
6 confusion **7** roughly **8** unconventional **9** transitional **10** thrive

II **1** in progress **2** dedicated to **3** am equipped to **4** on a scholarship
5 getting stuck in **6** call on **7** headed to **8** keep up with
9 cope with **10** hand out

PART V Text Translation

Text A

运动员是否会成为更出色的学生？

娜塔莉·吉尔

1 赶最后的交作业期限和赶着去上课是许多学生经历的最吃力的锻炼形式。而要兼顾攻读学位和当职业运动员两方面，这事儿光想一想就足以让我们有些人捏一把汗。

2 但是证据表明，平衡两者有益于提高学习成绩和体育成绩。研究发现，兼顾"两份事业"能够让人更有动力去训练、备战，激发运动员的智能并帮助解压。

3 兼顾运动和学习的学生是否真的更出色呢？

4 根据拉夫堡大学伊恩·亨利教授的观点，在运动之外发展其他兴趣有助于运动员"正确对待训练和战绩，更有效地应对诸如失败和伤痛等运动中的挑战"。

5　在大学里参加体育运动的机会很多，英国有一些世界级的体育院校。在过去的十年间，拉夫堡大学在英国大学体育协会（BUCS）的排行榜上一直名列前茅，该排行榜根据体育成绩来给院校排名。在上周的英联邦运动会上，拉夫堡大学派出了25名学生运动员参赛，并引以为豪。

6　"他们每周的压力都很大，所以优秀的运动员极有条理，极其自律，时间安排上非常高效，而这些都是对他们学业有用的技能，"巴斯大学的体育系主任史蒂夫·巴德利说。他的大学有11名在校生参加了英联邦运动会。

7　自律十分有助于提高学习的专注度，摆脱拖延症。"写论文时容易走神，但是假如你养成了专心致志的习惯，明白自己必须有效地利用时间，那么这项技能就可以沿用到学习上，"巴德利说。

8　代表根西岛参赛的杜伦大学地质系学生卢克·贝尔顿，在英联邦运动会的游泳项目上打破了两项本岛纪录。他说运动帮他成为更出色的学生。

9　"当我需要做功课时，我就坐下来着手做。我并不比你们一般人少做多少，因为该做的我都不落下，所以到目前为止我的学习成绩没有受到影响。也许我课程相关的阅读量不及其他同学，但是我认为在现阶段这不算什么大问题。"

10　在体能上突破自己的极限也增强了他对学习的投入和韧性。"对于我不喜欢的功课，它能帮我坚持完成。有时候你要在泳池中完成一小时的魔鬼训练，但是你坚持做了。做完之后，你就会感觉很棒。"

11　人们常常建议学生们参加锻炼，因为它能改善情绪。"人们说身体健康，头脑也就健康，这话一点不假，"杜伦大学体育、音乐和戏剧部主任昆汀·斯洛珀说。

12　该大学有四名学生参加了上周的英联邦运动会，而且90%的学生参加体育运动。"我们和咨询服务部门紧密合作，该部门的主任告诉我们，我们的学生心理很健康，因为他们积极参加体育运动。假如某天我们跑了步，那么这一天接下来的时间中我们会感觉更好。"

13　根据英国大学体育协会（BUCS）去年所做的研究，在大学中参加体育运动还能增加学生的就业机会。

14　"用人单位说，参加体育运动的学生具备公司所需的特质，尤其是兼顾学习和其他兴趣的能力，比如为参赛而训练，以及团队合作精神和决策能力，"伯明翰大学竞技体育部主任亚历克斯·泰勒如是说，该大学有6名在校学生参加了英联邦运动会。

15　即使参加体育中非体能竞技的活动——从当委员会的志愿者到当教练——也获得了发展领导技能的机会。

16　"这些素质在职场上一直很重要，在竞争激烈的毕业生就业市场上日益受重视，"巴德利说道。

17　学生运动员也可能更擅长沟通和团队合作。"在七人制橄榄球中，你经常接触到新的队友，因此你必须学会如何与其相处，才能打出最好的赛绩，"埃克塞特大学医学生卢克·特里哈恩说。他在英联邦运动会上代表威尔士参加了七人制橄榄球比赛。

18　埃克塞特大学橄榄球运动主任基思·弗莱明说，"两者兼顾最重要的就是要做到以尽可能最好的成绩毕业，而不是牺牲一方来保另一方。"

19 虽然决定兼顾运动和学习两方可能会令关切的导师们担忧，但是像贝尔顿和特里哈恩这些达到英联邦运动会水准的运动员范例表明，只要专心投入并保持正确的态度，就有可能在两个领域都成为佼佼者。

Text B

告别运动：一位大学生运动员的最大挑战

普里姆·席瑞皮帕

1 我怀念网球的队友之情。我怀念竞赛。我怀念赛前的忐忑。我怀念大胜后特别是全队大胜后的肾上腺素狂飙。我甚至怀念输球后的痛苦。

2 但我并不怀念之后发生的事。我称之为转折点。

3 我从7岁起开始打网球。到我12岁时，家里做出了重大牺牲，一家分居两地，从而让我能追求打网球甚至可能转为职业球手的梦想。母亲和我搬到了位于佛罗里达州的善道泉网球学校，而父亲留在密苏里州工作，养家糊口，同时照顾我的哥哥。我最终赢得了全国前十的排名，得到了随美国国家队出征的名额。毕业后，我拿到了网球奖学金进入杜克大学就读。

4 我的大学经历很有收获，但也是我人生中最困难的阶段之一。作为一名学生运动员，我一直竭力兼顾学习和运动两项重担。追求完美的我努力跟上班里的同学以及十佳球队的队员们。

5 大学阶段已然不易，但没有人提醒我前面还有一个更大的挑战：告别我钟爱的运动，转型进入"现实世界"。这一转型给我心理上和情感上造成的创伤，对我的世界是一次巨大冲击。

6 对于绝大多数学生运动员而言，这一转折点不可避免。根据美国大学体育协会网站统计，在所有在高中阶段就参加运动竞赛的学生中（大约740万名运动员），有百分之二会获得大学的奖学金。而这百分之二的人中（在美国大学体育协会中约有46万名），只有不到百分之二会成为职业运动员。其余百分之九十八的人只得自谋出路。对于一生都在按照严格日程投身体育的运动员来说，这样的现实不免令人畏惧。

7 苏·恩奎斯特曾是加州大学洛杉矶分校赫赫有名的垒球运动员兼教练，现在是一名大学和企业的绩效顾问。她说，完成进入现实世界的转变对每个人都是一场心理上的挑战。她说，最重要的是运动员"要真正明白，当你步入职场后就不再会有真正的轻松，并且要明白自己需要不断进步。"

8 "你要适应这种不适应。"

9 每个人的道路不尽相同。这里讲讲我自己，以及其他一些运动员，在这条路上探索时碰到的情况。

10 对我而言，在这个转型阶段最不适应的时刻是从赛场上退下来。它比任何输球或伤痛更令人痛苦。我经历了各种情绪：悲伤、愤怒、自卑、内疚、迷茫和孤独。这些情绪持续了好几年。而且一名运动员参赛的级别越高，退役的困难就越大。

11 2003年从杜克大学毕业三个月后，我开始朝一个新的目标努力，想当一名体育主持人，但是面对人生中失去的东西，内心仍在挣扎。这种痛苦犹如失去挚爱之人。

12 当我在北卡罗来纳州的罗利市一家电视台实习时，挣每小时8美元的工资，干着接接电话和发发稿子的活儿，而我的很多朋友仍在职业巡回赛上驰骋征战。我为我的朋友们高兴，但是看到他们能继续他们的运动梦想却让我痛苦。放弃网球和作为一名明星运动员的身份是我所做过的最艰难的事。

13 我剩下两种选择：我可以沉溺于痛苦中，依旧恋恋不舍地回望身后已合上的大门，或者可以凭借当运动员时学到的本领，接受挑战，努力奋斗，重塑自己。

14 一朝上赛场，终生会拼搏。

15 "要知道奇迹的发生不是靠比赛，而是靠你自己，"苏·戈登说道，她曾是杜克大学女篮队员，现任美国国家地理空间情报局的副局长。"让你在体育上成功的一切素质也能让你在任何奋斗中成功，只要你把它们发挥出来。"

16 研究表明，学生运动员，特别是女性，充分具备应对人生挑战的素质。例如，根据盖洛普调查，相比非学生运动员，曾经的学生运动员在许多方面都更为出色，包括目的性更强，在社区和社会上的幸福指数更高。

17 "你远比自己想象的更能应对现实世界，"凯莉·古德曼说，她曾是杜克大学女足队员，现任威廉与玛丽学院运动员培养部助理主任。"你已经具备了征服职场的所有技能：时间管理、有效沟通、职业道德、团队精神。要对自己有信心。追随自己的热情，哪怕它引你走向一条不寻常的道路。"

18 虽然我的比赛岁月已成过往，但是作为一名运动员，我所学会的和养成的本领帮助我跨入了人生的新阶段。

6 HUMANS AND NATURE

Humans exert great pressure on the natural world. Habitats and species can be affected by all kinds of human activities. Our thoughtless actions have made air and water become polluted, rivers dry up, seasons arrive unseasonably, and species die out. How can we reduce our threat to nature? Should we treat animals and plants fairly and with concern for their interests and welfare? This unit will help us reflect on our relationship with nature. Text A discusses what hidden lessons people are giving to their children through their attitude toward other life forms, and the negative effects of these lessons. Text B tries to validate the idea that nature brings people together. After learning this unit, you are encouraged to think about these questions: Do you agree to the authors' ideas? Why do you think it is important to protect nature? What can we do to protect it?

In this unit you will:

1 Learn what hidden and negative lessons people are giving to their children through their attitude toward other forms of life;

2 Learn how nature can bring people together;

3 Reflect on the importance of building a harmonious relationship between man and nature;

4 Learn how the suffixes -ic, ish, and -ous combine with nouns to form adjectives;

5 Learn some nouns and verbs that regularly occur together;

6 Learn to use the structure "*can't over + verb*", or "*can never over + verb*"; "*can't ... enough*", or "*can never ... enough*"; and "*can't ... too ...*", or "*can never ... too ...*";

7 Learn collocations of "retain/maintain/contain + noun" by using CADEL;

8 Learn how to write the introduction of an essay;

9 Learn to understand and create some warning signs expressing prohibition and obligation.

Sayings

Learning objectives:

- Get a general idea of the unit
- Get inspirations from the sayings
- Get useful advice and guidance from famous people or books
- Learn to develop a positive attitude toward life

Teaching steps:

1 Ask students to translate the two sayings into Chinese.
   Reference translations for the sayings:

   - 天地与我并生，万物与我为一。 ——庄子
   - 自记事以来，大自然就一直带给我慰藉、灵感、冒险和快乐；大自然就是一个家、一名老师、一位伴侣。 ——洛林·安德森

2 The first saying is quoted from Zhuangzi (or Chuang-tzu, "Master Zhuang"), a late 4th century B.C. Chinese Daoist philosopher. For this quote, tell students that it is important for man to live a way of life in tune with nature. A harmonious relationship between man and nature allows biodiversity to be valued, conserved, restored and wisely enjoyed. Man should not see himself as separated from nature. By protecting nature and preserving the environment, man is preserving himself and saving his own life.

3 The second saying is quoted from Lorraine Anderson, an American writer and editor. For this quote, tell students the significant role nature plays in our life. Not only does nature provide us water, food, oxygen, light and many other things that we need to survive on this planet, but also is a source of comfort and healing, a source of joy and relaxation, and a source of new ideas to stimulate innovation and novel approaches to solve problems. Whenever we want, nature is there to cater to our various needs.

Lead-in

Learning objectives:

- Learn the names of some common insects
- Share ideas about insects and people's living environment

Teaching steps:

1 Make a brief introduction to the unit and explain its learning objectives.
2 Ask students to do Exercise I and learn the names of some common insects.
3 Ask students to work in pairs. Give them about 10 minutes to talk about the questions in Exercise II. Encourage them to engage in the discussion actively.

Reading to Learn

Text A

Hidden Lessons

Learning objectives:

- Learn what hidden and negative lessons people are giving to their children through their attitude toward other forms of life
- Analyze the structure of the text
- Learn to use examples, stories and reasons to argue for one's point of view
- Learn to use some new words and expressions correctly

Teaching steps:

1   Introduce the topic of Text A. Ask the question: What hidden lessons does city life teach us? Please read the text to find out what the author has to say about it.

2   Ask students to go through the whole text and divide it into three parts. After that, ask them to look at the Text Organization exercise to check if they have made the same division. The text can be divided as follows: Part 1 (Para. 1), Part 2 (Paras. 2–8) and Part 3 (Paras. 9–11).

3   Help students recognize that this is an argumentative text, with rich use of examples, stories and reasons as supporting details. Help students review what they have learned about supporting details in Unit 5 of Book 1.

4   Go to Part III Detailed Study of Text A. Help students understand difficult sentences in the text accurately. Introduce important new words and expressions with explanations and examples.

5   Ask students to do the exercises following the text.

Critical Thinking

Learning objectives:

- Raise awareness of the need to protect nature
- Gather ideas about how to increase green spaces in cities
- Understand the importance of green and sustainable development
- Boost the sense of national pride and encourage environmentally friendly actions

Teaching steps:

1   Ask students to read the questions first and then give them some ideas on how to approach each question.

2   For Question 1, encourage students to think about the importance of creating more green spaces in cities and the measures that can be taken. You can guide them with these questions: How can more green spaces improve the environment in cities? How can they help develop better neighborhoods and communities? How can they improve the well-being and health of

city residents? To encourage students to talk about what measures to take, you can give students some relevant words and phrases, such as "urban gardens", "pocket parks", "mini forests", etc.

3   For Question 2, get students to understand the importance of green and sustainable development. First, ask students to explain the meaning of the slogan, and then ask them to discuss the importance of green development and the ways to achieve it. You may use the following words and phrases to guide students: reduce carbon emissions, switch to clean energy sources, improve energy efficiency, mitigate climate change, educate people about the importance of sustainable development to their lives, live a greener lifestyle, etc.

4   For Question 3, encourage students to discuss why it is important to protect natural wonders and how to protect them. You may name one or two natural wonders in China as examples first, such as Zhangye Danxia National Geopark in Gansu, and Huanglong National Geopark in Sichuan, and then ask students to name as many others as they can. The reasons for protecting natural wonders can include: Natural wonders provide unique ecosystems; they represent the timeless beauty of nature; they are home to diverse wildlife; they provide opportunities for outdoor recreation and help develop tourism. As to how to protect natural wonders, encourage students to talk about how they can change their own behavior to minimize the harmful impacts on natural wonders.

5   Ask students to work in pairs or in small groups to share their opinions. Encourage each pair or group to present their favorite ideas in class.

Corpora in Language Learning

Learning objectives:

- Learn to search CADEL for collocations of "retain/maintain/contain + noun" by using the "Concordance" function of AntConc

- Learn to complete the given sentences with *retain/maintain/contain* based on the contexts in which they appear

Teaching steps:

1   Ask students to search CADEL for nouns that collocate with *retain/maintain/contain* by using the "Concordance" function of AntConc. Ask students to identify the nouns that begin with the given letters.

2   Ask students to sort the search results by setting KWIC sort.

3   Discuss the use of the collocations "retain/maintain/contain + noun" and give the Chinese translations of these collocations.

4   Compare the use of *retain*, *maintain* and *contain* and explain how to complete the given sentences with these verbs.

Writing

Learning objectives:

- Learn how to write the introduction of an essay
- Analyze examples to see how the tips introduced in this part are used

Teaching steps:

1 Introduce the importance of writing an effective introductory paragraph for an essay.
2 Introduce the functions of an introductory paragraph.
3 Introduce the tips for writing an effective introduction.
4 Ask students to analyze two examples to see how the tips introduced in this part are used.

Language Functions

Learning objectives:

- Learn some warning signs expressing prohibition and obligation and their sentence structures
- Learn to create some warning signs by using the sentence structures introduced

Teaching steps:

1 Introduce the importance of warning signs expressing prohibition and obligation.
2 Introduce the sentence structures expressing prohibition and obligation with examples.
3 Ask students to do Exercise I to get familiar with some warning signs.
4 Ask students to create some warning signs by doing Exercise II.

Reading to Explore

Text B

How Nature Brings Us Together

Learning objectives:

- Learn how the shared experience of natural wonders can bring people closer
- Learn more about how to argue for a point of view with supporting details
- Learn more about how to write the introduction of an essay
- Learn to use new words and expressions correctly

Teaching steps:

1 Ask students to read the text and finish the exercises following the text before class.
2 Check answers to the exercises.
3 Ask students to tell the main idea of the text.
4 Ask students to discuss whether they agree with the author, and why.

This text tries to convince us that the shared experience of natural wonders can bring people closer. The writer tries to argue for his idea from three aspects. First, when we witness a natural wonder together with others, we forget our ages and social strata. We are reminded of the interdependence of all life, and are intuitively drawn together. Second, the shared experience of natural wonders also brings out our better selves. Whenever we see something exciting in nature, we are eager to enjoy the moment together with others. Third, nature can even bring us closer to people we may never meet. In a word, nature is a great equalizer. Shared appreciation of the wonders of nature can help to heal the social divide which prevents the building of a harmonious society.

PART III Detailed Study of Text A

Hidden Lessons

Understanding the Text

Part 1 (Para. 1)

Ask students to read Para. 1 and do two things:

1 Answer the question: Which sentence expresses the author's point of view? (The last sentence: There's nothing wrong with that, of course, but in such an environment, it's very easy to lose any sense of connection with nature.)

2 Go to the Text Organization exercise and complete the main ideas for Part 1.

Part 2 (Paras. 2–8)

Paras. 2–3

Ask students to read Paras. 2–3 and go to the Text Organization exercise to complete the main ideas for Paras. 2–3 in Part 2.

Paras. 4–6

Ask students to read Paras. 4–6 and do two things:

1 Answer the question: What supporting details does the author give to argue for his point that we humans have been deeply embedded in and dependent on nature in history? (Question 3 in Exercise I of Reading Comprehension) (The supporting details he gives are: When plants and animals were plentiful, we flourished. When famine and drought struck, our numbers fell accordingly.)

2 Go to the Text Organization exercise and complete the main ideas for Paras. 4–6 in Part 2.

<u>Paras. 7–8</u>

Ask students to read Paras. 7–8 and do two things:

1　Answer the question: Why is it still important for us to sense our place in nature even though we have modern cities and advanced technology now? (Question 4 in Exercise I of Reading Comprehension) (It is still important for many reasons, but two important reasons are: 1) Almost all scientists were fascinated with nature as children and retained that curiosity throughout their lives, which helped them to develop science. 2) Our sense of connection with nature can greatly affect our actions.)

2　Go to the Text Organization exercise and complete the main ideas for Paras. 7–8 in Part 2.

Part 3 (Paras. 9–11)

<u>Para. 9</u>

Ask students to read Para. 9 and do two things:

1　Answer the question: Why will children who understand their place in the ecosystem feel physical pain when seeing forests being clear-cut? (Question 5 in Exercise I of Reading Comprehension) (Because they will understand that trees are an extension of themselves.)

2　Go to the Text Organization exercise and complete the main ideas for Para. 9 in Part 3.

<u>Paras. 10–11</u>

Ask students to read Paras. 10–11 and go to the Text Organization exercise to complete the main ideas for Paras. 10–11 in Part 3.

Language Points

1　**In spite of** the vast **expanse** of **wilderness** in this country, most Canadian children grow up in **urban** settings. **(Para. 1)**

Paraphrase: Although this county has vast areas of wild fields, most children in Canada grow up in towns or cities.

in spite of: regardless of; despite 尽管

In spite of his ill health, my grandfather is always cheerful.

expanse: *n.* a wide and open area (of land, sea, etc.) （陆地、海洋等的）广阔的区域

Birds are flying above the earth across the **expanse** of the sky.

wilderness: *n.* a large area of land that has never been developed or farmed 荒野，不毛之地

Over 90 percent of the region has been labeled as **wilderness** that requires the most strict protection.

urban: *adj.* relating to towns and cities 城镇的，城市的

More than 13 million new jobs were created in **urban** areas last year.

2　**In other words**, they live in a world **conceived**, shaped and dominated by people. **(Para. 1)**

Paraphrase: To put it another way, they live in a world that is designed, produced and controlled by people.

in other words: expressed in a different way; that is to say 换句话说；也就是说

They asked him to leave. **In other words**, he was fired.

conceive: *v.* form or devise (an idea, a plan, etc.) in the mind 想出；构思；设想

Ancient Chinese philosophers **conceived** the idea of "datong", meaning great harmony, the idea of coming together rather than splitting apart.

3　Even the farms **located around** cities and towns are carefully **groomed** and **landscaped** for human convenience. **(Para. 1)**

Paraphrase: Even the farms that are close to cities and towns are carefully designed to make them look attractive to provide convenience for people.

locate: *v.* put or build sth. in a particular place 把……设置在；把……建造在

Large retail chains usually only **locate** stores in areas of high population density.

be located around sth.: be in a particular position or place 位于……附近

Most of the projects I've been involved in **are located around** Shanghai.

groom: *v.* look after (a lawn, ski slope, or other surface) 照料（草坪、滑雪坡或其他表面）

You should **groom** the ski slope before the competition.

landscape: *v.* make a piece of land more attractive by adding plants, paths, etc. 给……做景观美化，给……做园林美化

The shopping street has a nicely **landscaped** environment and some decent statues.

4　In city apartments and **dwellings**, the presence of cockroaches, fleas, ants, mosquitoes or flies is guaranteed to elicit the spraying of insecticides. **(Para. 2)**

Paraphrase: In the living spaces of cities, whenever cockroaches, fleas, ants, mosquitoes or flies appear, it is certain that people will kill them by spraying insecticides.

dwelling: *n.* a house, apartment, etc. where people live 住宅，寓所，住处

Some 3,000 new **dwellings** are planned for the area.

5　Mice and rats are poisoned or trapped, while the gardener wages a never-ending struggle with weeds and slugs. **(Para. 2)**

Paraphrase: Mice and rats are poisoned to death or caught by traps, while the gardener never stops fighting against weeds and slugs.

6　We have modern chemical **weapons** to **fight off** these **invaders** and we use them **lavishly**. **(Para. 2)**

Paraphrase: We have modern chemical products to fight these enemies away and we use these products in large quantities.

weapon: *n.* an action, piece of equipment, etc. that you can use to succeed in doing sth. 武器，手段，工具

Discipline was the new coach's secret **weapon**.

fight off: keep sb./sth. away by fighting or opposing them 抵挡；阻止

A little garlic and some precautionary steps may be all it takes to **fight off** those insects.

invader: *n.* 侵略者，侵犯者

Some plant and animal species, once thought harmless, have turned into aggressive **invaders**.

lavishly: *adv.* in large quantities; plentifully 大量地

We should try consciously to save money and avoid spending **lavishly** on unnecessary things.

7　We worry when kids roll in the mud or **wade** through a **puddle** because they'll get "dirty". **(Para. 3)**

Paraphrase: We feel worried when our kids play in the mud or walk through a small pool of water because they will get dirty.

wade: *v.* walk through water that is not deep 趟水，涉水

He **waded** across the stream over the stones and disappeared into the forest.

puddle: *n.* a small pool of water, esp. of rain-water on the road 水坑；雨水坑

The little girl picked up a small pink starfish in a **puddle** of seawater.

8 Children learn attitudes and values very quickly and the lesson in cities is very clear — nature is an enemy; it's dirty, dangerous or a **nuisance**. **(Para. 3)**

Paraphrase: Children acquire attitudes and values very quickly and the message they get from cities is very clear — nature is an enemy; it's dirty, dangerous, or annoying and unpleasant.

nuisance: *n.* a person, thing or situation that annoys you or causes problems 讨厌或麻烦的人（事物、情况）

An unreasonable landlord could become a **nuisance**.

9 So **youngsters** learn to **distance themselves from** nature and to try to control it. **(Para. 3)**

Paraphrase: So young people learn to keep themselves away from nature and to try to control it.

youngster: *n.* a child or young person 孩童；年轻人

For years yoga has been widely practiced all over China, especially by **youngsters**.

distance oneself from sb./sth.: become less involved or connected with sb. or sth. 使自己与……保持距离，疏远（某人）；不介入（某事）

I always try to **distance myself from** people who make me feel inadequate and unconfident.

10 I am astonished at the number of adults who are sick of or terrified by snakes, spiders, butterflies, worms, birds — the list seems endless. **(Para. 3)**

Paraphrase: I am shocked at the number of adults who are very annoyed by or terribly afraid of snakes, spiders, butterflies, worms, birds — the list could continue endlessly.

11 If you **reflect on** the history of humankind, you realize that for 99 per cent of our species' existence on the planet, we **were** deeply **embedded in** and dependent on nature. **(Para. 4)**

Paraphrase: If you think carefully about our human history, you will realize that for 99 percent of our existence on the earth, we were deeply involved with and dependent on nature.

reflect on sth.: think deeply or carefully about sth. 认真思考；深思

We should **reflect on** what aspects of the work we enjoyed and what we would prefer to avoid.

embed: *v.* put sth. firmly and deeply into sth. else, or be put into sth. in this way （使）嵌入；把……插入

The team's ultimate goal is to **embed** sensors in the robotic arm that can send signals back to the brain.

be embedded in: 嵌入；根植于

These fossils **are embedded in** hard sandstone.

12 When plants and animals were plentiful, we **flourished**. When **famine** and **drought** struck, our numbers fell accordingly. **(Para. 4)**

Paraphrase: When plants and animals existed in large numbers, our population increased. When famine and drought hit, our population would decrease as a result.

flourish: *v.* develop well and be successful 繁荣，兴旺，成功

In order for creativity to **flourish**, teachers must develop students' ability to generate original ideas.

famine: *n.* a lack of food during a long period of time in a region 饥荒

If harvest fails, **famine** is sure to follow.

drought: *n.* a long period of dry weather 旱灾，干旱

The region experienced serious **drought** in recent years, but farming and gardening continued to thrive.

13 We remain every bit as dependent upon nature today — we need plants to fix photons of energy into sugar molecules and to **cleanse** the air and replenish the oxygen. **(Para. 4)**

Paraphrase: Today we remain as dependent on nature as before — we need plants to change photons of energy into sugar molecules, and to clean the air and keep the oxygen supply.

cleanse: *v.* make sth. completely clean 使清洁，清洗

His body needed to be bathed in warm water to **cleanse** sweat and dirt away.

14 It is **folly** to forget our dependence on an intact **ecosystem**. But we do whenever we teach our **offspring** to fear or reject the natural world. **(Para. 4)**

Paraphrase: It is foolish of us to forget our dependence on a complete ecosystem. But whenever we teach our children to feel afraid of or stay away from the natural world, we forget this fact.

folly: *n.* (an act of) stupidity 愚蠢；蠢行

It is the height of **folly** to ignore the lessons of history.

ecosystem: *n.* 生态系统

We should treat the lakes, ponds, forests, farmlands and grasslands as a whole **ecosystem**.

offspring: *n.* a child or children of a particular person or couple 子女；子孙；后代

Since ancient times, the Chinese have been very serious about the naming of their **offspring**.

15 The urban message kids get **runs** completely **counter to** what they **are born with**, a natural interest in other life forms. **(Para. 4)**

Paraphrase: The message that kids get about nature from urban life is totally in opposition to what they are born with, a natural interest in other forms of life.

run counter to sth.: be the opposite of sth. 违背……；与……背道而驰

The company tried to impose a policy that **ran counter to** the wishes of the employees.

be born with sth.: have a particular type of character, disease, etc. since birth 生来就有某种性格（疾病等）

The little boy **was born with** weak sight and hearing.

16 Just watch a child in a first encounter with a flower or an ant — there is instant interest and **fascination**. We condition them out of it. **(Para. 4)**

Paraphrase: You just need to watch a child who sees a flower or an ant for the first time — he/ she will show an immediate interest. We adults change them and make them lose the interest.

fascination: *n.* the state of being very interested in sth. 着迷，迷恋

The objects and artworks included in the exhibition are reminders of Chinese people's centuries-old **fascination** with tea.

17 The result is that when my 7-year-old daughter brings home new friends, they **invariably**

shrink in fear when she tries to show them her favorite pets — three beautiful salamanders her grandfather got for her in Vancouver. **(Para. 5)**

Paraphrase: The result is that when my 7-year-old daughter brings home her new friends, they will always step back quickly in horror when she tries to show them her most liked pets — three beautiful salamanders her grandfather got for her in Vancouver.

invariably: *adv.* never changing; always the same 始终不变地；总是

People visiting a royal palace from the Qing dynasty would **invariably** be greeted by a pair of stone lions at the gate.

shrink: *v.* move back or withdraw from sth./sb., esp. through fear or disgust 退缩；畏缩

The woman **shrank** in horror at the sight of the stray dog.

18 And when my 3-year-old comes wandering in with her treasures — spiders, slugs and sowbugs that she catches under rocks lining the front **lawn** — children and adults **alike** usually respond by saying "**yuk**". **(Para. 5)**

Paraphrase: And when my 3-year-old daughter walks around and comes in carrying her treasures — spiders, slugs and sowbugs that she has caught under the rocks surrounding the front lawn — both children and adults usually respond by saying "disgusting".

lawn: *n.* 草坪，草地

The man accidentally killed a rabbit while mowing the **lawn** in front of his house.

alike: *adv.* in the same way 同样地，同样都

I read extensively on Chinese history and literature, written by Eastern and Western authors **alike**.

yuk: *interj.* (*also* **yuck**) used to show that you think sth. is very unpleasant 呸，讨厌（表示强烈的厌恶）

"Oh, **yuk**!" She snatched the cake off the counter and threw it into the trash can.

19 I can't **overemphasize** the **tragedy** of that attitude. For, **inherent** in this view is the assumption that human beings are special and different and that we lie outside nature. **(Para. 6)**

Paraphrase: It is not enough no matter how much I emphasize the danger of such an attitude. Because, what is naturally implied in this view is the idea that human beings are special and different, and that we can exist without nature.

overemphasize: *v.* place excessive emphasis on 过分强调，过于重视

The current attitude toward gifted children **overemphasizes** IQ and neglects many basic life skills.

tragedy: *n.* a very sad event or situation 悲惨的事；不幸；灾难

We shouldn't forget that war is a **tragedy**, and that damage caused by war is often irreversible.

inherent: *adj.* existing as a natural or permanent feature or quality of sb. or sth. 内在的；固有的；本来的

We should enhance our capacity to deal with uncertainties **inherent** in business operations.

20 Yet it is this belief that is creating many of our **environmental** problems today. **(Para. 6)**

Paraphrase: But it is such a belief that is causing many of our environmental problems today.

environmental: *adj.* concerning or affecting the air, land, or water on Earth 自然环境的；生态环境的

In recent years, **environmental** protection has been given increased importance in China.

21 Does it matter whether we sense our place in nature **so long as** we have cities and technology? **(Para. 7)**

Paraphrase: Is it still important for us to understand our place in nature provided that we have modern cities and advanced technology?

so long as: on condition that; provided that 只要；如果

Successful entrepreneurs should be respected **so long as** their wealth has been acquired legally.

22 Yes, for many reasons, **not the least of which** is that virtually all scientists were fascinated with nature as children and retained that curiosity throughout their lives. **(Para. 7)**

Paraphrase: Yes, it is still important for many reasons, and the essential reason is that nearly all scientists were greatly interested in nature when they were young and remained that way all their lives.

not the least of which: 其中最重要的是

I am doing the job for a variety of reasons, **not the least of which** is that I want to make some extra money for traveling.

23 But a far more important reason is that if we **retain** a spiritual sense of connection with all other life forms, it **can't help but** profoundly affect the way we act. **(Para. 7)**

Paraphrase: But a much more important reason is that if we maintain a spiritual sense of connection with all other forms of life, it will certainly deeply affect our way of action.

retain: *v.* keep sth. or continue to have sth. 保留，保有

The company has effectively **retained** customers through its sophisticated after-sales service.

can't help but do sth.: be unable to prevent oneself from doing sth. 忍不住做某事，不能停止做某事

Every time the team lost a game, he **couldn't help but** feel very disappointed.

24 Whenever my daughter sees a picture of an animal dead or dying, she asks me fearfully, "Daddy, are there any more?" At 7 years, she already knows about **extinction** and it frightens her. **(Para. 7)**

Paraphrase: Whenever my daughter sees a picture of an animal that is dead or looks dying, she asks me in a fearful tone, "Daddy, are there any more?" Though she is only 7 years old, she already knows that certain species could die out and it makes her frightened.

extinction: *n.* when a particular type of animal or plant stops existing 灭绝，绝种

These birds once were on the edge of **extinction** due to the destruction of their environment.

25 The vast **flocks** of migrating waterfowl in the fall, the determined salmon returning thousands of kilometers — these images of nature have inspired us to create music, poetry and art. **(Para. 8)**

Paraphrase: The large groups of waterfowl that are migrating in the fall, the salmon that are swimming thousands of kilometers with determination to return to their original waters — these images of nature have given us inspiration for creating music, poetry and art.

flock: *n.* a group of sheep, goats, or birds of the same kind 一群（羊或鸟）

From dawn to dusk he could be seen chasing off the **flocks** of birds that came to feed on his crops.

26 And when we struggle to retain **a handful of** California condors, it's clearly not from a fear

of **ecological** collapse, it's because there is something **obscene** and frightening about the disappearance of another species **at our hands. (Para. 8)**

Paraphrase: And when we try hard to protect a small number of California condors, it's obviously not because we are afraid of ecological breakdown, but because it is something shameful and terrifying if we have caused the extinction of another species.

handful: *n.* an amount that you can hold in your hand 一把（的量）

She picked up another **handful** of sand and let it run through her fingers.

a handful of sth.: a very small number of people or things 几个人（或物），少数人（或物）

There are **a handful of** studies indicating that later entry into formal schooling positively influences academic measures.

ecological: *adj.* 生态的

Studies show that **ecological** problems can be reduced by living simpler, gentler, more spiritual lives.

obscene: *adj.* extremely unfair, immoral, or unpleasant 不公平的；不道德的；可憎的

Some people feel using animals' skins for fur coats is **obscene**.

at sb.'s hands: caused or done by a particular person 某人导致；出自某人之手

I did not expect such unkind treatment **at your hands**.

27 If children grow up understanding that we are animals, they will look at other species with a sense of **fellowship** and community. **(Para. 9)**

Paraphrase: If children grow up knowing that we human beings are animals, they will then look at other animals with a sense of friendship and community.

fellowship: *n.* a feeling of friendship resulting from shared interests or experiences 友情，友谊

The camp activity provided an opportunity for parents and their children to build **fellowship** with other families.

28 If they understand their ecological place — the **biosphere** — then when children see the great **virgin** forests of the Queen Charlotte Islands being clear-cut, they will feel physical pain, because they will understand that those trees are an extension of themselves. **(Para. 9)**

Paraphrase: If they understand their place in the ecological system — the biosphere — then when children see the great primitive forests of the Queen Charlotte Islands being damaged completely, they will feel pain in their body, because they will understand that those trees are an extension of themselves.

biosphere: *n.* the part of the world in which animals, plants, etc. can live 生物圈

Pressures on food supplies and on the entire **biosphere** can be worsened by climate change.

virgin: *adj.* in an original or natural condition; untouched 原始或天然状态的；未开发的

Destruction of **virgin** forest in that country is forbidden on a permanent basis.

29 When children who know their place in the ecosystem see factories **sending out** poison into the air, water and soil, they will feel ill because someone has **violated** their home. **(Para. 10)**

Paraphrase: When children who understand their place in the ecosystem see factories producing poisonous waste into the air, water or soil, they will feel sick because it's like someone has broken into their home.

send out sth.: produce a signal, light, sound, etc. 发出（信号、光、声音等）

After a few days of inquiries, the bureau **sent out** a request for information from the company.

violate: *v.* do sth. that makes sb. feel that they have been attacked or have suffered a great loss of respect 侵犯，侵害

This factory will face fines up to 500,000 yuan for **violating** the waste disposal rules.

30 Those of us who are parents have to realize the **unspoken**, negative lessons we are conveying to our children. Otherwise, they will continue to ruin this planet as we have. **(Para. 10)**

Paraphrase: We as parents must realize the hidden, negative lessons we are giving to our children. Otherwise, they will continue to damage the Earth as we have.

unspoken: *adj.* not said for other people to hear 未说出的

His face was expressionless, but Alex felt the **unspoken** criticism.

31 I have struggled to cover my **dismay** when Severn and Sarika come running in with a large wolf spider or when we've **emerged from** a **ditch** covered with leeches. **(Para. 11)**

Paraphrase: I have tried hard to hide my unpleasant feelings when Severn and Sarika run home with a large wolf spider or when we have got out of a ditch that has leeches spreading over the surface.

dismay: *n.* the feeling of shock and discouragement 惊愕；气馁；灰心

To my **dismay**, I discovered that the wrapping paper I had bought was only enough for me to wrap one gift.

emerge: *v.* appear or come out from somewhere 浮现，出现

Today in China, many new ways of celebrating the Spring Festival are **emerging**.

emerge from: 从……出来，从……显现

It was great that a few key ideas had **emerged from** the meetings last week.

ditch: *n.* a narrow channel dug at the side of a field, road, etc. 沟，渠

She almost stepped into a **ditch** while walking on the country road in the dark night.

32 But that's nature. I believe efforts to teach our children to love and respect other life forms are **priceless**. **(Para. 11)**

Paraphrase: But that's nature. I believe our efforts to teach our children to love and respect other forms of life on the Earth are extremely valuable.

priceless: *adj.* extremely valuable 无价的；极其珍贵的

It is **priceless** to have a trusted board of advisors to guide you through the tough decisions of your business.

PART IV Keys to Exercises

Lead-in

1 A bee   B ladybird   C ant   D butterfly

Reading to Learn

Reading Comprehension

I   1 It's easy for children to lose any sense of connection with nature.

2 Nature is an enemy, and it's dirty, dangerous or a nuisance.

3 When plants and animals were plentiful, we flourished. When famine and drought struck, our numbers fell accordingly.

4 It is still important for many reasons, but two most important reasons are:
   1) Almost all scientists were fascinated with nature as children and retained that curiosity throughout their lives, which helped them to develop science.
   2) Our sense of connection with nature can greatly affect our actions.

5 Because they will understand that trees are an extension of themselves.

II   **1** D   **2** C   **3** A   **4** B   **5** B

III   **Text Organization**

1 shaped and dominated by people

2 lose any sense of connection with nature

3 chemical products

4 Nature is an enemy; it's dirty, dangerous or a nuisance.

5 embedded

6 a natural interest

7 condition

8 environmental problems

9 a spiritual sense of connection

10 the way we act

11 inspiration

12 fellowship and community

13 unspoken, negative lessons

14 avoid giving these hidden lessons

15 love and respect other life forms

Language in Use

Words and Expressions

I   **1** dismay   **2** shrank   **3** lavishly   **4** obscene
    5 invariably   **6** inherent   **7** nuisance   **8** conceived

II   **1** distance himself from   **2** reflect on   **3** are embedded in
     4 not the least of which   **5** run counter to   **6** emerged from
     7 a handful of   **8** at their hands

III **1** are fascinated with   **2** can't help but   **3** flourished   **4** environmental
5 extinct   **6** tragedy   **7** wilderness   **8** ecosystem
9 flocks   **10** priceless

Word Formation

1 childish   **2** mountainous   **3** scenic   **4** stylish   **5** glorious
6 courageous   **7** alcoholic   **8** bookish   **9** spacious   **10** photographic

Collocation

1 crawling   **2** barked   **3** jumped   **4** singing   **5** wove
6 blew   **7** rolling   **8** swam   **9** climbing   **10** stung

Grammar and Structure

1 You can't be too careful / You can never be too careful

2 I can't overemphasize / I can never overemphasize

3 can't be too diligent / can never be too diligent

4 can't give him enough praise / can never give him enough praise / can't praise him enough / can never praise him enough

5 can't be overemphasized / can never be overemphasized

6 You can't pay the chief engineer enough / You can never pay the chief engineer enough

7 We can't overstate / We can never overstate

8 You can't be too prepared / You can never be too prepared

Translation

I **1** 任何实验研究都有局限性，其中最突出的是可参与实验的人数的多少。

2 我们需要让经理们具备应对全球化世界固有挑战的能力。

3 对于那些热爱原始荒野的人而言，这个偏远而人口稀少的岛屿是一年四季的天堂。

4 他对传统和人际关系的评述往往与当时的惯例相悖。

5 进入餐厅时，我们不由自主地注意到食物背后所蕴含的灵感。

II **1** I try to distance myself from strangers rather than engage with them like other members in the department.

2 He has been reflecting on the nature of art, and will never stop doing so as long as he is practicing it.

3 No single approach can resolve the problem of educational imbalance. In other words, different approaches have different functions.

4 One of the greatest challenges facing many small Chinese cities today is how to attract and retain skilled workers.

5 Whether it's a domestic or foreign-invested enterprise, once it has violated the law, it will be punished.

III "Harmony" is at the core of traditional Chinese culture. Chinese people often say: "Man is an integral part of nature." As a result, they are in constant pursuit of harmony between humanity and nature. Confucianism holds that all creatures stem from nature, and stresses that kindliness should be shown to people and all other creatures. Taoism believes that harmony between nature and humanity is more important than other relations. Today, the Chinese people are also carrying forward the "harmony" idea, recognizing that the construction of a harmonious society is highly related to environmental protection, because when the environment is damaged, people's lives will be seriously affected.

Corpora in Language Learning

I (There can be more than one answer to some questions here, and to each question only one answer is provided for reference.)

Verbs	Nouns or noun phrases	Chinese translations
retain	warmth	保持温度
	belief	保持信仰
	information	保存信息
	talent	留住人才
	right	保留权利
maintain	conversation	保持对话
	contact	保持联系
	relationship	保持关系
	focus	继续关注
	leadership	保持领先地位
contain	emotional content	包含情感内容
	information	包含信息
	hidden messages	包含隐含信息
	proteins	含有蛋白质
	matter	含有物质

II   **1** maintaining/retaining   **2** retain   **3** maintain   **4** contain   **5** maintain

Writing

I **Strategy to capture the reader's interest:** using a startling statistic.

Sentence that introduces the subject: "*This money could have been saved if computer users had a better knowledge of how to install a program.*" The subject to be discussed is: how to install a program.

Tone of the essay: friendly, informative, and professional, as can be judged from the last two sentences.

Thesis statement: "*Most programs require three fairly simple steps, each accompanied by a few precautions.*" The thesis also maps out for the reader the main points (underlined here) that will be discussed in the essay.

II **Strategy to capture the reader's interest:** using a question.

Sentence that introduces the subject: "*You don't need to be a doctor or firefighter. All you have to do is set aside approximately one hour to donate blood.*" The subject to be discussed is: donating blood.

Tone of the essay: formal, persuasive, and professional, as can be judged from the last sentence.

Thesis statement: "*Through donating blood, you can benefit patients and society and truly make a difference.*" The thesis also maps out for the reader the main points (underlined here) that will be discussed in the essay.

Language Functions

I
1 非公莫入
2 非请莫入
3 火车运行时请勿开门
4 无通行证者，禁止通行
5 禁止鸣号!
6 请在此等候咨询
7 请勿自行从此书架上取书
8 此处禁止扔垃圾
9 消防出口，保持通畅
10 禁止拍照!
11 请勿触摸
12 除装货外，禁止停车

Reading to Explore

Reading Comprehension

I 1 D   2 C   3 A   4 B   5 B
II 1 F   2 F   3 T   4 T   5 T
III A 5   B 7   C 3   D 6   E 11 & 12
       F 4   G 8   H 4 & 13

Words and Expressions

I 1 marvel   2 mutual   3 generous   4 remote   5 anonymous
    6 witnessed   7 occupied   8 startled   9 profound   10 magical

1 in place   **2** came by   **3** were tucked away   **4** bring out   **5** came across
     6 called out   **7** came up to   **8** reach out to   **9** vie for   **10** passed by

PART V   Text Translation

Text A

隐性的教育

大卫·铃木

1   尽管这个国家有广阔的荒野，大多数加拿大儿童却是在城市环境中长大的。换句话说，他们生活在一个由人类构思、塑造和主宰的世界中。即使是位于城镇周围的农场也都经过精心修葺和景观设计，以方便人们使用。当然，这也没什么不对。但在这样的环境中，人们很容易失去与大自然的联系。

2   在城市公寓和住宅中，蟑螂、跳蚤、蚂蚁、蚊子或苍蝇的出现必定会招致杀虫剂的喷洒。大小老鼠被毒死或捕捉，园丁们则与杂草和鼻涕虫进行着永无休止的斗争。我们拥有对抗这些入侵者的现代化学武器，并且大肆使用。

3   当孩子们在泥泞中打滚或在水洼里趟水玩时，我们会很担心，因为他们会弄"脏"。孩子们对于态度和价值观学得很快，城市里的教导非常明确——自然是敌人；它肮脏、危险或让人烦恼。因此，年轻人学会了远离自然，并试图驾驭自然。我很惊讶有那么多成年人厌恶或害怕蛇、蜘蛛、蝴蝶、蠕虫、鸟——诸如此类，不胜枚举。

4   如果你认真思索人类的历史，你就会意识到，我们人类在这个星球上的存在，99％靠的是深深植根于自然并依赖于自然。当植物和动物充足时，我们人类就兴旺发达。当饥荒和干旱来袭时，我们人类数量就会减少。如今，我们依旧一样依赖大自然——我们需要植物将带能量的光子转化为糖分子，需要植物来净化空气、补充氧气。忘记我们对完整生态系统的依赖是愚蠢的。然而每当我们教导我们的后代去恐惧或厌恶自然世界时，我们恰恰忘记了这一点。孩子们从城市中所获取的信息完全违背了他们的天性——对其他生命形式的天然的兴趣，这一点只要观察一下孩子第一次看见花或蚂蚁时的样子就能知道——他们会立刻产生兴趣并入迷。我们把他们调教得失去了天性。

5   其结果就是，当我7岁的女儿把新朋友带回家，并试图向他们展示她最喜欢的宠物——她爷爷从温哥华给她弄来的三只美丽的蝾螈时，他们总是吓得往后退缩。当我3岁的孩子带着她的宝贝——她从前院草坪边的石块下抓来的蜘蛛、鼻涕虫以及潮虫回家时，孩子们、大人们都会说"真恶心"。

6   这种态度的悲哀我再怎么强调也不为过。因为，这种观念本身的假设是，人类很特殊、与众不同，我们存在于自然之外。然而，正是这种观念造成了我们今天许多的环境问题。

7   只要我们有城市和技术，是否了解自己在自然中的位置这一点还重要吗？是的，很重要。原因很多，其中最突出的就是，几乎所有科学家从小就对自然着迷，并毕生保持着这份好奇心。然而，

还有个更重要的原因，如果我们保持与其他所有生命形式的精神联系，这自然而然会深刻影响我们的行为。每当我女儿看到一只动物死亡或濒临死亡的照片时，她都会害怕地问我："爸爸，还有更多的这种动物吗？"她只有7岁，就已经懂得物种灭绝，并感到害怕。

8　秋天大量水鸟迁徙，坚定的三文鱼不远千里洄游——这些大自然的景象激发了我们创作音乐、诗歌和艺术的灵感。当我们竭力保护为数不多的几只加州秃鹰时，显然不是由于害怕生态崩溃，而是因为如果又有一个物种在我们手中消失是可耻又可怕的事。

9　如果孩子在长大的过程中懂得我们人类属于动物，他们就会带着一种同伴和社区的意识看待其他物种。如果他们了解自己的生态地位，即生物圈，那么当孩子们看到夏洛特皇后群岛的原始大森林被砍伐殆尽时，就会感到切肤之痛，因为他们会明白这些树木是他们自身的延伸。

10　如果孩子们明白自己在生态系统中的位置，那么当他们看到工厂向空气、水和土壤中排放毒物时，就会感到难受，因为他们的家园遭到了侵犯。为人父母的一定要意识到我们正在传递给孩子们的未明说的、负面的教育。否则，他们将像我们一样继续破坏这个星球。

11　要避免提供这些隐性的教育并不容易。当塞文和萨丽卡拿着一只巨大的狼蛛跑进来，或者当我们从一个满是水蛭的泥沟里出来时，我会努力掩饰自己的惊愕。不过这就是大自然。我相信，教导我们的孩子爱护和尊重其他生命形式，这种努力是无价的。

Text B
大自然如何拉近人与人的距离

格雷格·西曼

1　最近，当我乘坐小渡轮回岛上的家时，船长向分散在船舱四周的乘客喊道，有一群虎鲸正在经过。

2　突然间，每个人都从座位上站起来，冲向右舷的窗户往外看。有扇窗户旁有位年长的绅士安静地坐着，没注意到这个消息。我看到一个小女孩冲向那扇窗户，停了一下，然后一脚踩到那位先生的大腿上向窗外看。一开始那位先生吓了一跳，但当看到人们为什么突然骚动时，他缓和了下来。他俩赶紧也冲出去看，这时鲸鱼正好从船后经过。

3　鲸鱼一走，船舱里的社交气氛就变了。那位年长的绅士和年轻父母中的一位聊着天，而小女孩则竭力向他展示她正在读的一本书。船舱里的气氛活跃了起来。我可以看出，目睹鲸鱼这一经历是如何让渡轮上的人们亲近了起来。

4　与他人分享自然奇观总是会提升你的体验。在自然面前，所有人，无论是何年龄段和社会阶层，都变得平等。当我们目睹大自然的奇迹时，就会意识到所有生命都是相互依赖的，我们就会本能地走到一起。

5　分享自然奇观的体验也让我们发现自己更好的一面。当我们感受鹰从头顶飞过所带来的兴奋时，我们希望别人也拥有和我们同样的美好体验。在那一刻自然而然地想让别人加入进来。

6　几个月前，我们一家有幸游览了夏威夷——一个满是自然景点的仙境。虽然我们游览的每一处都出乎意料地美，但令我惊讶的是陌生人所表现的友好及熟络。他们会走过来，告诉我们那些别致之处，比如隐藏的瀑布、安静的泳池、通往特别景点的最佳路径等。人们似乎不遗余力地与我们分享他们的发现。

7　在夏威夷大岛的植物园中，自然植物群的规模之大、种类之多令我们惊叹。当我与几位场地管理员分享我的兴致时，他们让我召集朋友们，几分钟后在"转弯"处与他们见面。在那里，我们看到了一个装有几只金刚鹦鹉的大型户外笼子。一名场地管理员进到笼子里，当两只金刚鹦鹉飞到他肩膀上后，他花了20分钟给我们展示了一场"驯鸟表演"。这些神奇的鸟儿充满智慧和魅力，给我们留下了深刻印象。这位管理员感受到我对花园的欣赏，就特地向我们展示了他的"孩子们"，这令我感动不已。

8　有一天我在一个小海湾游泳时，有个陌生人走上前来，给我们讲述他晚上和蝠鲼一起游泳的经历，称这是一次心灵的体验。他和我们聊天，就如同我们是他久违的朋友一样。他对和蝠鲼一起游泳仍感到极度兴奋，一心想着要把这次经历告诉别人。他需要分享他在大自然中的深刻体验。

9　大自然甚至可以拉近我们同那些可能永远不会相见的人的距离。

10　几年前，我去了位于加拿大崎岖西海岸的美丽的温泉湾。这是一个偏远而原始的区域，拥有通往大海的天然温泉池，森林覆盖的山脉一直向下绵延至海浪不绝的太平洋海岸，令人印象深刻。在这个神奇的地方还隐藏着六个露营地，但都没有人。

11　在岩石环抱的温泉池中泡了很长时间后，我们走进了森林，发现了一处露营地。在那里的一个临时火坑旁，放着一瓶未开封的葡萄酒。这瓶酒是留给下一个来这里的人的。酒瓶上还有张匿名字条，上面写着"和我们一样享受这里吧"。

12　拿着那瓶酒站在那里，我和我的同伴们明白了为什么前面的露营者会如此慷慨。这儿的美激励人心，发现它的美时，内心的喜悦被点燃。那些露营者是在和我们分享快乐呢！在无言的默契中，我们将那瓶酒放回了原处，没有打开，把那份感受传递下去。分享在这片天然的世外桃源中的乐趣，这一体验比任何一杯酒都更让人心满意足。

13　大自然是一位平衡大师。在体验大自然之美时，不管是富人还是穷人，都没有区别。所以，今年夏天，当我们前往最喜欢的大自然目的地时，请记住，每一次与他人接触、共同欣赏自然奇观的机会，都有助于愈合造成我们公民社区分裂的社会鸿沟。

14　就让大自然成为我们增进理解和友谊的使者吧。

7 STARTING A BUSINESS

PART I Introduction

One thing many successful entrepreneurs have in common is that they made an early start with their business attempts. The most famous examples include Michael Dell, who started his computer business in a university dorm, and Steve Wozniak, co-founder of Apple, who built his first computer while at university and started an Apple shop in a garage together with Steve Jobs. The lesson you can learn from these humble beginnings is that there's no need to wait until your studies are over before you can begin your journey as an entrepreneur. This unit aims to encourage an entrepreneurial spirit in you as university students. Text A will help you learn about how to start a business at university and what it takes to make it a success. Text B will inspire you to seek business success through sharing one success story. Thanks to the development of modern technology, do you think young people now have far more business possibilities than previous generations? If you want to become a successful entrepreneur, how are you going to prepare yourself from now on?

In this unit you will:

1 Learn how to start a business at university and what it takes to make a start-up a success;
2 Learn a success story and some advice for achieving business success;
3 Reflect on how to prepare oneself for entrepreneurship;
4 Learn how the suffixes *-ify* and *-ize* combine with a noun or an adjective to form a verb;
5 Learn what nouns the verb "receive" often collocates with;
6 Learn to use the different forms of the sentence structure "there + be";
7 Learn verb phrases of "go + adverb/preposition" by using CADEL;
8 Learn to write the conclusion of an essay;
9 Learn to describe or introduce a business.

PART II Teaching Suggestions

Sayings

Learning objectives:

- Get a general idea of the unit
- Get inspirations from the sayings
- Get useful advice and guidance from famous people or books
- Learn to develop a positive attitude toward life

Teaching steps:

1 Ask students to translate the two sayings into Chinese.
   Reference translations for the sayings:

   - 千里之行，始于足下。 ——老子
   - 你不必是伟人了才开始去做，但你一定得开始去做才能成为伟人。 ——吉格·金克拉

2 The first saying is a quote from Laozi, a great ancient Chinese philosopher. For this quote, tell students the importance of taking small steps. Reaching big goals in life takes dedication, and often the sheer scale of the task can be frightening, which stops people from even trying to start. Small steps are important. Not only do they allow people to set out on their journey, but they also make tasks attainable, boost people's confidence, and provide them opportunities to learn and adjust till they finally achieve the big goal.

3 The second saying is quoted from Zig Ziglar, an American motivational speaker. For this quote, tell students the importance of getting started and taking actions if they want to achieve greatness in life. They can start their career journey as early as they like, rather than wait till they obtain excellent credentials. All the great human beings of the world were once ordinary. They started as an ordinary human being, but with their hard work, they achieved great heights in life.

Lead-in

Learning objectives:

- Learn some tips for starting a business
- Learn about the advantages and disadvantages for college students to start a business.
- Learn ways to balance academic study and running a business

Teaching steps:

1 Make a brief introduction to the unit and explain its learning objectives.
2 Ask students to do Exercise I and learn some tips for starting a business.
3 Ask students to do Exercise II. Encourage them to talk about if they intend to start a business while at college and why.

Reading to Learn

Text A

Starting a Business at University

Learning objectives:

- Learn how to start a business at university and what it takes to make the business a success
- Analyze the structure of the text
- Learn to use signal words for time to outline the steps of doing something and narrate a story
- Learn to use some new words and expressions correctly

Teaching steps:

1   Ask students to skim Text A for the main idea first. You can begin by asking two questions: What steps should you follow to start a business at university? What does it take for one to make a new start-up a success? Give students a minute to think about the two questions, and then ask them to go through the text and search for the answers.

2   Ask students to divide the text into three parts. After that, ask them to look at the Text Organization exercise to check if they have made the same division. The text can be divided as follows: Part 1 (Para. 1), Part 2 (Paras. 2–9) and Part 3 (Paras. 10–11).

3   Help students to identify that the text has three main points in the body. The first is about the basic steps of starting a business at university. The second is about the reasons why the second year of college is the best time to start a business at university. The third is the author's narration about how he achieved initial success in his business. Help students review how to use the chronological order to write about a process and narrate a story.

4   Go to Part III Detailed Study of Text A. Help students understand difficult sentences in the text accurately. Introduce important new words and expressions with explanations and examples.

5   Ask students to do the exercises following the text.

Critical Thinking

Learning objectives:

- Learn to create innovative ideas
- Learn how to prepare oneself for entrepreneurship
- Improve understanding about the challenges in starting a business and the ways to overcome them

Teaching steps:

1   Ask students to read the questions first and then give them some ideas on how to approach each question.

2   For Question 1, ask students to think of a problem they may have in their daily life, and

encourage them to talk about how they would like to solve the problem and how possible it is to develop that solution into a business.

3   For Question 2, ask students to discuss how to develop entrepreneurship. You can guide them to focus on talking about what skills they should learn, what events they should participate in, what student groups they can join, and what categories of books they should try to read, etc.

4   For Question 3, make students understand the challenges in becoming an entrepreneur. You can guide them to focus on a few main types of challenges, such as deciding on a business or product, securing the financial support or funding to get started, figuring out how to manage and streamline workflow, developing marketing strategies, etc.

5   Ask students to work in pairs or small groups to share their opinions. Encourage each pair or group to present their favorite ideas in class.

Corpora in Language Learning

Learning objectives:

- Learn to search CADEL for verb phrases of "go + adverb/preposition" by using the "Concordance" function of AntConc
- Learn to complete the given sentences with verb phrases of "go + adverb/preposition" based on the contexts in which they appear

Teaching steps:

1   Introduce how to search CADEL for verb phrases of "go + adverb/preposition" with "go *" as the search term by using the "Concordance" function of AntConc. Ask students to identify the verb phrases that match the definitions.

2   Ask students to sort the search results by setting KWIC sort.

3   Ask students to discuss the use of these verb phrases and complete the given sentences with these verb phrases based on the contexts in which they appear.

Writing

Learning objectives:

- Learn how to write the conclusion of an essay
- Learn how the conclusion writing tips are used through an example

Teaching steps:

1   Introduce the importance of writing a strong conclusion for an essay.

2   Introduce the tips for writing an effective conclusion.

3   Ask students to look at an example to learn how the tips are used.

4   Ask students to analyze the conclusion of Text A of this unit and strengthen their understanding about how to write the conclusion of an essay.

Language Functions

Learning objectives:

- Learn to describe the size, ownership, scale, category and operation state of a business
- Learn some words and sentences often used to introduce a product or service of a business
- Learn some words and sentences often used to introduce the founding and development of a business

Teaching steps:

1   Ask students to read the introductory part of Language Functions first.
2   Introduce the words and sentences listed in this part for describing or introducing a business.
3   Ask students to do Exercise I to get familiar with the language tips.
4   Ask students to practice using the language tips by doing Exercise II.

Reading to Explore

Text B

How My Success Story Is a Tale of Two Cities

Learning objectives:

- Learn a success story and some success advice from the author
- Learn more about how to narrate a story in chronological order
- Learn more about how to write the conclusion of an essay
- Learn to use new words and expressions correctly

Teaching steps:

1   Ask students to read the text and finish the exercises following the text before class.
2   Check answers to the exercises.
3   Ask students to retell the story in the text briefly.
4   Ask students to discuss whether they want to start a business at university and what they think is most important for business success.

Summary of Text B

In "How My Success Story Is a Tale of Two Cities", the author tells us his own success story. He succeeded in two cities — in both his hometown Sioux Falls and New York. He first started his business in his hometown, Sioux Falls, a small city in South Dakota. After achieving success, he, like other entrepreneurs, wanted to fish in a bigger pond and accomplish higher goals. So he went to New York to try his luck. Being big, brash and bold, New York was very different from his hometown, but he found it a nice and exciting place.

He tried to adapt himself to the new surroundings, and finally succeeded in New York as well. The message the author wants to share with the reader is that no matter where you work or develop your career, you should never forget your roots or where you came from. At the same time, you should be authentic and follow your heart. Only in this way can you stay strong in the face of difficulties and finally achieve success.

PART III   Detailed Study of Text A

Starting a Business at University

Background Information

1 **University Compare:** 大学比较网（英国）

University Compare is a free university comparison website founded in 2012 by UK entrepreneur Owen O'Neill. The website aims to provide information on universities in the United Kingdom, helping prospective university students to choose which university they wish to attend through searching about degree courses in each university, university reviews and student advice, etc. Today, University Compare is one of the most used services by students in the UK.

2 **Lynda.com:** Lynda 在线教育网（美国）

Lynda.com is now a subsidiary of LinkedIn, with the name LinkedIn Learning. It is an American massive open online course website offering video courses taught by industry experts in business, software, technology, and creative skills. It was founded in California in 1995 by Lynda Weinman, a special effects animator and multimedia professor, as online support for her books and classes. In 2002, the company began offering courses online. In 2015, it was acquired by LinkedIn, an American business and employment-oriented online service.

Understanding the Text

Part 1 (Para. 1)

1 Ask students to read Para. 1 and answer the following question:
Why does the author think the best time for young people to set up a business is at university?
(Question 1 in Exercise I of Reading Comprehension) (Because at university, not only do you have more free time, but also research facilities are easily available to you.)

Part 2 (Paras. 2–9)

Paras. 2–4

Ask students to read Paras. 2–4 and do the following tasks:

1 Go to the Text Organization exercise and complete the main ideas for Paras. 2–4 in Part 2.

2 Answer the question: What are the two most valuable resources can market validation save for you? (Question 2 in Exercise I of Reading Comprehension) (The two most valuable resources are time and money.)

Paras. 5–6

Ask students to read Paras. 5–6 and do the following tasks:

1 Go to the Text Organization exercise and complete the main ideas for Paras. 5–6 in Part 2.

2 Answer the question: How can you get the capital to start your business? (Question 3 in Exercise I of Reading Comprehension) (You can get the capital through friends and family, crowdfunding, a bank loan, or university entrepreneurial loans.)

Para. 7–9

Ask students to read Paras. 7–9 and do the following tasks:

1 Go to the Text Organization exercise and complete the main ideas for Paras. 7–9 in Part 2.

2 Answer the question: According to the author, what did it take to achieve the first milestone for his website? (Question 4 in Exercise I of Reading Comprehension) (It took risk, hard work, and vision to achieve his first milestone, from spending his term loan developing his website, to missing his first four months of student socials, and then to continuing to work on the product despite other people's disapproval.)

Part 3 (Paras. 10–11)

Ask students to read Paras. 10–11 and do the following tasks:

1 Go to the Text Organization exercise and complete the main ideas for Paras. 10–11 in Part 3.

2 Talk about how the author concludes the text. (The author concludes the text by highlighting the benefits of starting a business at university, and by giving a final thought-provoking remark.)

Language Points

1 At university, you **have** the gift of time and research **facilities on your side**. (**Para. 1**)
Paraphrase: While you are at university, you not only have more free time, but also can use research facilities more easily.
have sth. on your side: have an advantage that increases your chances of success 有某方面的优势
Although she doesn't have much experience, she **has youth and enthusiasm on her side**.
facility: *n.* rooms, equipment, or services that are provided for a particular purpose 设施，设备
Our hotel offers convenient leisure **facilities** such as the swimming pool, exercise room, tennis courts and outdoor barbecue area.

2 First things first, if you're thinking of starting a business, it means you have an idea and, **more likely than not**, this product or service is already out there and is already trading. (**Para. 2**)
Paraphrase: First of all, if you are thinking of starting a business, it means you have an idea for a certain product or service, and most probably, this product or service already exists and is in the market being sold or bought.

more likely than not: most probably 很有可能

More likely than not, the number of international students in our university will continue to increase in the coming years.

3   Most successful companies generally enter the market second and learn from their competitors' mistakes. Market **validation** is a great way for you to save two most valuable resources: time and money. **(Para. 2)**

Paraphrase: Most successful companies usually enter the market later than others, and they learn from their competitors' mistakes. Your observation of how well their products or services have been received by the market is a great way for you to save two most precious resources: time and money.

validation: *n.* proving or supporting the truth or value of sth. 验证；证实

In order to ensure that the computer systems work in the way anticipated by the users, it's required that a **validation** process be set in place.

4   If you have **assessed** your competitors and feel like you still have a **significantly** different and better product or service, then it's about time you **map out** the business in a **viable** way, where it's easy to assess each area of the market. **(Para. 3)**

Paraphrase: If you have evaluated the products or services of your competitors and still feel that your product or service is very different and much better, then you can begin to plan your business carefully and in a practical manner, so that it's possible for you to analyze each aspect of the market.

assess: *v.* make a judgment about a person or situation 评价，评定

An experienced real property agent can properly **assess** the value of a home and determine a fair market rent.

significantly: *adv.* in an important way or to an important degree 重大地；显著地

The student's essay has been **significantly** improved after the revision.

map out: plan carefully how sth. will happen 仔细策划，计划

It takes a lot of brainpower to **map out** a practical career course for yourself.

viable: *adj.* sound and workable 切实可行的；可实施的

It took him eight months of hard work before coming up with a **viable** plan acceptable to all stakeholders.

5   You'll soon realize there are a number of problems you have to face in the early stages of your setup, whether it be lack of capital, knowledge, or support. **(Para. 3)**

Paraphrase: You will soon realize there are many problems you have to deal with in the beginning stages of setting up your business, no matter the problem is lack of money, lack of knowledge, or lack of support from others.

6   If you can, you should quickly prioritize what is required. That way, you'll be able to **cater for** your weaknesses and have a much stronger company start. **(Para. 3)**

Paraphrase: If you can, you should quickly decide what is more urgently needed, so that you will deal with the most urgent things first, and less urgent things next. That way, you will be able to make up for your weaknesses and give your company a much stronger start.

cater for: provide with what is needed or required 提供所需；满足需要

The building is well equipped and designed to **cater for** both management and technical staff.

7　Once you have a very basic business plan **in place**, and have **calculated** your customers, competitors and **clients**, you'll most likely notice that it requires a **substantial** amount of time to make this idea a reality and create a viable and **profitable** business. **(Para. 4)**

Paraphrase: Once you have made a very basic business plan, and have evaluated your customers, competitors and clients, you will probably begin to recognize that it requires a huge amount of time to realize your idea and create a business that is workable and able to make a profit.

in place: existing and ready to be used 准备就绪的

We now have adequate systems **in place** to deal with different health care problems.

calculate: *v.* guess sth. or form an opinion by using all the information available 估计；预测；推测

It's difficult to **calculate** the long-term effects of these policy changes.

client: *n.* sb. who gets services or advice from a professional person, company, or organization 客户，顾客；委托人

Social workers must always consider the best interests of their **clients**.

substantial: *adj.* large in amount or number 大量的，多的

Without a right business model, companies can lose a **substantial** amount of profit.

profitable: *adj.* producing a profit or a useful result 可获利润或好处的；有利可图的

It is usually more **profitable** to sell direct to the public.

8　Being a previous dorm-room company starter myself, I realised the best time to **embark on** your **venture** while at university is **in the midst of** your second year. **(Para. 5)**

Paraphrase: Being a person who started a business in the dormitory room of a university myself, I came to learn that the best time to set up your business while at university is during the second year.

embark: *v.* go on board a ship or a plane 上船；上飞机

Millions of Europeans **embarked** for America in the late 19th century.

embark on: start to do sth. new or difficult 开始，着手（新的或艰难的事情）

The student **embarked on** her art studies after years of pursuing other goals.

venture: *n.* a new business activity that involves taking risks（有风险的）商业，企业

While it's true that launching a **venture** requires entrepreneurs to take risks, they also need to take steps to minimize risks.

midst: *n.* the middle part 中部；中央；中间

Suddenly, from the **midst** of the crowd came an unexpected answer to my question.

in the midst of: happening during sth. 在……进行过程中；正值……发生的时候

We are now **in the midst of** the Spring Festival holiday, so people are busy greeting or visiting relatives and friends.

9　Not only do you have less term-time scheduled lectures, but you should also be a more independent adult than you were the previous year. **(Para. 5)**

Paraphrase: Not only do you have less lectures that you have to attend in the term, but also you are more grown-up, and thus should be more independent than you were in the first year.

10 This combination of being more **responsible** with extra time will allow you to look at the bigger picture and begin your journey without the **distraction** of £1.50 **vodka**-double student Wednesdays. **(Para. 5)**

Paraphrase: The combination of the two things you now have, namely, a stronger sense of responsibility and more free time, will enable you to broaden your mind and start your business journey without being carried away by other things, like the wine promotion program specially offered to students — students can get a double amount of vodka on Wednesdays for only £1.50.

responsible: *adj.* sensible and able to make good judgment so that one can be trusted 有责任心的，可信赖的，可靠的

I hope my children will become **responsible** people who meet commitments and are generous to others.

distraction: *n.* sth. that stops you paying attention to what you are doing 使人分心的事物

One of the easiest ways to reduce **distractions** is to keep your cell phone out of reach while working.

vodka: *n.* 伏特加（俄罗斯烈酒）；一杯伏特加

The company boasts that its production process is organic and produces a higher quality **vodka**.

11 If you are serious about your venture, assess your market, create a small business plan, and then source extra capital (whether it be through friends or family, **crowdfunding**, or a bank loan) to make your idea a reality. **(Para. 6)**

Paraphrase: If you are serious about setting up a business, then just go ahead to evaluate your market, make a small business plan, and raise more capital money — whether the money is obtained through friends or family, crowdfunding, or borrowed from a bank — to realize your idea.

crowdfunding: *n.* the process of getting a large group of people to finance a particular project 众筹，集资

After the **crowdfunding** project was put online, we hit 80 percent of our target amount in less than one hour.

12 There are actually university **entrepreneurial** loans you can access too. **(Para. 6)**

Paraphrase: Actually, you can also borrow money from your university — universities normally have loan programs for students who want to start a business at university.

entrepreneurial: *adj.* having the qualities that are needed to succeed as an entrepreneur 具有创业素质的

The HR department was asked to find a sales manager with **entrepreneurial** mindset.

13 Unfortunately, your idea will never **be taken seriously** unless you have at least attempted to make it work with what you have got. **(Para. 6)**

Paraphrase: However, your idea will never be regarded as important unless you have at least tried to make it function properly with all that you have.

take sth. seriously: regard sb./sth. as important and worth treating with respect 认真对待某人或某事物

During the weeks I was in the small town, I got to know an easygoing young man who **took** his job **seriously**.

14 The real challenge is this: you'll have to do this on **minimal** income while at university, bringing the true entrepreneurial spirit out to play. **(Para. 6)**

Paraphrase: The real difficulty is this: you'll have to do this with very limited sources of money while at university, so it's necessary that you fully show the spirit of a real entrepreneur.

minimal: *adj.* smallest in amount or degree（量或程度）最小的，最低的

We do hope and pray that the property damages from the flood will be **minimal**.

15 Back in late 2010 when my website — higher education comparison site University Compare — was a mere **beta version**, I spent my entire first-term second-year loan on a few developers, developing my first **concept** of the site. **(Para. 7)**

Paraphrase: Back in late 2010 when my website — higher education comparison site University Compare — was only at the testing stage, I spent all my first-term loan of the second year on a few web developers, developing my first idea about the website.

beta: *n.* the preliminary or testing stage of a software or hardware product 软件或硬件产品的初始或测试阶段

The new video game is still very much in **beta** and is scheduled for a release next year.

beta version: the version of a new product, esp. computer software, that is almost ready for the public to buy or use, but is given to a few customers to test first （计算机软件等新产品上市前的）测试版

Users can try out a **beta version** of the software via the firm's website.

concept: *n.* an idea of how sth. is, or how sth. should be done 概念，观念；想法

In the 1980s, the Internet was still a distant **concept** for most of the world.

16 Once the site was live, I began looking into **analytics**, understanding my user, and joined the online education website, Lynda.com, a website dedicated to educating users in digital, social marketing and business management. **(Para. 7)**

Paraphrase: Once the site was put into use, I began doing analysis, trying to understand my user. I also joined the online education website, Lynda.com, a website that is devoted to educating users in digital, social marking and business management.

analytics: *n.* the method of logical analysis 分析方法

The dean said students would be given the option to major or minor in business **analytics**.

17 **From** there **onwards**, every problem I faced, I went to Lynda to learn about the problem so I could fix it myself. **(Para. 7)**

Paraphrase: From the day I joined the website, whenever I had a problem, I went to Lynda to search for information so that I could solve the problem myself.

onwards: *adv.* directed or moving forward 向前；前进地

A clear purpose of life will make you full of passion and drive you ever **onwards**.

from … onwards: continuing from a particular time 从（某时）起一直

From now **onwards** my teacher will be stricter.

18 I worked extremely hard over the next two years, with many late nights drinking energy drinks and weekends staying in developing University Compare so that it was one step ahead of the competition. **(Para. 8)**

Paraphrase: I worked extremely hard during the next two years. For many nights, I worked so late that I drank energy drinks to feel more energetic, and for many weekends, I simply stayed in my dorm, developing my website University Compare so that it had an edge over other similar websites.

19 Eighteen months later, I met my very first **angel investor** through a co-worker and received a £20,000 **investment** at a £100,000 **valuation**. **(Para. 8)**

Paraphrase: Eighteen months later, I met my very first investor through a person who worked together with me, and received an investment of £20,000 based on a judgment of my website worth £100,000.

angel: *n.* sb. who is very kind, very good, or very beautiful 安琪儿，天使（指仁慈、善良或美丽的人）

"Be an **angel** and get me a cup of coffee," my sister begged me after she came back from her morning run.

investor: *n.* sb. who gives money to a company, business, or bank in order to get a profit 投资者
China's business environment and stable industrial supply chain have won widespread recognition from foreign **investors**.

angel investor: an individual who provides funding to a new or young company, usu. in exchange for shares in the company 天使投资人

investment: *n.* the money that you invest, or the thing that you invest in 投资额；投资物
Investment is up by 6% after adjustment for inflation.

valuation: *n.* a professional judgment about how much sth. is worth （专业的）估价，估值
Experts set a high **valuation** on the painting though it was the work of a young artist.

20 The rest, as they say, was history. **(Para. 8)**

Paraphrase: Everything that had happened before I met my angel investor, as they say, belonged to the past.

Note: This sentence implies that after my website received a large amount of investment from an angel investor, it got a totally new start, and everything that had happened before the investment simply belonged to the past.

21 What people don't see is that it took **risk**, hard work, and vision to achieve my first **milestone**, from spending my term loan — when it should have been used for rent, to missing my first four months of student socials, and then to continuing to work on a product when many people were telling me it was a "waste of time." **(Para. 9)**

Paraphrase: What people don't realize is that it took risk, hard work, and the ability to plan the future to make my first big success, from spending all my term loan money — when it should have been used for paying the rent, to not being available for any student social activities for the first four months, and then to continuing to work on a product when many people were warning me that I was just wasting my time.

risk: *n.* the possibility of meeting danger or suffering harm, loss, etc. 危险；风险

The patients should be made aware of the **risks** involved with an electric shock treatment.

milestone: *n.* a very important event in the development of sth. 重大事件，里程碑

Though the method was never used commercially in farming, the test itself was a **milestone**.

22 Starting a business at university isn't easy but it provides the best building blocks for any future **entrepreneur**. (Para. 10)

Paraphrase: It is not easy to start a business at university, but the experience provides the most essential knowledge for anyone who may become an entrepreneur in the future.

entrepreneur: *n.* 企业家

If you are an **entrepreneur** or small business owner, you certainly need to be a good decision-maker.

23 Early on, you'll learn the art of mastering time-keeping — and you'll never have a time in your life where you have minimal responsibility, independence, and some of the best facilities **on your doorstep**. (Para. 10)

Paraphrase: At an early stage, you will learn the art of time management — and you will never have another time in your life where you have little responsibility, much independence, and convenient access to some of the best facilities.

doorstep: *n.* a step just outside a door to a house or building 门阶

Remote sellers now provide "**doorstep** convenience", and that's why people are happy to pay freight charges.

on sb.'s doorstep: very near 在家门口；很近

My uncle opened his latest restaurant right **on his doorstep**.

24 So, never forget that **entrepreneurship**, as a career, is always a serious option. After all, how do you know you will not succeed if you don't even try? (Para. 11)

Paraphrase: So, never forget that starting a business and developing it into a career is always a choice you can seriously consider about. Anyway, you will not know whether you will be successful if you never try at all.

entrepreneurship: *n.* 企业家的身份或行为；企业家精神

Today, the Internet is playing an important role in supporting widespread **entrepreneurship** and innovation.

PART IV Keys to Exercises

Lead-in

I 1 Do what you love.
2 Keep a source of cash.
3 You need a team.
4 Get some clients; make the contacts.
5 Write it and plan it.

6 Do the research.
7 Get professional help.
8 Build your cash reserve.
9 Be professional.
10 Solidify your legal framework.

Script

Hi, this is John, he wants to start a business. But he doesn't know how to start his own business. That's why I'm sharing these ten tips for starting your own business.

Tip number one: Do what you love. The greatest driving power of an entrepreneur is the passion in them is born from their love for what they do. When starting your own business, you must be sure you love what you're doing as you will spend lots of time and energy starting a business and nurturing it to success.

Tip number two: Keep a source of cash. Start when you're still employed. When starting your own business, you need to know that profits will not start coming in right away. Having a job while you're starting your own business helps you in getting through the startup process with enough cash.

Tip number three: You need a team. There's a great strength in teamwork. You will always need some level of support when starting your own business. You may need to find a mentor, who can always guide you and give you invaluable advice. You can also subscribe to a consultancy firm who care enough to know you are just starting a new business.

Tip number four: Get some clients; make the contacts. You should not wait to start your business officially before you start getting your clients or customers or building the necessary network around your business. Doing this will give you some assurance that you are creating a business with a market.

Tip number five: Write it and plan it. Creating a business plan is highly important. It helps you understand and investigate your new business idea. A solid business plan will help you see and separate reality from expectations.

Tip number six: Do the research. Writing a business plan means you are ready to do a lot of research, asking questions, surfing the Internet, and reading some books. When you're starting your own business, you should be well-informed about your industry, competition, customer behavior, market risk and opportunities.

Tip number seven: Get professional help. You do not have to be an expert in everything about your business. Although you may have to multitask yourself when starting your own business, you will still have to use some professional services.

Tip number eight: Build your cash reserve. Financing is a critical part of your business success. When starting your own business, you can save up if you can, or approach potential business investors and lenders. You must be open to different ideas of raising your capital. Normally, traditional lenders do not like new ideas. This means a lot of risk for them. They always love businesses with proven track records.

Tip number nine: Right from the blow of the whistle, be professional. Starting off, your business should show professionalism. This will require getting all the accoutrements（装备）like a business card, a website if you can afford it, a business email address and treating customers in a highly professional manner.

> · And tip number ten: Solidify your legal framework. Getting your business fully complied with available laws can save you from a lot of headaches and financial trouble in the near future. Does your business need to be registered? Do you need a legal framework for your employees? What about your tax issues? You can contact a legal expert for you to have the right information and build your legal framework.

Reading to Learn

Reading Comprehension

I 1 Because at university, not only do you have more free time, but also research facilities are easily available to you.

2 The two most valuable resources are time and money.

3 You can get the capital through friends and family, crowdfunding, a bank loan, or university entrepreneurial loans.

4 It took risk, hard work, and vision to achieve his first milestone, from spending his term loan developing his websites, to missing his first four months of student socials, and then to continuing to work on the product despite other people's disapproval.

5 To summarize the text by pointing out the benefits of starting a business at university, and emphasizing again the advantages of doing it then.

II 1 C   2 A   3 D   4 B   5 A

III Text Organization

1 time and research facilities
2 idea
3 significantly different and better
4 business plan
5 make your business idea a reality
6 the second year
7 responsibility
8 crowdfunding
9 a bank loan
10 University Compare
11 competitive
12 angel investor
13 entrepreneur
14 serious option

Language in Use

Words and Expressions

I 1 responsible   2 assess   3 milestone   4 substantial
5 facilities   6 distraction(s) 7 calculated   8 viable

II 1 have … on your side 2 cater for   3 on your doorstep   4 in the midst of
5 map out   6 took … seriously 7 from … onwards   8 more likely than not

III 1 concepts   2 embark on   3 ventures   4 investments

5 entrepreneurial   6 profitable   7 minimal   8 assess

9 in the midst of   10 substantial

Word Formation

1 stabilize   2 glorify   3 standardize   4 justify   5 identify

6 legalized   7 prioritize   8 simplify   9 classify   10 dramatized

Collocation

1 receive a benefit   2 receive information   3 receive training

4 receive medical treatment   5 received recognition   6 receive e-mails

7 receive guests   8 receive gifts   9 receive signals

10 received an injury

Grammar and Structure

1 there was no one waiting for him there

2 there is going to be (will be) heavy rain tomorrow morning

3 There may be some students who don't like the movie

4 There are lots of people who can help you

5 There is only a pen and two grammar books on the desk

6 There being a subway station near my house

7 there was a truck collecting rubbish outside

8 there being a second chance for me to attend such a big event

9 there to be no argument about its new admission policy

10 there would have been far more injuries in the accident

Translation

I 1 我原以为德国队会赢，但四年内第三次进入半决赛的爱尔兰队有经验上的优势。

2 过去众所周知，东北地区是中国的重工业基地，而今它正处于巨大的变革之中。

3 这家服装公司自2013年开始雄心勃勃地扩张店铺，仅五年就将店铺数量翻了一番。

4 错误可以成为学习的良机，从而改进寻找可行解决方案的过程。

5 这些统计数据有一段时间没更新过了，因而利润分析很可能不准确。

II 1 Gifted learners could also experience learning difficulties if their needs are not catered for.

2 The statistics show that the admission revenue brings a substantial amount of money to the amusement park.

3 The medical association decided to assess the quality of health information available on the Internet.

4 This conference mapped out a blueprint for China's development over the next 30 years and beyond.

5 All countries must take environment issues seriously, for tackling pollution is a battle mankind must win.

III The China International College Students' "Internet+" Innovation and Entrepreneurship Competition is a major innovation and entrepreneurship competition for college students worldwide. The Competition aims to stimulate college students' enthusiasm for innovation and entrepreneurship, to promote international integration of innovation and entrepreneurship education, to encourage the exchange of resources related to innovation and entrepreneurship, as well as to build a cooperation platform for college students to deal with global challenges. Started in 2015, the Competition has attracted active participation of college students from China and abroad each year. As a result, many high-quality projects have stood out. The Competition has greatly boosted the number of business start-ups and created huge numbers of jobs.

Corpora in Language Learning

I

Verb phrases of "go +adverb/preposition"	Definitions
go about sth./doing sth.	begin to do sth.
go after	go in search of
go against	be opposite to sth.; not fit or agree with sth.
go ahead	proceed with a plan of action
go beyond	exceed
go for	choose sth.; try to have or achieve sth.
go on to do sth.	continue to do sth.
go over	examine, or think about sth. very carefully
go through	experience sth. especially sth. unpleasant

II **1** go ahead **2** go about **3** go on **4** go beyond **5** go for
     6 going against **7** going after/going for **8** go over **9** go through **10** go through

Writing

The author concludes the article by using two of the components introduced in the writing skills.

1 He summarizes two main points of the body paragraphs: "Starting a business at university isn't easy", and "you'll never have a time in your life where you have minimal responsibility, independence, and some of the best facilities on your doorstep." One main point that is not summarized is about the steps of starting a business.

2 He demonstrates the significance of starting a business at university by two steps: First by highlighting the benefits of starting a business at university: "it provides the best building blocks for any future entrepreneur. Early on, you'll learn the art of mastering time-keeping", and then by encouraging students to embrace entrepreneurship as a choice: "So, never forget that entrepreneurship, as a career, is always a serious option. After all, how do you know you will not succeed if you don't even try?" The two steps make the conclusion strong and also enlightening to the reader.

Language Functions

I Bob Evans Restaurants is a <u>chain</u> of <u>family style restaurants founded and headquartered</u> in Columbus, Ohio, which <u>owns and operates</u> nearly 500 locations in 18 states, primarily in the Midwest, mid-Atlantic and Southeast regions of the United States. As a <u>private</u> company <u>owned</u> by Golden Gate Capital, Bob Evans Restaurants <u>is focused on providing quality food and hospitality</u> to every guest at every meal, each and every day.

Reading to Explore

Reading Comprehension

I **1** C **2** D **3** D **4** A **5** C

II **1** T **2** T **3** F **4** F **5** T

III **A** 2 **B** 6 **C** 10 **D** 4, 8, 10
  E 1 **F** 12 **G** 7 **H** 11

Words and Expressions

I **1** located **2** brash **3** diminished **4** obstacle **5** authentic
  6 subsided **7** persona **8** rough **9** steady **10** roaming

II **1** ring true **2** at the core of **3** let go of **4** get immersed in
  5 dip my toes in **6** go back to **7** leaving behind **8** adapt to
  9 has referred to **10** knocked down

PART V Text Translation

Text A

在大学期间创业

欧文·奥尼尔

1   在大学期间创业是最艰难的事情之一，但这也是史上年轻人创业的最佳时期。在大学里，你拥有时间和研究设施方面的有利条件。

2   首先，如果你正在考虑创业，这意味着你有一个想法，而且你想到的产品或服务很可能已经有了并且已经在买卖。然而，这并不意味着它不会成为一个未来价值十亿美元的公司。通常大多数成功的企业都是后来才进入市场的，并从竞争对手的错误中吸取教训。市场验证是你节约两项最珍贵的资源的好方法：时间和金钱。

3   如果你对竞争对手进行了评估后，仍然认为你的产品或服务与他们的截然不同而且更好，那么

你差不多就要规划业务了，规划要有可行性，即易于评估市场的每个领域。你会很快意识到，在创业初期你必须要面对很多问题，不管是资金、知识还是支持的短缺。可以的话，你应该快速确定所需要做的事项的优先顺序。这样你就能弥补自己的弱项，使公司在创业起步时变得更强。

4　一旦你有了基本的创业规划在手，并且对顾客、竞争对手和客户也做了预估，你很可能就会意识到，要将想法变为现实，创建一个可行的又能盈利的公司，需要花费大量时间。

5　作为一名从宿舍起步的创业者，我认识到大学期间开始创业的最佳时机是在二年级。那时不仅学期规定安排的课程较少，而且你也应已成长为比前一年更独立的成年人。有了更强的责任心和更多的空闲时间，你的视野会更加宽广，并且在开启创业旅程时，不会受学生周三花1.5英镑就能获得双份伏特加酒这些杂事的干扰。

6　如果你对创业是认真的，那就评估一下市场，制定一个小型的商业计划，然后寻找额外资金的来源——无论是通过朋友或家人、众筹还是银行贷款——来让你的想法成为现实。实际上你也可以利用大学创业贷款。很遗憾，除非你已至少尝试过靠手头的资源来实现自己的想法，否则它永远不会得到别人的重视。真正的挑战是：在大学，要靠最低的收入来做到这点，你要发挥真正的创业精神。

7　回想2010年底，当我的网站——高等教育比较网站"大学比较网"——仅仅还处在测试阶段时，我把我二年级第一学期的贷款全部花在了几位网站开发人员身上，以将我的第一个网站理念付诸实施。网站一上线，我就开始做研究分析，了解用户，并加入了在线教育网站Lynda.com。Lynda网是一个致力于在数字、社会营销以及商务管理方面对用户开展教育培训的网站。从那以后，每遇到一个问题，我都会到Lynda网进行了解，以便自行解决。

8　在接下来的两年里，我特别努力地工作，很多个深夜都在喝能量饮料，周末也闭门不出，专心开发"大学比较网"，要在竞争市场中领先一步。十八个月后，我通过一名同事认识了我的第一位天使投资人，以十万英镑的估值获得了两万英镑的投资。其余的，如他们所说，已成为历史。

9　人们没有看到的是，我顶着风险、努力工作、精心规划才实现了第一个里程碑。我花费了本应用于支付房租的学期贷款，缺席了前四个月的学生社交活动，坚持做一个产品，哪怕许多人对我说这是"浪费时间"。

10　在大学创业不容易，但它为成长为未来的企业家提供了最好的基石。很早你就学会掌控时间的艺术——并且你一生中永远也不会再有这样的一段时光，在此期间你不用承担多少责任，又能享受独立自由，还能就近利用一些最好的研究设施。

11　在大学一年级结束时，学校将帮助你准备开始思考未来的职业。所以，千万不要忘记，创业作为一种职业，始终是个值得认真考虑的选项。毕竟，你如果连试都不试，怎么知道自己不会成功呢？

Text B

我的成功故事为什么是部双城记

杰弗里·海兹勒特

1　这是最好的时代，也是最坏的时代……算了，我毕竟不是查尔斯·狄更斯，但我要给你讲个故事——我自己的故事。我因不同的身份而为人所知——名人堂的演讲家、电视/电台节目主持人、前首席营销官和企业家。我的职业使我有机会无数次周游世界各地。

2 作为创业者，我们总是在寻找下一个要创造的东西，或者下一片要征服的世界。对于这一召唤我们必须做出响应，因为它是我们之所以成为人的核心。有时候，响应这一召唤意味着寻找更好的生活，并抛弃我们所熟知的一切。但是，我们绝不能忘记我们来自哪里。无论你闯荡多远或者认为自己有多成功，忘本会——而且定会——削弱你的成功。

3 这是一部双城记，这两座城市帮助塑造了我经营业务的方式。

4 我来自南达科他州的苏瀑市，一个很多人在地图上都找不到的地方，但它过去是——现在仍然是——我的家。在那里，我开始创业，学到了一些至今仍然受用的经验教训。在我的《思考重要，行动更重要》一书中，我提到了要在更大的池塘里钓鱼。虽然在小池塘里做一条大鱼完全没问题，但是一旦你征服了那个池塘，你下一步要干什么？你需要去哪儿实现更大的目标呢？

5 如果我们渴望在大池塘里获得成功，我们需要不断问自己这些问题。我们就是这样成长的，这种成长的一部分就是适应你周围的环境。我曾多次说过——适应、改变或灭亡！这些话在我日常的商务生活中仍然是真理。然而，适应或改变并不意味着为了成功，你必须放弃你所知道的一切或者改变你本来的面目。

6 人们总是问我，"成功的秘诀是什么？"我的回答总是一样，"做真实的自己！"这话听起来很简单，但说到底就是要忠于自己和自己骨子里坚信的东西。我在《道德经》中看到了这句话："胜人者有力，自胜者强"，我认为这句话很贴切地体现了这个含义。

7 纽约，一座如此美好的城市。纽约很大、很高调也很大胆——基本就是你在电视和电影里看到的那样。但这座城市有一种特质，这种特质只有一些人可以体验，可以理解的人则更少。这座城市到处是每天上班、创造奇迹的人。无论是在上城区的写字间还是在苏豪区的创业公寓，都是故事发生的地方。

8 这里就是我的更大的池塘。我或许已在苏瀑成就了我的大角色，但在纽约我则让这一形象更臻完美。在这里，你的态度需要和这座城市的精神相匹配，所以，当我在做电视节目或哥伦比亚广播公司（CBS）的Play.it播客节目时，我必须大胆而高调。我是在适应我的环境，但没有真正失去自我或忘记我的根。

9 从一个小镇来到纽约对任何人来说都会是一种文化冲击——我也如此。但是，一旦你沉浸到日常的城市生活当中，这种冲击感就会消退，而你就成为这座城市律动的一部分。作为这座大城市的一名创业者，我坚守我的信念——做真实的自己。

10 不管是在美国小城镇还是大都市，经商都没有一个万能的模式。没有哪种模式放之四海而皆准，但有一点是真的，那就是，总有更大的事业可以成就。这也是我很久以前就决定要走的路。我在苏瀑获得了成功，然后我就说，"为什么不试试整个州？"所以我去做了，再然后我又意识到还有其他49个州我可以去尝试，于是就有了纽约的故事。

11 不要以为你可以轻松打入当今最大、竞争最激烈的市场。障碍会有，陷阱会有，你跌倒和失败的次数也会很多。但这算不了什么。重要的是你所获得的经验教训，你被击倒后如何爬起来，又是如何继续前行的。

12 我这里的总结就是：无论你是在苏瀑、纽约还是在你所处的任何城市经营生意，你成功的基础都将是诚实和真实。要去适应，开拓新的视角。就我个人来看，永远都不要忘记自己的根，不要忘记你来自哪里。当你在汹涌的大海中航行时，它将是那稳固可靠的锚。

8 THE TRUTH ABOUT SMILES

PART I   Introduction

When we spread the lips and turn up the corners of the mouth, we smile. Smile can express joy, satisfaction, liking, acceptance, kindness, politeness or even say hello. Text A is about how the meaning of smiling varies in different cultures. Text B is about some unexpected effects of trying to look happy by putting on a smile in the workplace. We will discuss some cultural differences that may lead to cross-cultural misunderstandings, reflect on how to improve our communication skills to avoid misunderstandings and conflicts in everyday life and how to build more harmonious relationships with others. Hopefully, these two texts will help us understand some hidden truths about smiles and become more competent in our everyday communication — verbally or non-verbally.

In this unit you will:

1   Read a passage about cultural differences in smiling and the misunderstandings they may cause;

2   Read a passage on some undesired effects of putting on a happy face in the workplace;

3   Reflect on the importance of being aware of cultural differences and mastering effective communication skills to resolve misunderstandings;

4   Learn how the adjective *minded* can be used with adjectives or nouns to form compound adjectives;

5   Learn how the word "relationship" can collocate with verbs, adjectives, and nouns;

6   Learn how the word "it" can be used as the introductory subject;

7   Learn verbs ending with the root "pose" by using CADEL;

8   Learn to write an exemplification paragraph;

9   Learn to describe people's character and personality traits.

PART II Teaching Suggestions

Sayings

Learning objectives:

- Get a general idea of the unit
- Get inspirations from the sayings
- Get useful advice and guidance from famous people or books
- Learn to develop a positive attitude toward life

Teaching steps:

1 Ask students to translate the two sayings into Chinese.
Reference translations for the sayings:

- 爱人者，人恒爱之；敬人者，人恒敬之。 ——孟子
- 温暖的微笑是善意的通用语。 ——威廉·亚瑟·沃德

2 The first saying is a quote from Mencius, a Chinese Confucian philosopher during the Warring States Period. The quote suggests that the way you treat others determines the way others will treat you. A person who loves others is often loved by others, and a person who respects others is often respected by others. You can introduce a similar quote by Lin Bu（林逋）, a famous poet of the Northern Song dynasty: "A gentleman's way of life is to get along well with others, be generous to subordinates, and treat people who have made mistakes with a forgiving attitude（和以处众，宽以待下，恕以待人，君子人也）." You can ask students to think about how to show respect for others.

3 The second saying is quoted from William Arthur Ward, an American writer. For this quote, tell students the importance of smiles in our interpersonal communication. A kind and open smile often paves the way for making new friends and brightening everyone's day. Even when language barriers prevent verbal communication, a smile will more often than not show your kindness and willingness to get along with everyone nearby. To build a more harmonious society, we should give more compassion, gratitude and love to others. You can encourage students to think about how to get along with others in family, in school, in the workplace and in public.

Lead-in

Learning objectives:

- Get familiar with some adjectives of emotions
- Explore the meaning of a smile in the Chinese culture

Teaching steps:

1 Make a brief introduction to the unit and explain its learning objectives.

2 Ask students to do Exercise I.

3 Encourage students to role-play more daily situations and use proper adjectives to describe the emotions involved.

4 Ask students to do Exercise II. Ask students about their understanding of the meaning of a smile. Compare students' answers, trying to summarize the meaning of a smile in the Chinese culture.

Reading to Learn

Text A

The Meaning of a Smile in Different Cultures

Learning objectives:

- Learn new words and expressions to describe facial expressions and their underlying feelings and emotions
- Interpret the meaning of a smile in different situations and cultures
- Learn about how to include examples in a paragraph to support an idea

Teaching steps:

1 Introduce the topic of Text A: The meaning of a smile in different cultures.

2 Ask students to check the word list and see what words they do not know. Then explain the new words and expressions to students.

3 Ask students to read the first sentence of each paragraph and guess what each paragraph is about. Refer to the Text Organization exercise.

4 Go to Part III Detailed Study of Text A.

5 Ask students to do the exercises following the text.

Critical Thinking

Learning objectives:

- Reflect on cultural differences that may lead to misunderstandings in cross-cultural communication
- Learn to improve one's communication skills to prevent and resolve misunderstandings and conflicts in everyday life
- Discuss how to build harmonious relationships with others

Teaching steps:

1 Ask students to read the questions first and then give them some ideas on how to approach each question.

2 For Question 1, ask students to analyze some typical examples of cultural differences they know. For example, silence is valued and appreciated in Japan, while in Europe and North America it may cause embarrassment. In Mediterranean European countries and Latin America, it is normal, or at least widely tolerated, to arrive half an hour late for a dinner invitation, whereas in countries such as Germany and Switzerland this would be extremely rude. In Africa, telling a female friend one has not seen for a while that she has put on weight means she is physically healthier than before, whereas this would be considered as an insult in Europe, North America and Australia. Encourage students to give more examples to raise their awareness of cultural differences.

3 For Question 2, ask students to think about some cases of misunderstandings and conflicts between roommates in college and the ways to resolve them. For example, most roommate conflicts involve incompatible lifestyles, different habits, or different perspectives. To resolve these issues, you should first of all realize the cause(s) of the problem. Take some time to do some self-reflection, and you may have a clearer look at the root of the problem. Find a private place to talk openly about the problem, which can lead to a solution. If you've realized that the problem comes from you, then you must be willing to admit your faults and genuinely apologize to your roommate(s).

4 For Question 3, first introduce the quote by Mencius "Good timing is not as good as being advantageously situated, and being advantageously situated is not as good as having harmonious people." Then ask students to think about the importance of having a harmonious relationship with others and how to build it. To build harmonious relationships with others, you need to fully understand what they think or feel; to communicate honestly, openly and sincerely with them; to express admiration and appreciation for their talents, qualities, and accomplishments; to support them with kind gestures; to accept the fact that we are all different and respect these personal differences.

5 Ask students to work in pairs or small groups to share their opinions. Encourage each pair or group to present their favorite ideas in class.

Corpora in Language Learning

Learning objectives:

- Learn to search CADEL for verbs ending with the root "pose" by using the "Concordance" function of AntConc

- Learn to search CADEL for collocations of "verbs ending with 'pose' + noun/preposition" and translate these collocations into Chinese

- Learn to complete the given sentences with verbs ending with the root "pose" based on the contexts in which they appear

Teaching steps:

1   Ask students to search CADEL for verbs ending with the root "pose" by using the "Concordance" function of AntConc. Ask them to identify the verbs which complete the given collocations, using the given first letters as a hint.

2   Ask students to sort the search results by setting KWIC sort.

3   Explain the use of the verbs ending with "pose" and tell students how to complete the given sentences with these verbs.

4   Discuss the collocations of the verbs ending with "pose" with the retrieved nouns or prepositions, and ask students to translate these collocations into Chinese.

Writing

Learning objectives:

- Learn to write a paragraph of exemplification
- Learn to order examples logically and use signal words to introduce examples

Teaching steps:

1   Introduce the exemplification pattern in writing a paragraph and its two methods: the general-to-specific pattern and the specific-to-general pattern.

2   Introduce the ordering of several examples in one paragraph.

3   Introduce the words and phrases that indicate how each example is related to the topic sentence and to other examples.

4   Ask students to reflect on the use of exemplification in Text A. (In Text A, while some paragraphs provide several examples to illustrate the confusion caused by cultural differences, other paragraphs give one example only.)

5   Ask students to do Exercise I and practice identifying the topic sentence, the examples, and the signal words for exemplification.

6   Ask students to do Exercise II. Encourage them to organize their writing in the general-to-specific pattern, order examples logically and use signal words for exemplification properly.

Language Functions

Learning objectives:

- Learn to describe people's character and personality traits
- Understand the qualities that make one outstanding in different occupations

Teaching steps:

1   Ask students to read carefully the introduction on how to describe people's traits before doing the exercises.

2   Ask students to study carefully the list of descriptive adjectives.

3   Ask students to do Exercise I. Ask them to read aloud the sample, think of a friend they want to talk about and then use adjectives from the list to describe that friend. Encourage students to find synonyms and antonyms from the list and use them in their description.

4   Ask students to do Exercise II. Ask them to read aloud the sample and then choose an occupation they want to talk about.

5   After they are prepared, ask students to work in small groups and take turns to describe the qualities that make one outstanding in an occupation. Encourage them to guess the occupation that has been described, and then add some characteristics that the speaker did not mention.

Reading to Explore

Text B

Do You Expect Service with a Smile?

Learning objectives:

- Learn to understand new words and expressions through the context
- Learn to identify the most important information in a paragraph
- Learn about the differences between two varieties of emotional labor — surface acting and deep acting — and their effects
- Learn to give opinions on something

Teaching steps:

1   Ask students to read the text and finish the exercises following the text before class.
2   Check answers to the exercises.
3   Ask students to summarize the differences between surface acting and deep acting and the impacts on employees' health and work performance.
4   Encourage students to comment on the implications of these research findings.

Summary of Text B

This article reviews recent studies on the harmful effects of emotional labor. In the workplace, we often have to put on a happy face to please others, which is called "emotional labor". While surface acting changes our facial expressions without changing the real emotional state, deep acting does this by changing the genuine feelings. Empirical studies have discovered that surface acting leads to psychological problems such as strain and low job satisfaction, as well as physical problems such as headaches and chest pain. Despite some positive effects such as higher personal accomplishment and customer satisfaction, deep acting also results in greater emotional exhaustion and physical problems. This is because when emotional labor exhausts our mental resources and creates stress, we are more likely to act aggressively toward customers and colleagues. In conclusion, emotional labor impedes work performance, and we have to reduce employees' stress and aggression in order to boost productivity.

PART III   Detailed Study of Text A

The Meaning of a Smile in Different Cultures

Background Information

Journal of Experimental Social Psychology:《实验社会心理学杂志》

The *Journal of Experimental Social Psychology* is a bimonthly academic journal covering social psychology. It is published by Elsevier on behalf of the Society of Experimental Social Psychology (SESP) starting from 1965.

Understanding the Text

Part 1 (Paras. 1–3)

Para. 1

1 Ask students to read Para. 1 and answer the following questions:

  1) What is a common belief that people have about smiling? (How much people smile reflects their level of happiness with life.)

  2) What is the truth about the amount people smile, according to the author? (How much people smile is culturally-influenced rather than directly related to their level of happiness with life.)

  3) What example does the author give to prove this point? (The Swiss are reported to have the highest level of happiness in the world, but do not smile much.)

2 Ask students to offer some possible explanations for why the Swiss are unsmiling.

Paras. 2–3

1 Ask students to read Para. 2 and answer the following questions:

  1) What is another common belief that people have about smiling? (Smiling is a genuine expression of our emotions.)

  2) What is the truth about smiling, according to the author? (Smiling is more a way of communicating with others that is strongly influenced by culture than a genuine expression of our emotions.)

  3) What example does the author give to prove this point? (In pro-smiling cultures such as the United States, smiling is regarded as a way to show one's respect for other people and to ease relationships, and so it is important to greet unfamiliar people with a smile. Smiling is also regarded as a way to assure other people that one is enjoying life and comfortable with situations.)

2 Ask students to discuss in pairs whether Chinese culture is a pro-smiling culture.

Part 2 (Paras. 4–8)

Para. 4

1   Ask students to read Para. 4 and answer the following questions:

　1)　What is the main point of this paragraph? (Differing cultural attitudes towards smiling can cause misunderstandings when we encounter people from a culture that approaches smiling differently.)

　2)　What example does the author give to prove this point? (Misunderstandings can happen between people from Japan and the United States due to their different cultural attitudes towards smiling.)

　3)　What different attitudes do Japan and the US have towards expression of feelings? (The American culture values open expression of feelings, while the Japanese culture values humility and the suppressing of emotions in order to improve interpersonal relationships and therefore avoids overt displays of emotion.)

2   Ask students to work in pairs to think of some possible examples of misunderstandings that result from different cultural attitudes.

Para. 5

1   Ask students to read Para. 5 and answer the following questions:

　1)　What is the first example the author gives to show difficult communication between Japanese people and Americans? (Some Japanese people find typical American facial expressions strange, with mouths slightly too open and the mouth corners raised too much.)

　2)　What is the second example the author gives to show difficult communication between Japanese people and Americans? (Japanese smiles are confusing for Americans because Japanese people are seen to smile not only when happy, but also when angry, sad or embarrassed.)

2   Ask students if they find these facial expressions strange and confusing.

Para. 6

1   Ask students to read Para. 6 and answer the following question:

　1)　What is another difference between Japanese people and Americans? (Japanese people are better than Americans at detecting whether a smile is genuine or false, because they tend to focus attention on the eyes rather than the mouth.)

2   Ask students to think about how they can tell true smiles from false ones.

Para. 7

1   Ask students to read Para. 7 and answer the following questions:

　1)　What example does the author give to show the effect of cultural differences in smiling? (Americans and Russians sometimes misunderstand one another.)

　2)　What different cultural approaches do these two countries have to smiling? (To Russians, smiling when greeting a stranger is insincere and smiling when carrying out serious work is inappropriate. In contrast, Americans consider it important to greet unfamiliar people, especially customers, with a smile to show respect.)

2   Ask students to discuss in pairs what is the appropriate way in Chinese culture to greet people.

Para. 8

1   Ask students to read Para. 8 and answer the following questions:

    1) What example does the author give to show the effect of cultural differences in smiling? (The difference between traditional Indian culture and Western culture in terms of how much smiling is appropriate for a bride on the wedding day.)

    2) Why did a modern-minded Indian bride quarrel with her photographer on the wedding day? (Question 5 in Exercise I of Reading Comprehension) (The two quarreled because the photographer held on to the traditional Indian culture which values female shyness, while the modern-minded Indian bride who was confident and assertive smiled more on the wedding day than expected.)

2   Ask students to discuss in pairs what is the appropriate emotional expression for brides and grooms in Chinese culture today.

3   Draw students' attention to the word formation of "modern-minded". Ask students to do the exercise of Word Formation.

Part 3 (Para. 9)

1   Ask students to read Para. 9 and answer the following question:

    1) What is an important part of adapting to a new culture? (Understanding how non-verbal behaviors and attitudes should be given and received.)

2   Ask students to pay attention to the last part of the last sentence. What rhetorical device is used here? (Metaphor.)

Language Points

1   In some parts of the world, such as America, smiling is much more common than in less emotionally **expressive** countries such as Japan. **(Para. 1)**

    Paraphrase: Smiling is much more common in some countries like America than in countries such as Japan where people do not show their emotions clearly.

    expressive: *adj.* showing very clearly what sb. thinks or feels 明确表现感情或思想的；富有表现力的

    Eyebrows are one of our most **expressive** facial features.

2   It seems the difference in the amount people smile **is** culturally-influenced rather than directly **related to** their level of happiness with life. **(Para. 1)**

    Paraphrase: It seems that the difference in how much people smile is decided by culture rather than directly connected with how satisfied they are with their life.

    be related to: be connected with 与……有关系的，有联系的

    Statistics show that workers' education levels **are** strongly **related to** their income.

3   ... yet visitors often report being surprised by how **unsmiling** the Swiss are. **(Para. 1)**

    Paraphrase: ... but visitors to Switzerland often say that they are surprised by how serious local people look without any smiles on their faces.

    unsmiling: *adj.* looking serious and unfriendly 面无笑容的，严肃的

Sociology research rates smiling people as more attractive than **unsmiling** people.

4 It seems that smiling is **more** a way of communicating with others — one that's strongly influenced by our culture — **than** a genuine expression of our emotions. (**Para. 2**)

Paraphrase: It seems that smiling is a way of communicating with others, which is largely decided by our culture, instead of a way of expressing our true feelings.

more … than: 与其说……不如说……

The words were spoken **more** in sadness **than** in anger.

5 **Pro**-smiling cultures such as the United States tend to see smiling as **a mark of respect** for another person. (**Para. 2**)

Paraphrase: In cultures that are in favor of smiling such as the United States, people smile in order to show respect for others.

pro-: supporting or approving of sth. 赞成；支持；亲

There are both **pro**-American and anti-American biases in Hollywood movies.

a mark of respect/honor, etc.: sth. that happens or is done to show respect, honor, etc. 尊敬/敬意等的表示

We presented the sponsor of the event a bouquet of flowers as **a mark of respect** for his generosity.

6 Smiling is a **diplomatic** tool to ease relationships, so it's considered important to greet people with a smile even if they are **unfamiliar** to you. That's especially true if the person is in a **superior** position, such as a customer. (**Para. 2**)

Paraphrase: Smiling is a tool that we can use to skillfully improve our relationships with others, so we consider it important to smile when we greet others even if they are strangers. People should do this especially when they are greeting somebody in a higher position, such as a customer.

diplomatic: *adj.* having or showing skill in dealing with people in difficult situations 灵活变通的；圆通得体的；策略的

The spokesman gave a **diplomatic** answer when he was asked about the likelihood of more policy adjustment in the near future.

unfamiliar: *adj.* not known to you 不熟悉的

When you see an **unfamiliar** word in a book, do not skip over it impatiently.

superior: *adj.* having a higher position or rank than sb. else 地位较高的，上级的

"You have disobeyed a direct order from your **superior** officer," he told her solemnly.

7 In smiling cultures, people will sometimes challenge those who are not smiling and ask why they are looking **miserable**. (**Para. 3**)

Paraphrase: In cultures where people smile a lot, people will sometimes ask those who do not smile why they look unhappy.

miserable: *adj.* extremely unhappy or uncomfortable 痛苦的；非常难受的；可怜的

Why do you make yourself **miserable** by taking on too much work?

8 People from these smiling cultures tend to feel wounded by encounters with unsmiling people, and they will commonly return from a visit to an unsmiling country slightly upset that people were not smiling more often. **(Para. 3)**

Paraphrase: People from smiling cultures often feel hurt when they meet people who do not smile. When they return from a visit to a country where people seldom smile, they usually feel a bit disappointed because they did not receive as many smiles from local people as they had expected.

9   People from Japan and the United States are often chosen as subjects for studies of smiling, as these cultures are seen as being at opposite ends of the **spectrum** in their attitudes. **(Para. 4)**

Paraphrase: Japanese people and Americans are often chosen by researchers to be the subjects in their studies of the smiling behavior, because Japanese culture and American culture are regarded as two extremes in all the cultures with sharply contrastive attitudes toward smiling.

spectrum: *n.* a complete range of a particular type of thing 范围；幅度

The two articles here represent opposite ends of the **spectrum** of public opinions.

10   Whilst the American culture values emotional openness and **broadcasting** feelings, the Japanese culture avoids **overt displays** of emotion. **(Para. 4)**

Paraphrase: While the American culture appreciates expressing emotions and feelings openly, the Japanese culture avoids showing emotions publicly.

broadcast: *v.* tell sth. to a lot of people 广为传播，散布

There is no need to **broadcast** the fact that the two companies will merge.

overt★: *adj.* done publicly, without trying to hide anything 公开的，不加隐瞒的

The author remains calm though there is much **overt** criticism on his recent work.

display: *n.* an occasion when sb. clearly shows a particular feeling, attitude, or quality 流露，显露

Her writing is a remarkable **display** of her natural talent.

11   Japan's culture tends to value **humility** and the **suppressing** of emotions in order to improve relationships with others, and **as a consequence**, fewer emotions are communicated using the mouth. **(Para. 4)**

Paraphrase: The Japanese culture often thinks highly of being modest and hiding emotions so as to build better relationships with others. Therefore, Japanese people seldom express emotions by changing the shape and position of the mouth.

humility: *n.* the quality of not being too proud about yourself 谦逊，谦恭

We need passion, faith and confidence, but not at the expense of **humility**.

suppress: *v.* stop yourself from showing your feelings 抑制（感情），忍住

While expressing emotions in a socially healthy way helps you connect to others, **suppressing** the emotions of sadness, anger or fear can be a symptom of depression.

consequence: *n.* 后果

Her investment had disastrous **consequences**: she lost everything she owned.

as a consequence: as a result 因此，结果

His departure from the position was totally unexpected and, **as a consequence**, no plans had been made for his replacement.

12   Cultures with such opposite approaches to smiling **are bound to** find this a **sticking point** in their communications. **(Para. 5)**

Paraphrase: As the two cultures are so different in their understanding of smiling, people from these two countries will certainly find this cultural difference an obstacle in their communications.

be bound to: be very likely to do or feel a particular thing 一定会做某事

Don't lie to your teacher. She **is bound to** find out about it.

sticking point: *n.* sth. that a group of people cannot agree on and that stops them from making progress 症结，障碍

The main **sticking point** in the negotiation was the question of taxes.

13 Some Japanese people have reported finding **typical** American facial expressions to be a little strange, with mouths slightly too open and the mouth corners raised too much. **(Para. 5)**

Paraphrase: Some Japanese people have said they found the facial expressions of average Americans a little strange — they keep their mouths a little bit too open and raise the corners of their lips too much.

typical: *adj.* having the usual features or qualities of a particular group or thing 典型的；有代表性的

A **typical** freshman schedule includes five required courses and one elective（选修课）.

14 And Japanese smiles can be just as **confusing** for outsiders. "Naki-warai"（泣き笑い）is a term used to convey crying while laughing and describes how Japanese people will be seen to smile when angry, sad or **embarrassed. (Para. 5)**

Paraphrase: And similarly, foreigners also find it difficult to understand the smiles of Japanese people. "Naki-warai" is a phrase used to mean "cry and laugh at the same time". It describes how Japanese people are seen to put on a smile even when they feel angry, sad or awkward.

confusing: *adj.* unclear and difficult to understand 令人困惑的，难懂的

If you find the instructions **confusing**, let me know and I'd be happy to help you.

embarrassed: *adj.* shy, awkward or ashamed, especially in a social situation 窘迫的，尴尬的

I felt **embarrassed** when I was asked to sing in front of a big crowd.

15 ... people from a Japanese cultural background may be better than Americans at **detecting** when a smile is genuine or false. **(Para. 6)**

Paraphrase: People growing up in the Japanese culture may do better than Americans when judging whether a smile is sincere or not.

detect: *v.* notice or discover sth., esp. sth. that is not easy to see, hear, etc. 察觉，发现

WHO will help to set up a disease monitoring system to **detect** and control outbreaks of infectious diseases.

16 It's thought the eyes may be better at **portraying** genuine emotion than the mouth, which may be why the Japanese can **distinguish** true smiles from false ones. **(Para. 6)**

Paraphrase: Japanese people think that eyes may reveal true emotions better than the mouth. This is probably the reason why the Japanese can recognize the differences between real smiles and fake smiles.

portray★: *v.* describe or show sth. or sb. in a particular way 描写；表现

The novel *A Dream of Red Mansions* **portrays** a large number of characters and depicts the living conditions of people from all walks of life in the feudal society.

distinguish: *v.* (**distinguish sth./sb. from**) recognize the difference between two people or things 区分，辨别

No one can **distinguish** one from the other because the twin sisters are identical in appearance.

17 Russian writers have often mentioned how **perplexing** the American smile is to them. The American **readiness** to smile is a sticking point for the less smile-ready Russians. (**Para. 7**)

Paraphrase: Russian writers have often mentioned how the American smile confuses them. Americans smiling so often is not understandable to Russians who smile much less.

perplexing: *a.* very puzzling 令人困惑的

Research funding for the **perplexing** and growing problem of kidney stone will be doubled over the next decade.

readiness: *n.* willingness to do sth. 愿意，乐意

The new manager expressed his **readiness** to accept any challenge.

18 Russians only smile to genuinely express a good mood or personal **regard** for an **acquaintance**. (**Para. 7**)

Paraphrase: Russians only smile in a sincere way to either express their good mood or show their respect when they meet someone they know.

regard: *n.* respect or admiration for sb. or sth. 尊重；尊敬；敬佩

Chinese people have high **regard** for Guan Yu, a military general of the late Eastern Han dynasty who is best known for his loyalty and righteousness.

acquaintance: *n.* sb. you know, but who is not a close friend 相识的人，熟人

Having worked here for twenty years, he has a wide circle of **acquaintances** in Shanghai.

19 Smiling when greeting a stranger would be seen as **insincere**. (**Para. 7**)

Paraphrase: If you smile when you say hello to a stranger, other people will think you are not being true but just pretending.

insincere: *adj.* pretending to be pleased, sympathetic, etc. 不诚恳的，虚伪的

A genuine apology benefits both parties. In contrast, an **insincere** apology can make matters worse.

20 Smiling when carrying out serious work would be seen as **inappropriate**. (**Para. 7**)

Paraphrase: If you smile while doing serious work, other people would think you are behaving in an unsuitable way.

inappropriate: *adj.* not suitable or acceptable 不合适的，不恰当的

The book contains violence and language that may be **inappropriate** for children under the age of thirteen.

21 Russian smiles are **reserved** for acquaintances rather than strangers. (**Para. 7**)

Paraphrase: Russians smile only to people they know — they don't smile to strangers.

reserve: *v.* use or show sth. only in one particular situation 留作，用于（特定场合）

The headmaster spoke in a soft tone of voice that she usually **reserved** for young children.

22 **No wonder** Americans and Russians sometimes may misunderstand one another. (**Para. 7**)

Paraphrase: It is not surprising that Americans and Russians sometimes may misunderstand each other.

no wonder (that): it is not surprising 不足为奇，难怪

You drank so much last night. **No wonder** you've got a headache.

23 With Indian culture valuing female **shyness**, a more serious expression has traditionally been the **norm**. **(Para. 8)**

Paraphrase: Because Indian culture considers it important that women should be shy, it is the tradition that Indian women put on an unsmiling face and appear reserved on the wedding day.

shyness: *n.* 羞怯，腼腆

When she took on the role of a teacher, her **shyness** went away.

norm: *n.* the usual or normal situation, way of doing sth., etc. 标准，规范

Video interviews are now the **norm** during the hiring process.

24 But that's changing now as Indian women are becoming more confident and **assertive**. One modern-**minded** Indian bride **clashed** with her wedding photographer when he told her to stop smiling so much on the big day. **(Para. 8)**

Paraphrase: But the tradition is changing now, because Indian women are becoming more confident and self-assured. One Indian bride with modern ideas argued with her photographer when he told her not to smile so much on the wedding day.

assertive: *adj.* expressing opinions or desires strongly and with confidence, so that people take notice 坚定自信的

You should be **assertive** when requesting a solution from the service team, but never be aggressive.

-minded: (combined with adjectives to form compound adjectives) having a particular attitude or way of thinking 有某种态度或思想的

She is a very serious-**minded** girl who studies hard to achieve her dream.

clash: *v.* two people or groups argue because they have very different beliefs and opinions 发生冲突；产生矛盾

Mr. White **clashed** with his boss over issues of security and emergency.

25 It's hard to **overcome** one's own cultural **conditioning when it comes to** the behavior of the lower parts of our faces. **(Para. 9)**

Paraphrase: When we are showing our facial expressions by moving the mouth, it is difficult to go against the long-time influence our own culture has had on us.

overcome: *v.* succeed in dealing with (a problem or difficulty) 解决，克服

Molly took swimming lessons this summer and finally **overcame** her fear of water.

conditioning: *n.* the training or experience that an animal or a person has that makes them behave in a particular way in a particular situation 训练；熏陶；条件作用

It is social **conditioning** that makes crying more difficult for men than for women.

when it comes to: when you are dealing with sth. or talking about sth. 在某个方面；说到某事

When it comes to vacations, I prefer the beach to the mountains.

26 Moving successfully into another culture and becoming culturally **fluent necessitates** understanding how **non-verbal** clues should be given and received. **(Para. 9)**

Paraphrase: In order to adapt to a culture different from our own and know that culture very well, it is necessary to understand how local people send and receive messages without the use of words or speech.

fluent: *n.* able to express oneself easily and articulately 表达流利的

Being **fluent** in a foreign language means that you can communicate freely with native speakers without having to constantly look for help.

necessitate: *v.* make it necessary for you to do sth. 使成为必需，需要

On the third day of our journey, the breakdown of the car **necessitated** a change in our plans.

verbal: *adj.* relating to words or using words 词语的；文字的

The test measures students' **verbal** skills, mathematical skills, and abstract reasoning skills.

non-verbal: *adj.* not using words or speech 非语言的

Non-verbal communication is the nonlinguistic transmission of information through the use of body language including eye contact, facial expressions, gestures and more.

27 Smiling is an important part of how we **come across** and how we understand the behavior and attitudes of others, which is why it's important to understand exactly what a smile is worth in the local emotional **currency. (Para. 9)**

Paraphrase: Smiling is an important part of how we make a particular impression and how we understand others' behavior and attitudes. Therefore, it is important to understand how significant a smile is in expressing emotions in the local culture.

come across: make a particular impression 给人以……印象；留下印象

Responding effectively to all the questions from the hiring manager, Bob **came across** well in the interview.

currency: *n.* the system or type of money that a country uses 货币；通货

The official name for Chinese **currency** is Renminbi, which is shortened to RMB.

PART IV Keys to Exercises

Lead-in

| 1 C   2 B   3 C   4 B   5 A

Reading to Learn

Reading Comprehension

| 1 The passage is mainly about cultural differences in smiling and the misunderstandings they have caused.

2 In pro-smiling cultures such as the United States, smiling shows one's respect for other people and eases relationship. Smiling also assures other people that one is enjoying life and comfortable with situations.

3 While the American culture values emotional openness and broadcasting feelings, the Japanese culture avoids overt displays of emotion. Japan's culture tends to value humility and the suppressing of emotions in order to improve relationships with others, and as a result, fewer emotions are communicated using the mouth.

4 They sometimes misunderstand each other because, to Russians, smiling when greeting a stranger is insincere and smiling when carrying out serious work is inappropriate, while Americans consider it important to greet people, even if they are unfamiliar to you, with a smile to show respect.

5 The two quarreled because the photographer held on to the traditional Indian culture which values female shyness, while the modern-minded Indian bride who was confident and assertive smiled more on the wedding day than expected.

II 1 C   2 B   3 B   4 A   5 C

III **Text Organization**

1 culture   2 culturally-influenced
3 Switzerland   4 communicating with others
5 the United States   6 approaches smiling differently
7 Japan and the US   8 tense relations
9 Russia and the US   10 inappropriate
11 there can't be enough   12 Indian and Western
13 non-verbal behavior

Language in Use

Words and Expressions

I 1 clash   2 overcoming   3 fluent   4 expressive
   5 superior   6 detect   7 suppress   8 portrayed

II 1 as a consequence 2 sticking point   3 is bound to   4 when it comes to
   5 came across   6 am comfortable with 7 are related to 8 a mark of

III 1 display   2 reserved   3 miserable   4 distinguish   5 insincere
    6 acquaintances   7 tend to   8 non-verbal   9 assertive   10 bound to

Word Formation

1 absent-minded   2 tradition-minded   3 health-minded   4 like-minded
5 simple-minded   6 budget-minded   7 career-minded   8 open-minded
9 noble-minded   10 safety-minded

| 1 blood | 2 steady | 3 maintaining | 4 interpersonal |
| 5 business | 6 bear | 7 family | 8 worsened |

Grammar and Structure

1   It is essential that schools develop not only students' academic ability but also their personal qualities and social skills.

2   More and more people find it of great help to master a foreign language.

3   It is a great pity that the committee has rejected the plan to repair the railroads connecting the two cities.

4   Researchers conclude that it is no good teaching babies to carry out simple movements by using milk as a reward.

5   In my opinion, it is wise of the government to impose speed limit on roads to reduce accidents.

6   It has not been made clear when the new road will be opened to traffic.

7   It is suggested by test results that some beer lovers are not really able to tell their favorite brand by taste.

8   It has never crossed his mind that employers often reject resumes with spelling mistakes.

Translation

I   1 在演讲中，演讲者描述了通过肢体语言来区分真实情感和虚假情感的方法。

　　2 难怪我们在办公楼里找不到人；他们都去开会了。

　　3 说到保持健康，人们普遍认为多吃蔬菜少吃肉很重要。

　　4 这两家公司都被消费者视为非常环保的公司，但它们的产品定价却截然相反。

　　5 庭审中的难点在于是否她所犯下的是个错误，而不是罪行。

II 1 It is perplexing to westerners that the Japanese smile when feeling embarrassed.

　　2 Outside the hospital, two parking spots are reserved for parents with babies.

　　3 The headmaster assured the parents that the school was bound to take their complaints seriously.

　　4 The traditional Chinese culture values harmony, courtesy, wisdom, and loyalty, which is displayed in China's foreign policy for dealing with international affairs.

　　5 In the 1970s, there was a sharp increase in China's birth rate. As a consequence, the country's population grew rapidly.

III Smiling makes you look more attractive, successful and approachable. It may also protect you from the common cold, lighten up your mood, and enhance your ability to deal with difficult situations. Have you ever been around someone who seemed to be smiling all the time? Chances are, you found yourself smiling as well. This is because smiling is incredibly contagious. Research suggests that happy people influence the people closest to them and increase positive energy. So, next time you're feeling down, seek out your happiest friend and let the smiles begin.

Corpora in Language Learning

I

Collocations of "verb ending with 'pose' + noun/preposition"	Chinese translations
compose emails/letters	写邮件/信件
dispose of files	处理文档
expose sb. to (danger, threat)	使某人暴露于/遭受(危险，威胁)
impose a fine/punishments/laws/limits	处以罚款/加以惩罚/执行法律/施加限制
pose a challenge/barriers/risks to sb./sth.	对……构成挑战/障碍/风险
propose a solution/approaches	提出解决方案/途径

II   **1** impose   **2** expose   **3** pose   **4** dispose   **5** compose

Writing

I   The first sentence is the topic sentence.

Two examples of useful and interesting courses are given: An Introduction to European Culture and American Society and Culture.

The transitional words and phrases used are "for instance" and "another".

Reading to Explore

Reading Comprehension

I   **1** C   **2** C   **3** B   **4** D   **5** C

II   **1** F   **2** T   **3** F   **4** F   **5** T

III   **A** 2   **B** 10   **C** 6   **D** 7   **E** 4

       F 12   **G** 3   **H** 9   **I** 6   **J** 8

Words and Expressions

I   **1** neutral   **2** proposed   **3** aggressive   **4** demonstrate   **5** supervisor

       6 bullying   **7** significance   **8** adjust   **9** exhaust   **10** amplify

II   **1** find out   **2** put on   **3** stir up   **4** to some extent   **5** the big picture

       6 be herself   **7** make sense   **8** on occasion   **9** give … a leg up   **10** used up

PART V | Text Translation

Text A

不同文化中微笑的含义

优素福·波哈那

1　在世界的某些地方如美国，微笑比情感内敛的国家如日本常见得多。似乎人们微笑的多少主要受文化的影响，而不是和他们的生活幸福水平直接相关。生活在瑞士的人们声称自己拥有世界上最高的幸福水平，但游客却经常因瑞士人不苟言笑而感到惊讶。

2　微笑似乎更多地是一种与他人交流的方式——一种受我们文化强烈影响的方式——而不是我们自身情感的真实表达。像美国这样崇尚微笑的文化倾向于将微笑视为尊重他人的标志。微笑是一种缓和人际关系的圆通的方法，因此即便是遇到不熟悉的人，微笑着向他们问好也被认为是很重要的。如果这个人身处优势地位，例如客户，则尤其如此。

3　另外，通过微笑使他人确信你很享受生活、舒适自在，也被认为是很重要的。在微笑文化中，人们有时会质疑那些不笑的人，问他们为什么一脸愁容。来自这些微笑文化的人们遇到面无笑容的人往往会感到受伤，当他们从某个不苟言笑的国家游览归来时常常会略感沮丧，因为当地人没有更多地微笑。微笑文化似乎认为他们有权期望别人对其报以微笑。

4　当我们遇到来自对微笑持不同态度的文化的人时，我们对微笑的不同文化态度会引起误解。日本人和美国人经常被选为微笑研究的对象，因为这两种文化对于微笑的态度被视为处于两个对立的极端。美国文化重视情感开放和情感外露，而日本文化却回避公开的情感表露。日本文化倾向于崇尚谦卑和抑制情绪，从而改善与他人的关系，因此很少用嘴巴传达情感。

5　对微笑持相反态度的文化必然会发现这是双方沟通时的障碍。一些日本人声称觉得典型美国人的面部表情有点怪异，嘴巴有点张得过大，嘴角上扬过高。日本人的微笑对外人来说同样令人困惑。"Naki-warai"（泣き笑い）（"哭笑"）是一个用来表达边笑边哭意思的词语，描述的是日本人在生气、悲伤或尴尬时如何看上去依然微笑。而他们快乐时也微笑，这自然令人困惑。

6　发表在《实验社会心理学杂志》上的研究表明，来自日本文化背景的人可能比美国人更擅长察觉微笑是真是假。日本人在表达自身情感或感知他人情感时往往把注意力集中在眼睛而不是嘴巴上。人们认为眼睛可能比嘴巴更能表现真情实感，这也许就是日本人能够辨别真假微笑的原因。

7　对待微笑的不同文化态度甚至可能导致关系紧张。俄罗斯作家经常提到美国人的微笑让他们感到多么困惑。美国人动不动就微笑的特点对于不善微笑的俄罗斯人来说是个沟通障碍。俄罗斯人只有在真正表达心情好或对熟人的尊重时才微笑。问候陌生人时微笑会被视为不真诚。开展严肃工作时微笑则被视为不合适，所以一位俄罗斯银行职员可能显得比一位态度友好的美国银行职员严肃很多。俄罗斯人的微笑是留给熟人而不是陌生人的——女服务员会对她的朋友而不是顾客微笑。难怪美国人和俄罗斯人经常彼此误解。

8　还有在某些特定的场合，有些文化认为微笑太多是不恰当的，而其他文化却认为微笑再多也不为过。印度新娘在婚礼当天并不总是像西方新娘那样面带微笑。印度文化欣赏女性的羞怯，因此较为严肃的表情已成为惯例。不过随着印度女性变得更加坚定自信，情况正在发生变化。一位具有现代意识的印度新娘与她的婚礼摄影师便起了冲突，因为他让她在这个重要的日子里不要笑太多。

9　当涉及脸的下半部分的动作时，我们很难克服自身的文化影响。要想成功地融入另一种文化，并在文化方面运用自如，就必须了解如何发出和接收非语言提示。微笑是我们如何表现自己、理解他人行为和态度的重要组成部分，因此准确理解当地情感体系中微笑的意义至关重要。

Text B

你期待微笑服务吗？

米尔达·佩尔米尼

1　人类一直对他人的情绪表达高度敏感。不出所料，研究表明我们更喜欢看起来快乐的人，而不是那些神情忧伤或不动声色的人。但是总是面带微笑的情感代价是什么？要求人们在工作中总是保持微笑是否公平？我们刚刚回顾了这个话题的相关证据，研究结果令人担忧。

2　我们之所以喜欢快乐的面容，是因为他人的积极情绪会立即提升我们自己的精神状态。例如，最近的一项研究表明，在快速约会中，表现积极的人能够更多激发他人的振奋情绪，并且更容易获得再次约会的机会。

3　但是，为了取悦他人而试图表现得开心的情绪后果是什么？阿莉·霍赫希尔德的开创性研究将这种"情绪劳动"分为两类："深层行为"和"表层行为"。当我们使用表层行为时，我们调整面部表情和身体姿态而不实际改变我们的情绪状态，例如，在并不感到快乐的时候依然保持微笑。

4　另一方面，深层行为是指我们试图通过想象能够激发正面情感或减少负面体验影响的事物来改变自己感受的行为。例如，在与难缠的客户打交道时，你可以想想即将到来的假期，或者找出他们身上你喜欢的品质。

5　这两种技巧都可以在一定程度上帮我们在家里和工作中建立更好的关系，但总的来说，深层行为有助于展现更真实的情感。事实上，最近的一项研究发现，采取深层行为的服务员往往获得了比别人更多的小费。

6　服务行业的员工显然承受着从事情绪劳动的压力——抑制或放大特定的情绪，使客户满意，鼓励他们再次光临。大多数关于情绪劳动的实证研究都发现了其负面影响。实施表层行为的人"戴上面具"，在表达的情绪和感受到的情绪之间会造成不利健康的内心冲突。对2011年95项研究的回顾表明，实施表层行为与情绪疲劳、紧张、工作满意度降低以及对工作单位归属感减弱相关联。表层行为还会造成身心失调问题，如睡眠障碍、头痛和胸痛。

7　另一方面，深层行为则与一些正面的结果相关联——例如更高的个人成就、客户满意度和对雇主的归属感。这可能是因为深层行为有助于表现更真实的情感，从而被客户和同事所欣赏。深层行为还可以帮助实现更有益的社交互动。但是，它也并不总是有益的。深层行为也会导致更重的情绪疲劳和更多的身心疾病。尽管研究人员的观点有所不同，但表层行为和深层行为似乎都对员工有害。

8　从更宏观的角度思考，如果情绪劳动使我们精疲力竭，并导致压力和紧张堆积，它就可能会对我们的人际关系产生负面影响。一些理论认为，意志力和自我调节要用到有限的心理资源储备，而这些心理资源是会消耗殆尽的。可以说，反复的情绪劳动会耗尽这些资源。结果，最轻微的诱因也可能会引爆敌对性反应，而做不到客气待人。

9　在过去十年中，我对职场霸凌进行了研究。我知道工作场所的敌对行为可能是由压力引发的。在有压力的情况下，我们会变得更加戒备、更加敏感，因此更可能表现出敌意。鉴于情绪劳动会产生压力和紧张，它自然也可能引发敌对行为。

10　我和我的同事决心查明真相。一开始，我们系统梳理了认为情感劳动与职场敌对行为有关的现有论文。我们回顾了专门关注情绪劳动和工作场所关系失常的12项最近研究（大多数发表于2015年和2016年）。

11　我们的文献综述尚未正式发表，但已经在最近的欧洲工作与组织心理学协会大会上宣读。文献回顾表明，在大多数情况下，表层行为与工作中针对客户和同事的敌对行为相关。在一项研究中，深层行为与对同事的敌对行为相关。有些案例中的敌对行为是由参与者自己报告的，还有些是由同事或主管报告的。

12　虽然我们知道情绪劳动可以助企业一臂之力，但实际上它可能会抑制业绩。如果我们认同每个人有时都需要做真实的自己，那么我们可能会减少职场中的压力和敌对行为——最终使之成为一个更快乐、更高效的地方。